DEDICATION

This book is dedicated to my family, friends, fellow teachers, teammates, students, employees, employers, and all those who have given me so much to remember and be grateful for.

WELL, AT LEAST I OWNED A ROLLS ROYCE

BY

DONALD P. MCKEAG

INDEX

FOREWORD

BY MIKE FOLEY

AUTHOR OF RESCUED HEARTS AND THE WAR YEARS

Okay, I'll admit it. When Don suggested the title for his book by explaining that he'd actually owned a Rolls Royce, I was smitten. Not in the way a boy might be smitten in first grade by a little pigtailed girl in the row by the blackboard, but the way you'd be smitten by the memory of something from years ago that still manages to tickle your fancy. In this case, I thought of the legendary image preserved on celluloid of a Rolls Royce transporting a diminutive and happy drunk, a filthy rich alcoholic devoid of any inspiration or ambition until he watched Liza Minnelli stealing neckties. I speak, of course, about the Rolls limousine in the movie Arthur and its venerable star, the late, great Dudley Moore.

You see, Don's Rolls Royce was first cousin to the one Lil' Arthur rode in while the quintessential curmudgeon John Gielgud, AKA Hobson, maneuvered through traffic in midtown Manhattan and in his most condescending, buttoned-up British manner, chastised his employer as one's father might do to a wayward child. Who can forget the scene where Arthur announces that he's going to take a bath and Hobson replies in perfect deadpan, "I shall alert the media."

However, unlike the Arthur character in the movie, Don McKeag wasn't born into money; he didn't have a huge inheritance with which to fund his zest for life. Let there be no mistake about Don's life and times; he had and still has a supreme zest for life as you'll read in the following pages.

So, along the way, while overdosing on zest, Don did what most of us only wish we had done. He lived the American dream, an abstract thought process where, on the one hand, he is a wildly successful entrepreneur with a storied and envious résumé, a determined man who has clawed his way to the top of the business mountain and met a complete cast of interesting characters along the way while, on the other hand, and when he least expected it, he lost his footing and tumbled into the deep valleys that surrounded his unflinching efforts.

But Don is resilient. Or is it stubborn? He didn't give up. He ran, hopped, skipped, and sometimes trudged along but forward, always forward. Because, like the true believers among us and to this very day, Don embraces and accepts, with all his heart and soul, that life is a journey, one fraught with opportunity and in many instances, failure. Too often it seems, one begets the other, and with this in mind, we can say that the story of Don's amazing life can be favorably compared to a nine-inning baseball game. There were innings when the opposing pitcher - life itself - struck him out with three 100 MPH fastballs down the middle; there were innings when Don loaded the bases then hit a grand slam.

Of course, the innings that brought Don's to the top of the business game were the most fun. They were the best. The ones where he struck out though, well, not so good.

The fun times saw him spill water on Dorothy Lamour; help the fetally-positioned George Gobel down from the top of a piano; enjoy a cigar with Arnold Schwarzenegger; watch comedienne Martha Raye, upon exiting the ladies room, decide to sing for her friends at an after-hours cocktail party in a deserted restaurant "Swanee, how I love ya, how I love ya"; share cocktails and lots of laughs with the late Ted Kennedy, the unchallenged king of the liberals, who knew that Don hosted a radio talk show with an unapologetic and decidedly conservative bent.

Figure that one out! Below you will read how easily Don blended in with Hyannis Port society and its mores. Then, in a flash, we will shudder in disbelief as his entrepreneurial empire comes crashing down in a heap, most often because of his own deeply inbred notion that haunts many Irish to this very day, a notion that speaks to a guilt-ridden and anti-successful life where one believes that if things are going too good, well, there must be something wrong. In short, Don shot himself in the foot so many times, and with such remarkable accuracy that the U. S. Marines, those artisans of exactitude, would stand and cheer had they only known.

In trying to consider a comparison to Don's life and times, I settled on what I believe is a perfect simile. Don is the silver ball flying around inside a pinball machine, bouncing off bumpers, being flipped about every which way, racking up points as bells ring in rapid harmony, falling into the hole and disappearing, only to be replaced by yet another silver ball.

Carefully crafted inside the words contained herein is a message, a borderline rags-to-riches type story that could easily have come from the Horatio Alger's famous pen. It's a bold and sincere message for anyone who ever wondered whether hard work, determination, courage, and honesty actually pay. Well, they do. And Don McKeag proved it. In a happy review of all that he has done (and not done), we can safely conclude that he is the kind of guy who will race up to the Pearly Gates in that Rolls Royce he owned, downshift his ride and skid, sideways, into a parking place right beside the desk where St. Peter stands, climb out and speaking to his life, exclaim, "Man, what a ride!"

CHAPTER 1

JOYRIDE TO DISASTER

Left: David "Lefty" McKeag, 1927
Right: Donald McKeag, 1957

In his poem "If," the British poet laureate, Rudyard Kipling, tells us:

"If you can dream and not make dreams your master;
If you can think and not make thoughts your aim;
If you can meet with Triumph and Disaster
and treat those two imposters the same, then"
yours is the Earth and everything that's in it, and -
which is more important - you'll be a man my son."

Dreaming is the easy part. It's becoming a man that's difficult and part of the challenge is that we are products of our parents' past, as well as those of our ancestors -- whether we like to admit it or not. Like many families, my ancestral heritage was somewhat colorful and probably shaped me, my interests and tendencies more than I could have dreamed possible.

My first real dream was to become rich and famous as a baseball player. Ever since I made Little League, I could see it all in my head: first a high school career, then getting a scholarship to play in college followed by heading for the big time. I could hear the crowds cheering as they watched me pitch and knew all that money and celebrity would earn me a house on the beach with a beautiful wife and kids, all of whom, like me, loved music, singing and of course, baseball.

My fondness for the sport was hardly coincidental as

my outgoing and handsome father, David "Lefty" McKeag, was one of the finest pitchers on the South Shore. Already well known for his success on the mound locally and in the Eastern League, he had signed a professional contract with the Boston Braves (now the Atlanta Braves), and pitched for their top minor league team in Hartford, Connecticut, making him somewhat of a local celebrity-hero.

After winning all nine junior varsity games as a sophomore at Weymouth High School and starting for the Junior Legion team during the summers, I dared hope that I, too, might become a professional ballplayer. In my junior year, Coach Jack Fisher named me the starting pitcher for the opening game against Brockton, a formidable rival and home town of boxing greats Rocky Marciano and later, Marvin Hagler. After pitching two innings in an intra-squad game the day before, coach told me to hit the shower, go home and get some rest before the next day's game. Although I was nervous, I felt pretty confident I could do well.

As I headed back to the locker room however, I was joined by another team mate, Doug MacLeod who, ironically, was heading home for a doctor's appointment. As we began walking towards the gym, Doug and I were joking around, relaxed and swaggering a bit. Suddenly, several members of the track team packed into a car, pulled up next to us and yelled, "Hey! Jump on the hood and we'll give you a ride!" Not wanting to look like chickens, both of us climbed on board.

But the moment the driver put the pedal to the floor I knew we were in trouble. Roaring ahead at top speed, the driver suddenly slammed on the brakes, screeching to a halt in front of the locker room. Dougie grabbed the car's aerial and front ornament but I had nothing left to grab. Bracing myself, I figured my only hope was to jump. But when I did, my spikes caught on the bumper and I was slammed onto the pavement, cutting my jaw and dislocating my right shoulder. Just before passing out, I could feel my shoulder bone scraping my right ear and being a right-handed pitcher, I knew right then that my dreams of a future in baseball were over.

Twenty years later, married and living on Cape Cod, I was playing tennis with a chiropractor friend and felt a nagging pain in my right shoulder. A day later in his office, he took a full body X-ray. Putting it under the clips at the top of the viewer, he leaned forward to take a closer look at my skull. When he asked, "How did you fracture your neck?" I was shocked. Then my mind flashed back to that terrible day in high school.

Assistant Coach Leo Hayes was in the locker room when the accident occurred and rushed to help. But there was no 911 in those days so when I came to and seemed fine, he didn't see the need for an ambulance. Instead, Coach Hayes stabilized my shoulder, put me in his car and drove to the South Shore Hospital, about twenty minutes away.

After standing in my uniform for twenty minutes

with blood on my jaw and my shoulder bone sticking out of my shirt, Coach Hayes complained that neither the nurses nor the doctors had responded. In a loud shout he demanded they do something but although a nurse stopped and apologized, she explained we'd have to wait until the doctor was available.

"Did they at least take an X-ray?" my chiropractor friend asked. "Nope," I said, and explained that by the time the doctor arrived and began manipulating my shoulder, the tissue around the joint had swelled so much he couldn't get it back into the socket. The pain was so bad I thought I was going to pass out again but finally he slipped it back in place. The doctor then placed my arm in a sling, patted me on the back, and said "You'll be okay, just keep ice on it." Coach Hayes drove me home with neither he nor I nor apparently the doctor ever knowing that in addition to my dislocated shoulder, I had also broken my neck.

After a short pause, my chiropractor friend looked at me and said, "Dislocating that shoulder may have been a blessing. With that kind of an injury, if you'd kept playing and re-injured your neck, you could have ended up crippled or paralyzed for life." After years of whining about that stupid accident I still had plenty of resentment over it. But those X-rays and my friend's words brought me back to earth. The bitterness over baseball was gone and suddenly I realized just how lucky I had been.

When I returned to school, several friends, fellow

students and even some teachers came up to me in the halls to say they were sorry. But it was my biology teacher, Mr. John "Jack" Delahunt, who still stands out in my mind. Gruff and tough with a pair of hands like meat cleavers, he liked to throw erasers at the pigeons when the windows of his third floor classroom were open. Someone was assigned to retrieve the erasers in the parking lot after class. Mr. Delahunt never talked much to students but as I left class that day, he called me back.

Coming from behind his desk, he put his heavy arm on my shoulders and said, "Don't let this get to you, Donny. You'll do fine. This is just a bump in the road." The last person I ever expected to show such concern was my biology teacher, Mr. Delahunt, and I never forgot it.

Having a professional ballplayer as a father was definitely a mixed blessing. I was awed by his past and proud to be his son but at the same time, felt I could never live up to him. His roommate with the Hartford Bees had been a Texan named Vernon Bickford who went on to the big club, pitched a no-hitter against the Brooklyn Dodgers, and went on to play in a World Series. My father on the other hand, by then thirty-nine years old, re-injured his arm and was released. My mother had told me how deeply disappointed Dad had been when he came home from Hartford and his baseball career meant a lot to me. But since he'd never attended my games or spent any time with me, I wasn't prepared for his reaction when Coach Hayes dropped me off from the hospital that day. When he saw my face bandaged and my pitching arm in a sling, his eyes filled with tears and it was the first time I'd ever seen him cry. I was already upset but when he said, "I'm sorry, Donny, but baseball was the only thing in life I could've helped you with," I was crushed.

Even a kid knows dreams mean nothing unless you make them happen. Playing for a good college, then making it even to the minor leagues is always a long shot but that was my dream. Now not only was that shattered for me, I'd also let my father down. Losing the chance to play baseball consequently hurt our relationship more deeply than it probably did for other fathers and sons. By becoming a star in baseball, I'd hoped to make Dad proud and also thought that my success might compensate for the pain and disappointment life had handed him. That didn't happen though.

Nearly two decades later, when I was thirty-two and married, I was the so-called clean-up hitter for the Gay Nineties softball team, a Cape restaurant I was working at for the summer. We were playing an off-Cape team from Dedham, Massachusetts one Sunday and since our games in the past had always been slow pitch, I would often hit home runs.

But on the only day my father came to a game, and with my father-in law no less, the rival team had a fast pitch ringer with them who refused to play slow-pitch. Rather than call the game off and look like wimps, our team agreed to play. Even with several former college players on our team, we weren't used to fast pitching and our timing was off. We only got three hits the whole game and I struck out twice then popped up in my final bat.

It sounds strange to be mentioning this, but when I heard my sixty-two year old father, yelling at me from his seat in the bleachers to "Shorten up on the bat!" all the disappointment of my high school years came flooding back and I was furious at Fate once again. The game meant nothing but I felt I'd failed my father once again.

I don't believe any son ever truly gets over being a disappointment to his father and that old wound has probably had a lot to do with why I've been competing so hard ever since – not in sports but in that very public male marathon called "Becoming A Success."

This memoir is about dreamers and their dreams as well as the highs and lows of that marathon, one I survived to run again and again after hitting the wall. Most of all it is a thank you to the many talented, brilliant, famous and sometimes obscure people I met along the way. The road was long and pitted with potholes, some of which I foolishly ignored and for which I paid a painful personal cost. Still, the journey has been worth it, if only because of the excitement of the race and the challenge of pitting hope, opportunity and hubris against the shenanigans of Lady Luck.

CHAPTER 2

FAMILY LEGACIES

L to R: Lilly McKeag, Florence McKeag, David McKeag
1914 – Blackpool England

I was born and grew up in Weymouth, Massachusetts, the second oldest settlement in northeast America. Its coastal area and proximity to Boston attracted a mixed population that included descendants of the original colonial settlers as well as immigrant families like the one from which I descended. Today the population is well over 50,000 but in the post-World War II years while I was a boy, Weymouth was a relatively small town of factories and homes.

Like most immigrants at that time, the McKeag and Wilson families had a strong work ethic. There was also inherent athletic ability and musical talent which if traced through my family's past could have been instructive to me. But I was too young at first and later too driven to take any notice.

In the fifties, life at home usually centered around the father. And David "Lefty" McKeag, was the man who would unwittingly mold my life in the image of his own. For centuries, stories have been written about father and son relationships. Plays and movies about them are performed all over the world and while some of this may have helped, I suspect that most fathers still remain oblivious to how much their lives affect those of their sons.

Tragedy was an event that seemed to run though my family history along with its handmaiden, fear. And both elements affected my father from an early age but I never understood that until well after his death.

According to my mother, my father's first bout with intense fear occurred on Tuesday, October 28, 1913, when he was only three years old. He, his mother, Florence Wilson McKeag, and his two-year old sister Lily, began a transatlantic voyage from England aboard the Cunard Line's RMS Franconia to Boston, Massachusetts, USA, and by all accounts, the vicious weather conditions during their crossing made it one of the worst on record. Huddling with other passengers in family groups as the ship tossed and turned through the North Atlantic along the same route taken eighteen months previously by the RMS Titanic, my family must have been terrified. According to family legend, the three were to sail the maiden voyage of the Titanic a year earlier, but cancelled the trip when Lily became ill.

In late autumn of 1913 my grandfather, David McKeag, Sr. stood on the dock at the Port of Boston awaiting the arrival of his wife and children on the RMS Franconia but when they finally arrived, their reunion was tense. The children were so traumatized they wouldn't talk. And after that my grandmother refused to ride in any kind of a boat for the rest of her life.

David McKeag Sr., was a talented master plasterer and hard worker but also had an affinity for "the drink." As the sole Irishman in the family, he resented being treated like an outsider by his English teatotaling in laws and felt they treated his Irish heritage as a curse. To make matters worse, David's five brothers and sisters, who were supposed to join him either in Weymouth or Quincy, remained either in their home town of Grey Abbey, Northern Ireland or in Blackpool, England, where they were working.

Feeling betrayed and abandoned, David severed all family ties to Ireland and began drinking more heavily. His marriage gradually deteriorated until things finally came to a head. During a night of carousing with friends, my grandfather became the victim of a bad railroad accident and lost his right leg. No longer able to work, his attitude became increasingly sour.

Other family traits – musical ability and the work ethic – were suddenly called upon to mitigate the family's dire financial situation. My grandmother, Florence Wilson, born in the seaside resort town of Blackpool, England, learned to play piano when she was just a little girl. During the late nineteenth century, Blackpool had built a replica of the Eiffel Tower which helped the town become a playground for the wealthy and popular tourist attraction for the middle class. As a twelve year old, Florence, worked in the tower selling scarves to tourists. And whenever Blackpool held a parade, she would be asked to play the piano on a horse-drawn wagon converted into a float while sitting on bales of hay. Later, she also earned money by playing piano in the pits of movie theaters showing silent movies.

Because jobs were so scarce in Northern Ireland, the William McKeag family had moved to Blackpool in the late 1800s hoping to find work. William's second son, David met Florence Wilson at that time and in June 1906 they wed. Seven years later, they had two children but the job market hadn't improved. Other Wilson family members had migrated to America in 1907 so David decided to join them. He sailed first and Florence came later with their two young children, my father, David Jr. and Lily.

Before moving to North Weymouth, the family settled in Braintree where David Sr. found employment as a plasterer. Florence played the piano for churches of all faiths and made extra money doing minstrel shows which were the craze at the time. However, not long after David Sr. lost his leg and job, the black-faced minstrel shows disappeared because of their racial overtones. Florence continued playing the piano for churches and other Weymouth organizations but also began taking in laundry.

Then came that blistering summer morning when my grandfather, her husband, dressed as if he were going to work, asked a friend to drive him to the Fore River Bridge. He said he wanted to watch the activity in the shipyard. But, as soon as his friend stepped away, he jumped off the bridge, leaving a wife and two children to fend for themselves. Friends said he felt guilty that he could no longer support his family, but more likely his suicide was prompted by alcohol.

David Sr. was only thirty-seven when he died and the family buried him in a Quincy cemetery, about a mile from the bridge and shipyard. Whether because it was a suicide or for other reasons known only to the family, his grave remained unmarked for over eighty years until I found it in 2003. There is now a small headstone with his name and dates on it beneath which I've added the word Forgiven. Although alcohol had ruined his life and created sadness and difficulties for the family he left behind, nearly fifty years later, when near death herself, my grandmother still asked that the name Florence McKeag be prominent on her gravestone, in addition to Horn, the name of her second husband.

A dozen years after her father, David Sr.'s death, Lily, my Dad's fourteen-year old sister, had developed into a happy, blonde, blue-eyed and beautiful girl. Life was going well until one sunny day when Lily was at the beach with friends and stepped on a tin can. When the cut became infected, gangrene set in and in 1925 there was no penicillin to save her. Near the end, her skin turned black and she began dying a slow and painful death. My grandmother Florence, blind and crazed with grief, insisted my father visit the hospital to say goodbye to his sister. Seeing her in that condition was such a shock that Dad ran from the hospital screaming and stopping only when he could no longer catch his breath.

Lily's death left my father as the last McKeag in the family and given the bias against the Irish at the turn of the century, no one told him about his Irish roots or that he had relatives in Ireland. Instead, he was told he was Scottish, a deception his mother's family justified because anyone Irish was presumed to be Catholic. Signs saying N.I.N.A. - No Irish Need Apply - were posted in stores, making it tougher for Irishmen to get jobs.

In 1926, like most of her family, my grandmother worked at Fore River Shipyard, where she met and married Alfred Horn, a kind and hardworking shipyard worker from Quincy. Within a few years, they had two daughters, Freda and Margery, but even though my father loved his sisters and his stepfather Alfred was good to him, Dad often kept to himself. By then, he was a rising star in baseball and that sport became his identity. Frequently he ate his meals and slept overnight at his friend Joe Kelly's house even though Grampa Horn was obviously so proud of him that he kept a scrapbook filled with pictures and articles throughout his baseball career.

I remember Grampa Horn as a quiet man who raised prize dahlias in the back yard. He was widely loved but one snowy night tragedy struck again. While walking home after playing cards with his friends at the town tavern, a passing car, unable to see through the snow, hit that good man and he died instantly. Once again, my grandmother was left to grieve.

When I was a small boy, my father was still playing baseball in the Boston Braves' organization and my parents would sometimes travel to Boston for weekends during the winter. My sister Judy and I would stay with Grammie Horn and often could hear her in the cellar shoveling coal into the basement furnace. After stoking the fire, she'd climb up the rickety narrow staircase, wash her hands, and make us breakfast or lunch. We soon learned to avoid the big heat register in the center of her tiny living room after burning our feet several times.

My grandmother made tea the old fashioned way with loose tea leaves rather than tea bags. And when we finished eating, she would read our fortunes from the designs made by the leaves in the bottom of the cups. Her old upright piano stood in the corner, always covered with the latest sheet music, and after a dessert of vanilla tapioca, she'd sit and play for us. Other than her piano, my grandmother had few material things. But having her play for us was something I'll never forget and it was a priceless gift.

Although the welfare department sent a small check every month, she still played piano for several churches for extra money but my father paid her major household expenses. At the time of David Sr.'s suicide, there was no health insurance, workman's compensation or paid sick days, so by the time Dad reached high school, he dropped out to work and help with expenses. Before long, however, he also became a baseball star. One night, after pitching a big game under the lights in front of two thousand people, a Yale graduate came to the bench and said if Dad would finish high school, he could get him into Yale. But by then it was too late. He was too old to qualify for admission and that missed opportunity would haunt him throughout his life. I believe Dad's lack of education always intensified his other insecurities.

Music, as well as baseball, was another important part

of his life. Grammie's half-brother, Uncle" Jack Brooks, a saddle maker and trumpet player back in England, brought his horn to her house one day and introduced my dad to the trumpet. After playing for a while, he handed the horn to my dad - who he called Davy - and showed him how to hold the horn and blow air through the valves. Dad was hooked.

Uncle Jack was quite an interesting character. Even as a little kid, I remember him telling me to make sure I visited "the most beautiful place in the world" before I died. It was Cape Town, South Africa where he stayed every winter in hotels who paid for his expenses by keeping their guests safe by killing the snakes around their premises.

Back in the 1890s, the most famous marching band in the world was The John Phillip Souza Band with its many brass instruments. Mr. Sousa wrote most of the marches himself and his band toured the world and entertained royalty. Today its songs are still part of our military musical heritage.

Mr. Nelson Bernier was the band's first cornetist. No one knew where Uncle Jack found him or how he got him to give young Davy lessons, but my uncle wanted to find out if his nephew had real talent before he went further with his training.

Consequently every Wednesday morning, Uncle Jack hired Mr. Bernier to take the trolley from Quincy and walk uphill to my grandmother's home at 14 Crescent Road in North Weymouth, to give young Davy his cornet lesson. My father's talent was immediately obvious and after studying for a short time but still taking lessons, he began playing in local bands and at Boston hotels. That is, unless he had a ball game to pitch somewhere.

Once Dad became a star however, with his name and picture appearing in newspapers, he thought about giving up the trumpet to concentrate on baseball. My father asked my grandmother to break the news to Mr. Bernier, but she refused, insisting she wasn't going do it. He'd have to tell him himself. After his next lesson, my father told the portly gentleman he was giving up his music and Mr. Bernier's eyes welled up with tears. Pleading with him not to give up the trumpet, the famous cornet player pleaded, "David, I'll give you lessons for free! You can't stop. You play with your soul! The trumpet will be with you long after baseball is gone. Please Davy, don't give it up." Seeing him so upset, Dad couldn't let him down and agreed to continue playing.

As a brilliant performer on the pitcher's mound, baseball made "Lefty" McKeag famous. But Mr. Bernier's prediction proved right. Long after baseball, Dad nourished his soul by continuing to play the trumpet and gave joy to others for many years.

When my parents began wintering in Florida, they became participating members of a non-denominational prayer group at a local church. Dad's seventieth birthday fell on a Sunday when I was still running the restaurant in Hyannis. But when I learned the church group had asked him to play the trumpet during the church service that day, I decided to book a flight and show up as a surprise. The church was overflowing and when that man with the white hair rose and began to play Amazing Grace, it was as if Gabriel himself were there. Every note was perfect.

When he finished, the church became eerily quiet and many eyes were wet; including mine.

My grandmother and father's musical talents carried into the next generation. My sister Judy started taking piano lessons when she was fourteen and three years later, began studying organ with Ira Bates, an organist and teacher famous for his recording of Stormy Weather. Ira had been appearing at the 1200 Beacon Restaurant in Boston for many years and would often ask Judy to sit in with him. Before she got married and left the area, I was always so proud to see her performing at other Boston area and Cape Cod restaurants.

For several years at home, we used to have jam sessions with Dad playing the trumpet, Judy on the piano, and me doing the singing. But once Judy began playing the organ, the piano remained untouched so I began tinkering with it.

Thanks to my grandmother, I'd inherited some ability to play a little by ear. I learned some chords but lacked the discipline to take lessons and practice. Besides, as a teenager my social life was more important! Dad would yell, "Donny! Get off that piano until you know what you're doing!" and of course he was right. So I took a few lessons, practiced just enough to get by, and began playing and singing in different bars and restaurants on Cape Cod. I knew I was capable of being much better, but people seemed to like what I did. Of course there were always pretty girls and enough noise in the room to take the focus off my music, but I would always regret not working harder on my talent.

After his father's suicide, the family warned Dad about the dangers of alcohol – a warning he heeded as a young man- and even though drinking and partying were always part of the music and sporting worlds, my father never touched a drop of alcohol during more than twenty years of playing professional baseball and playing trumpet in clubs and Boston hotels.

During World War II, Fore River built more ships than any other yard in the country. The yard workers were considered part of the war effort and exempt from the service, especially when, like my father, they were married with children. Dad worked in the machine shop, next to the same bridge his own father had jumped from twenty years earlier, and coincidentally, my mother's father, Murray Parker, was his boss.

He was also pitching for different local teams and playing trumpet other nights to make extra money. When I was older, my mother told me that when dad was playing trumpet in Quincy or Boston during the war years, so many men were away in the service that lonely women would sneak into his car and lock themselves inside after the band finished. They would try to get him to take them partying, but he would say no, come home and laugh when he told my mother about it. Years later, I asked relatives to confirm that story which they did; telling me that during those years Dad lived a wholesome, sober life and throughout his long baseball career, never ran around.

But something happened when he turned forty. No longer in the limelight as a baseball star, his life during the post-war years suddenly narrowed down to just running a small variety store seven days a week. Compounding that was the necessity of supporting a wife and two children. When the insidious demon called alcohol showed up, he was ill-prepared and everything changed. One night after work, he was invited to a Christmas party and decided to sample the spiked punch. It was Dad's first taste of alcohol and when nothing happened, he decided he liked it. After that, he'd occasionally stop for a drink with his buddies at the local bar and having a few drinks temporarily eased his unhappiness with life after baseball. But as his drinking increased his personality changed and problems began at home.

Dad was my boyhood hero but some of the things he'd witnessed when very young had left deep psychic scars. Among these were the terror of the ocean crossing, his father's drunken rages and subsequent suicide, his sister's ghastly death and the fact that he never finished school. His way of coping was to become angry. I loved him but his loud outbursts scared me to death and, like many other sons, for the rest of my life I would resent not having been able to live up to his expectations and my own.

At home there were nasty arguments, a drunk-driving episode, and finally, a deterioration of Dad's once impeccable personal appearance. I remember feeling my mother's discomfort when we were at a restaurant and he flirted with a waitress. Simultaneously, he also seemed to resent women. Sometimes, when just the two of us were in the car, he'd complain about women in general. I never thought I'd been affected but as events later proved, I, too, soon distrusted women.

As his drinking progressed, my father's moods grew unpredictable. Most days he would be super affectionate with me, my sister and my mother. Other times however, he'd seem indifferent. When we visited relatives during the holidays, I could never understand why he never hugged or showed any real affection to his sisters or especially his own mother. Even as a boy it seemed strange and made me uncomfortable.

Although my father loved his family and was outgoing, often the life of the party, he had his demons. Having watched his own dreams evaporate, he could never conceal his anger and disappointment with life for long. I think Dad was tormented by the thought that his life had ultimately been a failure and as a result, was never truly happy.

In the years after he'd stopped drinking, I'd try to talk with him about family matters or ask for advice. But in every conversation, something would set him off. He'd start yelling and that would be the end of the discussion. Finally, I stopped trying. His path should have been a warning to me, but it wasn't. I ended up following the same path he did and still have a hard time understanding why.

CHAPTER 3
BOYHOOD DAYS

Center: The author acting as MC for the Weymouth HS sports rally, 1957.

My grandparents' houses were less than a half a mile from each other but my mother and father didn't meet until both were attending nearby Athens Elementary School. In the first half of the twentieth century, many Weymouth residents worked for the Bethlehem Steel Company at Fore River Shipyard just over the bridge from North Weymouth into Quincy. My maternal grandfather, Murray Parker, headed the machine shop there and my father's stepfather, Fred Horn, worked there as a pipe fitter. Grampa Parker had a car but Grampa Horn did not and that, combined with their different jobs, meant my dad's family had a little less social status.

That never really mattered however and after my parents married, they built a house in South Weymouth on Blanchard Road a new street near the South Weymouth Naval Air Base. The base housed servicemen and provided hangars for old combat planes, new jet planes and blimps. As a boy I used to bike five miles with my friends to watch either the "Thunderbirds" of the Air Force or the Navy's "Blue Angels" present air shows. Even though we covered our ears, the noise was so loud they hurt. On our way home we'd stop before pedaling home for an ice cream cone at Kramer's Dairy Farm, next to the base and watch the cows and pigs roam around the barn.

The Weymouth Fairgrounds was down the street from our house and I always looked forward to its opening in the summer when there was horse racing. Since I loved horses, I'd get up at five am, hop on my bike and head down Ralph Talbot Street to clean the stables. Feeding and walking race horses never seemed like work to me and although I didn't get paid, someone always bought me a hot dog, a soda, and potato chips for lunch.

But when my Uncle Fred and Aunt Doris Klay finished building their summer cottage in Hyannis, my days at the Weymouth Fair were over and replaced with staying with the Klays on weekends on Cape Cod. In a short time, we grew to love the Cape and after the first two years, they sold the cottage and bought a larger house on Lake Wequaquet in Centerville where we spent many more happy times with them, swimming and water skiing. Thanks again to Uncle Fred and Aunt Doris, those were some of the best times in my life.

Then one autumn weekend as my aunt and uncle drove through Vermont, they decided to spend part of the next summer there. Their three week vacation in the mountains also gave me the opportunity to live and work on a farm.

During World War II many sons left the family farm to join the Service, which left the parents with empty bedrooms and little help in the fields. To offset the lost revenue and help fill the empty nests, some farmers' wives started what might have been the first country farm B&B's.

My aunt and uncle, along with their sons Rich and Ron, stayed at the Phillip Nelson farm in South Ryegate, Vermont near St. Johnsbury. The Nelsons raised Jersey cows and sold milk, cream and butter. Since Phillip's two brothers owned adjoining farms, the three families planted, harvested and maintained over a hundred acres of pasture land, fruit orchards and wooded areas.

The Klays enjoyed the summer of 1950 so much that they asked us to join them the next year. Mom and Dad liked the idea and the following August, we headed for the mountains and stayed through Labor Day. All kids slept on cots in a long room that was once the study but parents had their own bedroom. Every morning, Mrs. Nelson cooked a breakfast of eggs, bacon, and milk from the farm and her home-baked oatmeal bread was the best. I loved farming so much I'd get up at four a.m. to help Mr. Nelson bring in the cows for milking (not knowing they'd come in on their own), and that led my mother to ask "How come you can get up so early on the farm but are always late for school?"

Pitching hay, reaching under chickens to gather eggs and riding on the mower next to Mister Nelson was a wonderful life experience and for a while, I even thought of becoming a farmer. That is, until I saw Mr. Nelson working morning, noon and night every day but Sunday and came to my senses.

Sunday was barbeque time. Fresh ground hamburgers and hotdogs from the grille were served on fresh baked rolls with home-made pickles, corn on the cob and a salad with fresh picked lettuce, tomatoes, shucked peas, cucumbers and onions right out of the garden. Everyone prepared their own plates and sat at tables next to a man-made pool called The Ice Box fed by a mountain stream. If it got too hot and muggy we'd take a swim but could never stay in too long because the water was freezing even in the summer.

The Nelson's oldest son Lawrence had been a pilot in World War II and lost an arm and part of his leg when his plane was shot down over Germany. Often he came by on Sundays to enjoy the cookout and take a swim. But even though I was just a young boy, seeing him by the pool removing the leather straps on his prostheses, I understood he would never be able to run the farm. I can still remember that scene and how badly I felt for him and the Nelsons.

Twenty years later while I was teaching at Rockland High School, a town that still had farms, I was talking to my class about farming and asked the students how many had ever patted a cow, ridden a horse, or reached under a chicken to get a fresh laid egg. Out of all my classes, only three students had even petted a farm animal. Today's youth would benefit greatly from having more contact with nature and less with sex, drugs and video games. But nature isn't much of a priority today and I'm grateful to have had the chance to live and work on a farm.

CHAPTER 4
FORMATIVE PASSIONS

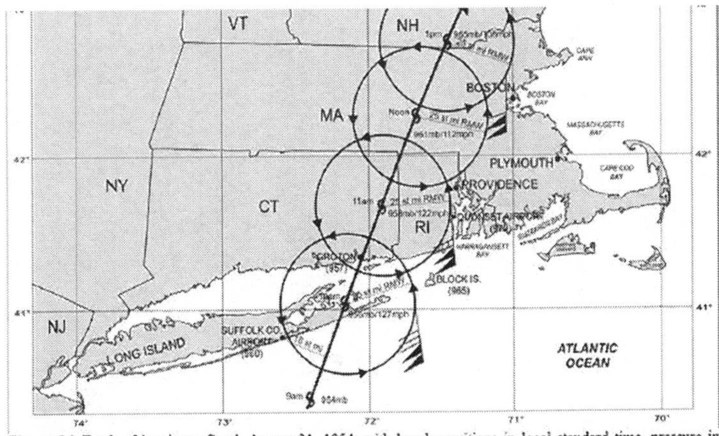

Figure 5.2 Track of hurricane Carol, August 31, 1954, with hourly positions in local standard time, pressure in millibars and SLOSH model maximum over water 1-minute wind speed in miles per hour. Circles represent location of maximum wind with radius given in statute miles. Wind vectors show where maximum wind is occurring at that time. Wind barbs in mph. http://www.aoml.noaa.gov

Hurricane Carol's devastating path from August 31, 1954.

Thanks to my aunt and uncle, Cape Cod was in my blood. But before long, the restaurant business would be as well. And that's probably because for some crazy reason, my father bought a restaurant in the spring of 1953; I only say "crazy" because he knew absolutely nothing about the restaurant business.

The Skipper Restaurant was a deceptively cute little place on South Shore Drive across from the town beach in South Yarmouth so after school let out, our family packed up and headed for the Cape. Mr. Arnold Burch, the original owner, built the place in 1950 to serve breakfast and lunch for guests staying across the street at his upscale beachfront property, The Yarmouth Seaside Village. He also owned The Colonial Candle Company in Hyannis but after a year, realizing he didn't want to deal with the restaurant, sold it. Dad was the third owner in three years which should have raised a red flag.

Hurricane Carol hit the Cape and Islands in late August 1954 just before Labor Day, causing massive damage and power outages and costing the region's businesses millions of dollars. After the storm went out to sea, leaving downed trees, stripped roofs and flooded streets, Mr. Burch arrived for breakfast, told my father that a light pole outside illuminating the Skipper was still on his electric bill and wanted Dad to pay him five dollars a month for the electricity. I was just a fourteen year old kid but after my father told him where he could put the light and the pole, I realized Mr. Burch had just given me my first glimpse of insensitivity and greed. No matter how much money he had or how successful he became, he would always be a miserable man.

Years later, when Mr. Burch put a shotgun to his head and pulled the trigger, I didn't feel a bit sympathetic. Now, though, I realize no one can ever really know another person's life, even if they seem to have it all superficially.

In those days, Cape Cod businesses depended on a ten-week summer season that began when school let out in June and ended on Labor Day. Business owners who didn't make enough money in the summer had a tough time surviving the winter. After suffering through two hurricanes in three years, Dad wasn't able to recover. He'd lost his shirt and about twenty pounds during that stressful time and finally, realizing how difficult the restaurant business was, especially a seasonal one, he threw in the towel. Reluctantly, we headed back home to Weymouth and although that restaurant had been unsuccessful, I knew I liked it.

The Skipper was a family project and I had enjoyed watching my mother, relatives (including my grandparents) and friends working together. Everyone pitched in painting the building inside and out, varnishing the furniture, cleaning and oiling the floors and hanging new wallpaper in the dining rooms. Mom was an expert at wallpapering and decorating but landscaping also needed to be done. Flower beds had to be planted, and window boxes filled so my sister Judy and I did that and more -- scrubbing kitchen equipment, stocking shelves, and washing windows.

The previous owner had hired an all-black kitchen staff from Roxbury and since they had worked at The Skipper before, Dad gladly welcomed them back. They lived in cramped quarters over the restaurant with no bathroom or air conditioning and had to use the outside staircase to get fresh air and for the bathroom facilities. While that meant going outside, they never complained and were good workers.

Sam Jones was the dishwasher and prep man. A kind and gentle man with piercing blue eyes and an easy smile, whenever we worked together on the dish machine he always made us fresh lemonade and we laughed a lot. I helped him scour the pots and pans, peel potatoes and do whatever else was needed. I served as the dining room busboy in the dining room but enjoyed being in the kitchen where the action was. As a result, I did both, an experience that later stood me in good stead when I owned my own restaurants. When Sam went for his mail at the post office, a mile or two down South Shore Drive, he took me with him. I was under the legal driving age, but sometimes he took a back dirt road and let me drive his gray, 1948 Plymouth coupe which made me feel like a big shot. Meanwhile our family car was a canary yellow, four-door, 1950 Studebaker Commander for which my father took a lot of razzing. People said they couldn't tell if he was coming or going because the front and the rear ends of a Studebaker were both shaped into a point.

When the power went out during that first hurricane, we stayed open. Dad knew the tourists staying in the waterfront hotels along the street were flooded out and since the roads were closed they had no place to go. Fortunately, the gas was still on in our kitchen so we could still cook and with lots of candles, could see well enough. But when anyone opened the front door, sea water poured in. Immediately I ran through the dining room, mopping like crazy, repeatedly emptying the bucket outside along with bussing tables and washing the dishes. Dad even went up on the roof one time to try to nail down some loose shingles.

In the aftermath of the 1953 hurricane, one man came across the street wearing only his underwear. The tide had pushed through the walls into his rooms sucking away all his clothes and luggage. Even his wallet was gone. But Dad didn't care. He found a chef's coat and pants for him to wear, gave him a seat at the bar, poured him a stiff drink and told him to relax. Even though the place was packed, my father took time to get the guy something to eat.

Despite the fact that his restaurant was going broke, Dad refused to charge that man and several others. During that wild and crazy night, we served over a hundred meals to many grateful people; Dad kept the restaurant open until the food and candles ran out, and I was very proud to be his son.

I can't remember any racial incidents at that time but being young, I never thought about it.

The kitchen crew stayed upstairs most of the time and never mixed with the staff. During their day off I'd watch them get into their cars and head off to parts unknown. That was how it was in the '50s. All I remember is that after we sold the place, I missed my friend Sam very much.

The actress Dorothy Lamour was staying at an elegant new hotel just down the street, called The Surf and Sand which was allegedly built inside and out using only mahogany wood. The morning she arrived at The Skipper she was wearing a black dress with a matching wide-brimmed hat while carrying a little white dog. Any fourteen year old kid would think it strange for someone to be eating breakfast with a dog in their lap but I felt more than that. I was so nervous when she sat down at her table, I spilled water on her. My father was upset with me but Miss Lamour just smiled and said "Honey don't you worry about it," sipped her coffee and ordered breakfast. Imagine anyone today being so classy and dressing that way just to have breakfast?

We lived in a trailer park the first summer but after that my parents rented a house on the street behind the restaurant. My sister Judy and I made friends with some kids living near us and when their parents had cookouts, our family was often invited. Everyone loved it when Dad brought his trumpet and even strangers showed up to see where the music was coming from. He always ended the night playing Taps and as the last note faded, everything fell silent. Then the whole neighborhood would erupt in loud cheering.

Dad had more bad luck when another hurricane hit the Cape the following summer. As the storm moved out to sea the power remained out, but I convinced some kids to go on a bike excursion to check out the damage. Several houses on the beach had been lifted off their foundations and were now in the marshes across the street. Boats were stranded all along Route 28, a good half mile away from the ocean. An inch or two of seawater was still on the roads and salt had killed shrubs and turned the green lawns brown.

Early the next morning, big trucks with cranes on them lumbered down the road to lift the beach houses back onto their foundations. After the trucks left, the homeowners cleaned up the mess and moved back in. Everything went smoothly and no one thought anything about it. That wouldn't happen today. It was too simple a solution and didn't cost people money.

During the 1950's, the only radio station on the Cape and the islands, Station WOCB, was located on Sea Street in West Yarmouth and owned by The New Bedford Standard Times newspaper. As our post-hurricane crew peddled down Route 28 passing stranded boats and damaged buildings, we spotted the radio tower on the horizon and decided to ride over there to see how it had handled the storm.

The Hayes family, from Brockton, lived down the

street from us and two of their daughters, Nancy and Joey, were members of our crew. When we arrived at the radio building, I saw a man inside sitting behind a microphone broadcasting the news and approached the window to sneak a peek. Nancy and Joey were afraid we'd get kicked off the property but the radio man was alone. Besides, the neighbors were so busy cleaning up they wouldn't have noticed.

Nancy Hayes would marry John Sununu, a governor of New Hampshire and Chief of Staff for President George H.W. Bush, and have eight children. And who would believe that forty years later, I'd be on the air doing a morning radio show in the same building, looking out the same window, at a tower still standing in the same place!

Vern Coleman, our station engineer, was a fifth generation Cape Codder from Hyannis who had returned to the Cape after a long career working for Boston radio and television stations. He now served as a consulting engineer for several different radio stations, ours being one. One morning I bumped into him in the hall after which we had coffee together. Somehow or other my 1954 hurricane story came up and after hearing my yarn, Vern sat back, smiled and proceeded to tell me he had been that twenty-three year old kid doing the news on the microphone that stormy day. Needless to say, we were both stunned by that crazy coincidence.

Although I didn't know it at the time, that summer would also give me a glimpse into my unsettling future with women. My first real girlfriend and two of her friends visited me at the restaurant and after our cooks made a picnic lunch for us, we went to the beach across the street. We had a great time swimming and talking that day, and it was the first time I'd ever thought of someone as my girl.

But when I returned home after the summer and stopped by her house after baseball practice a crazy thing happened. We were eating lunch in the kitchen when the swinging door flew open and her older sister walked in. Instantly I was smitten; her sparkling personality, beautiful figure and terrific smile immediately squelched the feelings I'd once had for "my girl." I knew it was stupid but after that, every time my girl and I were together, I kept thinking about her sister. Realizing how impossible the situation was and knowing how guilty I'd feel if I told her, I took the easy way out and just stopped seeing her.

So there it was. At fourteen, I was already on the path of becoming discontent in any relationship I'd have with women. And down the road, my life would suffer greatly because of it.

CHAPTER 5
A TEENAGER IN THE 50S

Singing Istanbul by the Four Lads in 1957 at Weymouth HS.
L to R: The author, Dick Hassan, Ken Ericson, Bob Nolan

Despite having an uneasy relationship with my father, my teenage years seemed fairly typical. Like other male high school students, I wanted a car of my own and was willing to work for the money to buy and support it. After school and on Sundays I worked as a soda jerk for my next door neighbor, Mr. Campbell, who owned Nash's Drug Store in Columbian Square, two blocks from our homes. The day I turned sixteen, the elderly lady working with me, knowing I was looking for a car, surprised me by saying she had one stored in her barn. It hadn't been driven for years but I could look at it if I'd like.

The car was a 1941 Plymouth four door sedan, the color of pea soup, and the moment I saw it I loved it. They called the rear doors suicide doors because they opened out to make it easier to jump. Even after all that time in storage, when I turned the key she started right up and ran like a top. The interior was in perfect shape; the chrome was beautiful with no rust, and the lady was only asking $100. When I said "Sold", she was happy for both of us. I knew I'd have to buy new tires because the rubber had dried out after being on blocks for so long. Mom gave me fifty dollars toward the purchase but also said that was it. From then on, I'd have to pay for all the expenses myself.

As soon as the car was registered, I called my best friends, Pete Stilphen and Donny "Jake" Jacobson, and they joined me for a cruise to Nantasket Beach. We cranked up the Mopar radio, went looking for girls and stopped at Joe's Clam Shack for a pint of fried clams that cost sixty cents. Gas was only seventeen cents a gallon then but we changed our own oil using the reconditioned green stuff in unlabeled long necked bottles that cost fifteen cents a quart. It all seemed so carefree in those days. We all had jobs and none of us drank or smoked.

Nantasket is part of Hull, Massachusetts and an easy drive or short sail from Boston. Across from the beach stood Paragon Park, a large amusement park that featured the usual rides including a fabulous roller coaster called Cyclone. Before the Southeast Expressway provided quicker access to Cape Cod, crowds of New Englanders visited for the weekend or for summer vacations. During the 1920's and 1930's, wealthy Bostonians and politicians, including the Mayor of Boston "Honey Fitz" Fitzgerald and banker Joseph P. Kennedy, owned beach houses and spent summers there. Little did I know that decades later, I would meet and be friendly with some of their family members on Cape Cod.

Ever since sophomore year in high school, my buddy Peter Stilphen had been president of the class and I had been vice president. Massachusetts then sponsored a program called "Boys State," which gave every town an opportunity for two high school boys to stay at the University of Massachusetts at Amherst, attend classes on government and participate in sporting events. Pete and I were chosen to represent the town of Weymouth and did well in the sporting events. Pete came close to two university records in track events and I did well in baseball and one race in track.

Coaches at UMass ran the games and after Boys State ended, would talk to some of us about going to school there. We were both approached but any opportunity I might have had ended after my shoulder injury. Unfortunately, Pete suffered the same fate later that summer during an unsupervised pre-season football practice. Both high school and college players were working out at Weymouth's Legion Field when Dick Lasse, a former Weymouth High lineman and teammate of future NFL hall-of-famer Jimmy Brown at Syracuse University, threw Pete a pass. Peter was one of the best backs in the state and could leap higher than most. But that time, when he landed with the ball cradled in his arms, we heard his knee pop and that ended his football career.

A good student who didn't drink or smoke, Pete would have received a full scholarship to almost any college he chose. But once again, Fate took it all away, then poured salt on the wound by having him elected captain of a team that would go undefeated as he watched from the bench. Today, his knee would have been repaired and he'd have been back playing football within a month.

The summer after high school graduation, my father got me a job at the Fore River Shipyard in Quincy where many members of my family had worked. The job was called a chipper and caulker and involved a noisy set of duties using an air gun with heavy duty chisels while working in the filthy inner bottoms of ships.

Fore River shipyard has a fascinating history. In the

late 1880's, Thomas A. Watson, the multimillionaire co-inventor of the telephone with Alexander Graham Bell, was fascinated with ships and their construction. After purchasing more than ten acres of waterfront land on Quincy Bay, he built and operated the Fore River Shipyard Company. But, after only fifteen years, in 1913, Watson became so bored he even pursued an acting career, and sold the yard to Charles Schwab, known today for financial investments and a PGA golf tournament.

After working for Andrew Carnegie in the iron and steel business, Schwab became President of Bethlehem Steel in Pennsylvania and during World War I hired twenty-three year old Boston banker, Joseph P. Kennedy, as his assistant general manager; the youngest man in the nation to hold such a position. Franklin D. Roosevelt was then assistant secretary of the Navy and helped assign more government contracts to Fore river than any other yard in the country.

But soon after the sale, Mr. Watson experienced seller's remorse and as he aged, became keenly aware of his mortality. He missed the activity around the shipyard and finally purchased several acres on a hill in North Weymouth overlooking Fore River and the yard. That became the Old North Cemetery, which he donated to the town, setting aside the best plots for himself overlooking Fore River and the shipyard, where he could watch the ships.

Coincidentally, my parents, grandparents and other

relatives are buried on that same hill just a few yards from Mr. Watson's grave. Several historically famous people have been laid to rest there as well. On the hill across the street are the graves of Abigail Adams' parents, the Reverend William Smith and his wife, and the house where Abigale was born is on the property at the bottom of the hill.

My job at the shipyard required me to wear goggles and long leather gloves every day. Regardless of the weather I had to crawl through those buffet holes above and below decks, carrying a bucket of chisels and dragging a one-hundred foot air hose behind me. The steel decks absorbed both heat and cold so they were hotter than hell in the summer and freezing cold in the winter. Most of the other workers hated the chippers because of the noise from the chisel guns but as a strong eighteen years old kid I could take it. The money was good but the job could be dangerous. One morning, I was pulling my hose over the deck when a tripod covering one of the buffet holes let go and I fell two floors into the belly of the ship. Some nitwit had taken the bolts welded to the deck that secured the tripod off the floor to use somewhere else.

During the fall, I scraped the side of my face and tore my leg up pretty good. Because there was only crawl space, I was strapped into a long, heavy wire basket and lifted out of the ship by Goliath, the largest crane on the entire eastern coast. Normally it was used for loading steel plates and other materials onto the ships' decks rather than rescuing an injured worker. Being lifted out of a ship by

Goliath was pretty scary but the view was spectacular and I became an instant celebrity. When the company gave me a week off with pay, I was delighted. Today, there'd be lawyers lined up outside my house looking for a big payday and I'd be called stupid for not suing the shipyard.

Earlier that spring I made the Weymouth Town Team as a first baseman and loved playing ball again. But when my mother asked what happened I lied. The injury looked worse than it was and I knew the truth would have frightened her. She would have made me quit my job at the Yard so I told her I'd done it sliding during the Town Team game.

Having that time off thrilled me. My friends picked me up every day and we'd head for Nantasket Beach; it was really tough sitting on a blanket watching pretty girls do their thing. Every day we'd go across the street to check out Paragon Park, buy hot dogs, cokes and ice cream then swim in the ice cold ocean. It was a blast!

But the week went by much too fast and when I returned to the yard, I found my job had been temporarily changed. I'd been assigned to the last riveting gang operating in the yard and that gave me my first look at corporate and union dishonesty and greed.

A new HTS welding system made rivets almost obsolete but the shipyard kept a five man crew on hand in case of an emergency. They needed one man and I was assigned as the catcher! Red hot rivets were dropped to me from the deck above which I'd catch in a scoop and hold them with tongs for the riveter to hammer them into the holes. The permanent crew never did that work.

For three weeks, we were told to punch our timecards on the rack assigned to the S.S. Springfield, a converted mine sweeper undergoing minor repairs. We were only five men, but for the entire time, we did nothing but punch in, stand around on the decks all day and collect a check. When she finally sailed out of the harbor, there wasn't a single rivet on the entire ship. At that time, I didn't know or care anything about government oversight or corporate ways. I never knew if the union was involved as much as management, but fifty years later, I'm sure they were both to blame for greed and selfishness continues to the present day.

Then I learned about strikes. Fore River Shipyard was then the area's largest employer and when they went on strike everyone lost, including the business community. The longer the strike lasted, the more everyone suffered. No matter what the final settlement, workers could never make up for their lost wages.

I watched hard-working men lose their homes, cars and have their trucks repossessed. Their kids had to drop out of college because union and management couldn't or wouldn't settle. But management and union negotiators never lost their jobs or paychecks. I can still see those fat union bosses walking around the yard with their thick black cigars hanging out of their mouths, telling the men how good the strike was going to be for them.

Many of the guys I worked with called me The Kid Some were former high school athletes I'd watched play sports at different gyms and fields. Others were also well known boxers. Mr. Louis Brouillard (Lou), a boss ship-fitter, was the middleweight champion of the world during the 1930's. But another boxer, Joe Rindone, was a gopher working in the "Y" department. (Some said the "Y" stood for, "Why should I have a job?") As a ranked middleweight, Joe had somehow fought the champion, Sugar Ray Robinson, a five-time champion in two different weight classes and probably the best boxer ever. The men said Joe got hit so many times he nearly got killed.

Mr. Brouillard kept to himself and never said much but Joe was a sad case. He was what's called "punchy" but always wore a tight black tee shirt and stayed in great shape. Often he strutted around the yard shadow boxing, talking to himself and doing little else.

Another shipyard boxer, Vetle A. "Ring" Larson, came to Quincy with his family from Gotenberg, Sweden at the age of sixteen. After he married, Ring moved to Weymouth with his own family and knew my father from the athletic world. Whenever he worked near my crew he'd look me up and we'd talk about Weymouth sports. His name "Ring" gave me a clue but he was such a modest gentleman I never knew he had been the New England Middleweight Champion in1932. He was also a first cousin of Ingmar Johansson, the heavyweight champion of

Sweden who defeated Floyd Patterson for the heavyweight championship of the world. Ring had been helping train Ingmar at the Clapp Memorial building in East Weymouth where we hung out as kids, the first time any foreign champion had trained in the U. S. before a major bout, and Ring was quite proud to be part of that.

Some of the guys in the yard loved to joke and one of their favorite subjects that summer was critiquing the sandwiches my mother made for my lunch which were always made from whatever was left in the refrigerator. It could be banana and onion, peanut butter and onion; jelly or fluff or olive; chipped beef and mayonnaise or plain mayonnaise with pickles. (One time it was cream cheese and onion with lime Jell-O and the guys went wild!) And they were always on that tasteless spongy Wonder Bread. Each week before she went grocery shopping, she'd clean out the refrigerator and whatever was left ended up in my sandwich. Then she'd put my lunch box in the refrigerator and go to bed. I never thought about it but it really was quite funny.

In those days, I thought everyone had baked beans on Saturday night. I remember helping my mother pick out the bad peas then watching her soak the rest in the bean pot before adding molasses and salt pork. So I was surprised when the guys thought my baked bean sandwiches were so funny. Every Saturday night, most of the family met at Grandma Parker's for baked beans with sliced ham and fresh baked oatmeal bread. I loved the leftover sandwiches because she made them with horseradish, pickles and ketchup mixed in with the beans and hopefully on the leftover homemade oatmeal bread.

Most of the men I worked with hated the shipyard and the ones closest to me kept harping at me to stay in school and make something better of my life. I watched them every day wearing their hard hats, filthy clothes and sweat soaked shirts. At lunch time on Wednesdays, the whistle would blow and their wives would come to the gate or fence, reach through and get their check. After lunch the whistle would blow again and everyone went back to work. In some ways, it was like prison except at three-thirty, you could leave. I appreciated the men's concern for me but still wasn't sure if I wanted to be in college if I couldn't play baseball.

And speaking of prison, I'm reminded of the time when I was working at the yard and playing baseball for the Town Team against the Norfolk County Prison inmates, just before I fell into the buffet hole. After being searched, we held our spikes in front of us and the players entered a steel cubicle one at a time. It was a sobering experience to have a guard holding a shotgun on you while looking into a mirror and having to circle around like a criminal.

Once the game started though, the prisoners in the stands cheered for us, I led off with a single then stretched it into a double. When their shortstop fell on top of me trying to make the tag, the umpires, who were prison guards, rushed over to grab the guy. It seems he had slashed the throats of his girlfriend and her mother so they were checking to make sure he didn't have a knife on him! After I scored and told the guys what had happened, I said I wasn't going near second base again! We were all laughing as I headed for the water bubbler, behind the backstop, to get a drink. But when a huge black inmate, covered with muscles from lifting weights every day, arrived at the bubbler the same time I did, I backed off and said, "You go ahead"

He smiled and said, "No man. You go first. I got twenty years to get that drink of water!" We both cracked up but on the way home I kept thinking about those men and what it would be like to sit in a prison for years with little or no hope for the future.

CHAPTER 6

THE COLLEGE YEARS

The author, pictured top center, as President of Kappa Sigma at UMASS Amherst, 1961

By 1957, it was time to choose a college. But money was still pretty tight at home after my father bought Barker's Stationary Store in Quincy. I had enjoyed Boys State at UMass in Amherst and it was one of the few schools my parents could afford, so when I was accepted there, I signed up. I also planned on supplementing my parents' costs with money I would earn from my summer job.

In those days, tuition was only $150.00 per semester but my first year was a disaster; although not because of money. As an entering freshman I hadn't picked a major but since math was my best subject, I decided to try mechanical engineering. It wasn't long before I learned it wasn't for me. The ever-changing formulas of that discipline and the need to carry a drawing board and slide ruler around the campus made me feel like a nerd.

Since I wasn't studying my grades were lousy. And I missed my girlfriend back home. Excited about returning home for Thanksgiving break, I stopped at a pay phone in Amherst to call her. When she answered, just hearing her voice made me feel better. But when I asked where she'd like to go that night, there was a long pause. Finally, she burst into tears and blurted out, "I'm pregnant!"

We'd never had sex so I was speechless. My knees buckled and I dropped the phone. Bolting out of the telephone booth, I staggered back to my car and sat there like a zombie for probably an hour. Her former boyfriend had played football at Weymouth High and was movie star handsome. He was a junior at the University of New Hampshire and when he came home and I was at UMass, they'd get together. I'd always been jealous of their previous relationship but since she and I had been talking about getting married and having kids, I never imagined she'd be seeing him, or anyone else, behind my back. In the 1950's, getting pregnant usually meant the couple would get married and they did. But soon after she had the baby, Pretty Boy left her and never became part of their son's life. I moved on but it was a bitter pill to swallow and a rough time in my life.

Like most kids growing up in the 1950's, my friends and I didn't drink or smoke. We drove around town in our old, usually white-wall tired cars, hitting the carhops and drive-in movies. We dated girls and had the same raging hormones as kids today but most of us settled for petting in the back seat rather than having intercourse. As a result, very few girls got pregnant. Besides it was frightening to contemplate early commitment to a wife and child and considered socially shameful in contrast to today's "enlightened" society.

I'd thought my girl felt the same way I did, but now felt betrayed and humiliated. As soon as I arrived home, I called my friend Santo and we went looking for the ex-boyfriend in vain. But as we drove around I knew my outrage didn't really come from any high moral ground. I was just pissed off at still being a virgin and worried what my friends and the other kids would think, especially since several of them were already sexually experienced.

Freshmen at UMass, along with most other colleges, weren't allowed to have a car on campus so I usually hitchhiked with Doug, a good friend and star basketball player from North Quincy. His girlfriend was a year older than him and upset he was away at college. One Sunday as we returned to school, he seemed down so I asked if anything was bothering him. His eyes welled up as he said his girl was pregnant and he planned to marry her right away. Several of my other friends at UMass were already married and living in married dorms off campus. When I saw those guys changing diapers it freaked me out. Once I saw how their college lives were compromised, my girlfriend's pregnancy by someone else suddenly felt like a blessing. I wanted a typical college life, not a married one, so the thought of having a sexual relationship at that time scared the hell out of me. And having a baby besides was unthinkable.

Kipling's poem warned about making dreams your master, and holding on to a dream that's over. Now that two of my dreams were gone and my father's drinking was creating tensions at home, my confidence was shot. After breaking up with my girl, I couldn't concentrate. My grades got even worse as I spent my time playing whist or listening to Frank Sinatra's album "Where Are You," feeling sorry for myself. Three songs on that album, " Witchcraft," "All the Way" and "Where Are You" were so etched into my brain, I played and sang them at every night club I worked, whether the people wanted to hear them or not.

Deciding to drop out of school before I flunked out, I returned to the shipyard that winter convinced it would only be for one semester and rationalizing that I could use the money and would return in the fall. My father was quite upset when I told him and I later found out he went to see my foreman and told him to give me the nastiest job in the yard hoping it would force me back to school.

On a freezing February morning, I found myself alone in the Hingham shipyard, working on a filthy, rusty oil tanker newly arrived from Sweden. As I tried to unload over a hundred iced up and salt covered Saab midget automobiles off the deck, the temperature was so cold my leather gloves kept sticking to the cars. Every time I tried to start one of the Saabs, it would stall. Then I thought of my friends back in college. My ass was frozen solid and I knew I'd had enough. My father's plan had worked and I knew it was time to return to UMass.

As I drove back to Amherst, I knew things would have to be different if I was to succeed. I needed a support system. Kappa Sigma Fraternity had asked me to join the previous year and many of my friends were already members. Some of them were former high school athletes who had encountered the same challenges I had in my freshman year. Now though, by living at the fraternity house and studying together at the library some of us made the dean's list. More importantly, we had great times, eventually graduated and became lifelong friends.

Founded in 1869 at the University of Virginia in

Charlottesville, Kappa Sigma Fraternity has initiated over 300,000 men on campuses in the United States and Canada. Over the years many alumni have become corporate and professional icons. Among them are musician Jimmy Buffet, former Senator Bob Dole, actor Robert Redford, Dallas Cowboys owner, Jerry Jones, entrepreneur Ted Turner, golfers Jay Haas and Curtis Strange, songwriter \ actor Hoagy Carmichael, White House correspondent Sam Donaldson, and award-winning war correspondent, Edward R. Murrow.

When I first joined Kappa Sigma, Jack Smith was house treasurer. Two years ahead of me he graduated and then went on to get his MBA at Harvard. After some years abroad straightening out their European market, Jack became the President and CEO of General Motors, then considered the biggest job in the world. But despite thousands of these success stories, the educational elite continue to demonize the fraternity system. Rather than being just a number in a dormitory, a young fraternity member has the opportunity to acquire some stability, experience a sense of belonging, and perhaps learn some social skills.

During my junior year, I was elected president of Kappa Sigma and put into a position of leadership which, while sometimes uncomfortable and unpopular, taught me a lot when I ventured into the business world. The movie Animal House, while hilarious at times, did a great disservice to fraternities by focusing only on the negatives. Struggling young men, like me, benefited greatly from the fraternity experience. I believe that were it not for Kappa Sigma, many of us would never have graduated.

When the celebrated genius, Albert Einstein, escaped from Germany and the Nazis in 1938, he came to America to accept a teaching position at Princeton University. When asked by the press what he thought of the college hierarchy in general, he replied, "Well, I find it to be mostly a quaint acrimonious community of demi-gods on stilts." Spoken like a genius. And I believe that observation still holds true for as many graduates today.

Like others in today's educational system, many college professors seem to have lost sight of what made America so successful. While living in a capitalistic society and making good money, they spend their time in ivy-covered towers built by successful capitalists, but all too often preach socialist ideas to young students with vulnerable minds.

* * * *

I still worked at my father's newly acquired Barker's Stationery Store in Quincy during school vacations. We sold office equipment, fine pens, paper products and greeting cards and I marveled at how many cards we sold during major holidays, especially Valentine's Day, Mother's Day and of course, Christmas. Sometimes the men heading home from work would stop at Sherry's Bar across the street for a taste then stop at the store to buy a Valentine's or Mother's Day card as a peace offering to their wives.

I was working at Barker's during the 1960 Christmas break and just a month before the inaugural celebration of John F. Kennedy, the new President of the United States, when my father said he wanted to show me something down the street at Montilio's Bakery Shop.

Because both Presidents John and John Quincy Adams were buried in a church in the center of the city, Quincy was known as The City of Presidents. Perhaps John F. Kennedy's love of history was what first brought Jackie there but when she discovered Montilio's Bakery, she began doing business with them and immediately after the election, returned to Quincy to ask the bakery to prepare the inaugural cake. When Dad and I arrived, people in white bakers' jackets were everywhere and all busily working. The place was buzzing in preparation for the completion of a huge cake. Large sections of it kept coming out of the ovens to be assembled and crated for shipment by rail to Washington. When completed, the cake was expected to feed over two thousand people.

I'd always presumed things went smoothly during that event. But years later during a conversation with George Montilio, by then the owner of the bakery, I heard the real story. Once the cake arrived in Washington and the White House staff learned that Montilio's wasn't a union shop, they refused to serve it. An alert Kennedy aide immediately called a union bakery to order another cake and both cakes were served to the huge crowd gathered on that blistery winter's night. But I still find it hard to believe that a simple mistake during the inauguration of a President wouldn't be considered an exception. If he was a Republican I could understand the union's actions. But the new President was a democrat!

* * * *

While my family had once owned a restaurant on Cape Cod, my first real job there was during the summer of 1959 after I left the shipyard. Hundreds, if not thousands, of college students from across the country came to Cape Cod and the islands each summer to earn money and party and not necessarily in that order. Landscapers, contractors, restaurants, motels, hotels, town beaches and even the police departments provided jobs for young men and women like me who rented cottages or houses for the summer to make money for college.

That first summer I was hired as a waiter at the Bake Master Restaurant on Rte. 28, South Yarmouth. It was a buffet operation with a cafeteria style menu that provided limited customer service so the tips were terrible. As waiters we had to wear brightly colored Calypso shirts with white three-quarter length pants that made us all look like Harry Belafonte wannabes on a bad night.

"Duke" Holmes owned the place and also ran the Cape Cod Taffy store next door. A CVS store now stands on the site but the taffy stand is still operating fifty years later. And it should be since the taffy was better than the food.

The Duke never bothered us, just stood in a corner, chewed on a toothpick, and stayed out of the way. "The Duke of Earl" was the number one song on the charts that summer and when the restaurant wasn't busy, and Duke was there, we'd sneak a forty-five record of the song onto the sound system. When the record came on and played throughout the restaurant all the waiters and bar tenders would chant "Duke, Duke, Duke" over and over again. Duke Holmes had a good sense of humor but we knew it drove him crazy.

After nine o'clock a cabaret group with some of the waiters sang show tunes and made extra money at it. Since there wasn't a spot in the act for me, I took a job at The Sandy Pond Club down the street, playing intermission piano for a rock and roll band, Beau James and the Playboys. This band, by the way, was the first on the Cape to have a black singer regularly appearing in a white bar.

The Sandy Pond Club was a former hunting lodge that became a longtime hangout for Cape natives and servicemen returning from WWII. The owner, Jack Smith, was more interested in playing cribbage at the bar than he was about business. A couple of UMass friends working there got me the piano job during intermissions and offered me a place to stay with them in a wonderful split-level house known as "Mother Lander's." Built by four single guys from Milton, the house had quality features like flagstone floors and counters; speakers (stolen from a drive-in theatre) were in the bedrooms hooked up to a stereo, and a bunk room out back slept up to ten guests. The guys had enjoyed many summers there until one of them got married and two others had steady girls. Since the women couldn't get along together, they rented the house to us.

While I liked working for "The Duke" even the extra money I earned at Sandy Pond job, barely enabled me to meet expenses that summer.

Then, in 1961, I met a waiter called Smokey who was working at another restaurant on the Cape and said they were hiring for the summer. It was the three-year old Gay Nineties Restaurant Cabaret and Black Horse Tavern, on Route 28 just down the street from the Bake Master. The owner and entrepreneur, John Kozelka, wanted to use the building as a museum to display his collection of antiques and vintage automobiles and had also built a mini-railroad that circled a pond in the back which was surrounded by quaint shops and a school house. For a small price of admission, families could take their kids for a ride on the train, buy them cotton candy or ice cream and then visit the museum.

John was from Willimantic, Connecticut and along with his brother Milton owned Republic Oil Company, a distributor of Texaco products. John owned other properties on the Cape but after two years realized his museum concept wasn't working. Since he lived on a street right behind the property he decided to convert the museum into a restaurant entertainment center thinking he would enjoy being able to watch the customers riding the mini-train from his back yard.

The Gay Nineties Restaurant offered a classic menu in a building filled with old and rare autos, a fully stocked blacksmith shop, period costumes and unusual antiques. Attached to the upstairs dining room, the Carousel Lounge contained a miniature carousel that played Victorian music for the customers waiting for dinner or just having cocktails.

Downstairs was the fun-filled The Black Horse Tavern which featured singing waiters and bartenders along with banjo, piano, and clarinet music. Assorted duos accompanied each waiter's singing style and after 9 o'clock the place was jammed. Everyone on staff wore uniforms. Waiters wore pink and white striped shirts with garters and bow ties: bartenders wore short-sleeved red checkered shirts with string ties and donned straw hats when called on to entertain. The waitresses wore red silk dresses with striped bustles and most wore their hair up with flat black hats topped by bows. Everyone looked great and the customers always felt they were part of another time.

Agnes Grady, Irish, buxom and gravelly voiced, managed the tavern and took charge of all hiring and firing. The moment she heard me say I sang and played the piano, she hired me. Sometimes Aggie could be gruff with people but her big heart and loyalty to the staff, especially the guys, more than made up for it. While serving as hostess, Aggie wore dresses reminiscent of Miss Kitty on the TV show

Gunsmoke. And with that loud whiskey voice, she could really belt out a song!

I'd been hired to wait on table upstairs but whenever they needed a piano player downstairs, Aggie grabbed me. Finally, I was teamed with Mike Lally, a wonderful entertainer from Brockton, Mass. who wore a handlebar mustache, played guitar, clarinet, flute and banjo, and thanks to his talent, I gained a friend and became a better musician. Mike had been a close friend of boxing champion Rocky Marciano, another Brockton man, and brought his instruments to all of Rocky's training camps to entertain the crew before each bout. He must have done something right because Rocky retired from boxing still undefeated.

Weymouth vs. Brockton on Thanksgiving Day was one of the biggest high school football games in the state. Both were Class A schools that had won league championships. Rocky attended that game every year I was in high school and I remember seeing him in the bleachers wearing a camel's hair topcoat. Knowing the men he'd fought and how tough he was, we were surprised he wasn't a bigger man. How many world famous athletes today would be attending their high school's football game on Thanksgiving Day?

In my senior year, Weymouth defeated Brockton 48 to 6, and was the last team to win the State Class A championship playing an all Class A schedule. I'd always regretted not playing football and being on that team with my friends. But my father had broken his collar bone playing end in high school before dropping out to work and while pitching in the minors, he told me he'd seen that players hindered by football injuries usually got cut from the team. Even so, I went out for football my junior year but always worried about getting hurt. I lasted three days until a pile up when I couldn't breathe told me I should quit.

* * * *

The Gay Nineties was a truly unique place. But the man standing at the door, playing the hurdy-gurdy with a live monkey on a leash, was something else.

Sigmund "Pop" Bednark was an eighty year old Polish-Russian immigrant, who, along with his son Raymond, had built the museum and railroad village for owner John Kozelka. A giant of a man, when he was dressed in that Swiss vest, mountain pants and an alpine hat, Pop looked as if he'd just stepped out of Hollywood's central casting.

Nights when I was waiting for parties to be seated in my station, I'd go outside to talk with him. Pop's ruddy, round face was always smiling (unless the monkey was acting up) and he was knowledgeable about so many things. I loved spending time with him and still remember the smell of his pipe. The customers loved Pop too, but the monkey didn't fare so well. After only two weeks, the creature got fired for biting some kids who were trying to pet him.

Jules Rykenbusch was another character and the fiery Frenchman and executive chef who presided over the kitchen as he had at the 1954 opening of Miami's famous Fontainebleau Hotel. Jules was tough on the wait staff but we got along great. I loved hearing him yelling and swearing in French and his talented crew on the line prepared some of the finest food I have ever eaten. He and his wife Lois owned a little house on Route 6A in Barnstable. Lois was a classical pianist living in Paris when Jules met her and she played the piano during the dinner hours upstairs at The Gay Nineties. She also ran a gift shop during the summer months. I loved working with Jules but one night, learned a lesson from him that people should remember when sending something back to the kitchen. I'm not talking about a legitimate complaint or when something is poorly prepared. I'm referring to the person who sends his meal back simply to call attention to him or herself.

On this particular night, the kitchen was backed up and customers were informed they could have free cheese and crackers with their cocktails, but dinner orders couldn't be taken and would be delayed. As it turned out, that wasn't good enough for the New Yorkers at one of my tables. Fifteen or so minutes after our announcement that group called the hostess over, whispered in her ear, and demanded that their orders be taken. Whatever they said worked because the hostess caved in and sent me into the kitchen to see Jules. After ranting with more French curses, he told me to "Go get their flukking order!"

Of course, one in the party had to order a large filet mignon, well done, which creates a problem for the kitchen and is always a no-no unless the meat is butterflied. (Cut in half and flipped over like wings.) When Jules saw the order he went crazy but George, the broiler man, threw the meat on the grille and tried to rush it along. When I placed the dish in front of the customer, he complained it wasn't cooked enough so back it went into the kitchen. As soon as Jules saw me, he grabbed the filet off the plate, yelled at George and threw it twenty feet past him where it bounced off the stainless steel refrigerator door and landed on the grungy floor.

George, who was wearing greasy, filthy shoes, jumped up and down on the filet. Spearing it with his long broiler fork, he put it back on the grille and sprayed oil over it. The flames engulfed the meat for a long moment before he slapped what was left onto a clean plate, added a sprig of parsley and without looking at me, yelled "Donny! Get this fucking thing out of here!"

I'd never seen anything like that in any kitchen where I'd ever worked. My lip was bleeding from biting it to keep from laughing and when I delivered what looked like a scorched hockey puck to the customer, he cut off a piece, took a bite, then looked at me and said, "This is perfect!" I lost it. Bolting through the dining room and out the front door, I went behind the building and laughed uncontrollably for at least ten minutes.

The following winter when I was visiting a friend on the Cape, I stopped at the restaurant to see John. When he asked if I knew any guys who might fit into our group the next summer, I told him some of my college buddies would love to join the ranks. Some of them couldn't sing a lick but their good looks and personalities made up for it and the customers loved hearing them massacre a song at the mike.

I've never heard of another job where waiters could drink beer while working, and not just any beer -- Heineken! For John and Agnes, nothing was too good for the boys. As long as he could sing his favorite song, Golden Days and have his boys backing him up John didn't care what we were drinking. And when we joined him in the chorus, he'd beam like a little kid.

Naturally shy and introverted, John loved having a bunch of wild and wacky guys around. We always included him in the group and knowing many of us had played sports, he and Agnes decided to have a Gay Nineties softball team. They bought the uniforms and equipment and on Sunday mornings we played at various fields around the Cape. Most teams were local firemen, summer cops or other musicians and restaurant employees from the Cape. But on occasion, there would be a team from "over the bridge," i. e., on the Boston side of the Cape Cod Canal.

Since we usually partied until at least two in the morning, the games were always slow pitch and started no earlier than 10:30 a.m. on Sundays. Occasionally John and Agnes would show up to cheer us on and in five years we only lost twice.

* * * *

One afternoon when I arrived for work John told me that the Red Sox icon, Ted Williams, was coming for dinner with his daughter and the managers of his baseball camp in Lakeville, Mass. He wanted me to wait on them and be sure to send them a drink on the house. I was thrilled at the prospect of meeting Ted, but had no idea what lay ahead.

By then he had been retired for two years and while a little heavy around the middle, Ted still looked fit enough to play. Rested, tanned and wearing his trademark blue blazer with an open-collared white polo shirt, he looked like a Greek god. The restaurant was buzzing with excitement. His party must have had a few before they arrived because Ted started getting loud the minute they sat down. Cheese and crackers were already on the table but after I brought their drinks, his daughter asked me to bring shrimp cocktails immediately. Apparently she wanted him to have something more solid than cheese and crackers and after I brought the shrimp, he settled down.

Then, out of the corner of my eye, I spotted a large woman pushing her way through the dining room, pen and paper napkin in her hand and heading for their table. I tried to intercept her but it was too late. Ted hadn't seen her and just as he raised a giant shrimp, dipped in cocktail sauce, to his mouth, she bumped him from behind. The shrimp fell off his fork covering his jacket and light tan slacks with bright red cocktail sauce.

Ted was furious but the woman wasn't fazed a bit. Handing him the napkin, she said, "Ted, Ted, Sign this napkin for my son Billy, will yah?" The room grew silent. Like everyone else, I waited to see his reaction. At first he just stared her down. Then, in a loud voice, he said "Lady! Get the f- - k away from me!"

Using the "F" word in public, especially in mixed company, was a no-no in 1962. Freezing in her tracks with her mouth wide open, the woman turned and fled. The room remained silent as Ted sat down and took a sip of his drink. Once I gave him a wet cloth to wipe off his jacket and pants, he started on the shrimp cocktail again, but was still miffed.

When I brought dessert a while later, I mentioned to Ted that I'd met him once before at a Fenway Park baseball clinic and we chatted a little about that and when I told him my father's baseball background, he became animated. After offering me a job at his camp, he asked for the check, gave me a big tip, and left. It was a memorable experience but it was then that I realized Ted Williams wasn't really interested in talking about anything except baseball.

Several Boston sports writers gave him a hard time over the years but most of it was about jealousy and Ted's refusal to flatter anybody. He was his own man and they couldn't stand it.

Another celebrity I waited upon was Frankie Fontaine, a TV personality known as "Crazy" Gugenheim on The Jackie Gleason Show. Dressed like a fat Buster Keaton, hat brim turned up, he deliberately looked goofy while singing in skits with Gleason playing Joe the Bartender and Charley Bratton. But when he began to sing his beautiful voice surprised everyone. When he arrived at the Nineties however, his face was bloated and beet red, and with his hair bleached blonde he was a sad sight. He also had a gambling problem. Gleason bailed him out twice but when he wouldn't stop, he was fired and they were about to take his house.

His career in shambles, Frankie, his wife and nine children were about to lose everything until Frank Sinatra, who was appearing in Boston, heard about their predicament. The crooner was a real contradiction. One day he'd do something nice for someone but the next day could cut the person's heart out. Sinatra first called Gleason to see if Fontaine was really an Italian, then bought the house back from "The Boys" and put it in the name of Mrs. Fontaine and the kids.

Years later when Jackie Gleason was starring with Burt Reynolds in the Smokey and the Bandit movies, I was tending bar in my new Hyannis restaurant when, for some reason, I mentioned to friends that I'd like to have a few drinks with Jackie Gleason. A little Irishman from Buffalo, Terry Kane, had become a friend and happened to be sitting at the bar just after he'd become the new manager of the nearby Dunfey's Hotel.

Hearing me say that, he informed us that while he was general manager of Chicago's Drake Hotel, Gleason was a frequent guest and notoriously abusive. Frequently he'd insult the staff, call for room service at three in the morning and make unreasonable demands. Everyone knew it was because of the booze, but Gleason never apologized, no matter how outrageous he'd been the night before, probably because he had been so drunk he didn't remember what he'd done. Later, I read a biography of his life that described his childhood poverty and inner demons. All his stardom and excessive boozing couldn't take away the pain and making all that money hadn't helped much either.

By then it had become an annual ritual for me to return to work on the Cape in summer. But finding a rental was becoming more expensive and difficult. The neighborhood had to be tolerant of cars arriving late at night and often leaving very early in the morning.

One winter, our perpetual group of summer roommates met in Boston for a birthday party when the subject of the following summer arose. I suggested to my friends that we buy a house instead of having to rent one each year. Nobody seemed interested so I asked them if I found a suitable house would they rent from me just for that summer. Paying the mortgage and taxes that first year worried me, but my friends agreed to be renters and I soon found a new three bedroom house that seemed perfect. It was in a wooded area of Centerville with over a half acre of land and deeded beach rights to Lake Wequaquet just a short walk away. It had a large living room with a fireplace, two bathrooms, a full cellar, and plenty of room for parking. The summer went well but living with friends and being their landlord, is never wise. The next summer, as previously agreed, my friends found a rental in South Yarmouth and I moved back in with them. As it turned out, I was able to rent the house for the summer at twice what I'd charged them!

Before buying that house, I'd asked my father if he could help with the down payment and for once, our discussion didn't end in a shouting match. Not only did he think buying the house was a good idea, he also agreed to loan me a thousand dollars. Then he shared with me one of the best things I'd ever heard him say. "You know Donny, one day you wake up and you're twenty-five. The next day you wake up and you're forty-five. Time goes by just that fast and what you do during those twenty years will usually determine how you will live the next twenty years."

My father had never talked to me like that before and I followed that advice for the next fifteen years. But once I was a big shot, I began doing things my way and paid a price for that.

CHAPTER 7

A COLORFUL YOUNG ADULTHOOD

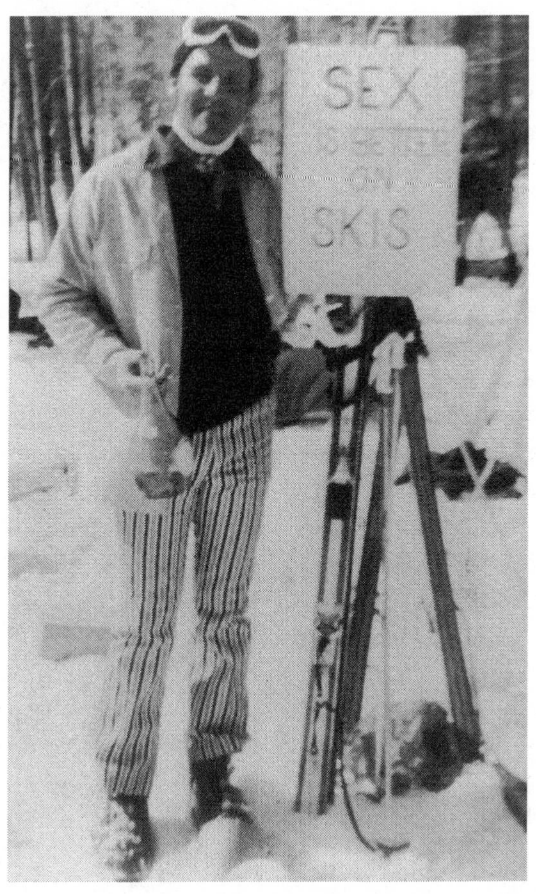

The author pictured at Wild Cat Mountain in New Hampshire, 1965.

After graduating from college with a degree in Business Management and a minor in English Literature, I went into business with my father. But father-son partnerships have a poor track record and too often don't survive because of personality conflicts. Ours was no exception but at that point in my life, I wasn't even sure I wanted a career in business anyway.

For two summers during high school, I'd been a park instructor and really enjoyed working with kids. Teaching and coaching seemed natural alternatives to the business world so I headed back to Amherst to get my teacher certification.

On November 22nd 1963, I was practice teaching at Pioneer Valley Regional High School in Greenfield, Mass, when two girls arrived late for class. Thinking they were testing me, I asked why they were late and when they said President Kennedy had just been shot I could feel my stomach and chest muscles tighten but couldn't digest the news. Hoping they'd made up the story, I said, "What a terrible thing to say!" which brought them to tears and sent them running down the hall. School was dismissed immediately and like millions of others in our country and throughout the world, I went home totally devastated.

One day in 1959, I'd seen John and Jackie Kennedy as they were leaving Sunday Mass at Saint Francis Xavier Church in Hyannis. Jack was still a senator and his youth, body language and sense of humor had impressed me even then. Jackie had a nice smile but seemed shy and uncomfortable around a crowd. Never could I have imagined a future where I would live on the same street with the Kennedys and be friendly with members of their family and friends so closely tied to that tragic day.

* * * *

In 1965, after completing teacher certification at UMass, I took a job as a reading teacher in Hingham. The school was only fifteen minutes from my house and had a terrific faculty and student body. But I wasn't really qualified to teach reading. I was a business school graduate with a minor in English. I believe the job was created by the Massachusetts Department of Education interested in increasing state requirements and enhancing public relations. But, my being certified to teach was good enough for the superintendent so I was hired.

During the first years as a reading teacher, I still enjoyed working summers on the Cape and continued playing piano at the Gay Nineties Restaurant. A group of fellow teachers and coaches from my UMass days continued to live together those summers and still partied until the wee hours while enjoying a carefree life. Despite the long nights, unless the weather was bad, we were always up for breakfast and off to the beach by ten a.m.

Although Sea Gull Beach was just a short walk from our house in West Yarmouth -- Saul Glisserman, our Jewish roommate, jokingly called it "Siegal Beach, the only Jewish beach on Cape Cod"-- once in a while we'd try a different place. Among our favorites was Nauset Beach in Orleans and known for its rough surf. One morning, after a heavy nighttime storm, someone suggested going there to bodysurf and as a treatment for our hangovers. Since we often played touch football and handball at the beach, we placed our blankets far away from the crowd. Nauset was the perfect place because it was long and rarely crowded. And we could take a break, jump in the surf and return to the competition without disturbing anyone.

During one such break, I noticed a well-built gray-haired man standing up to his knees in water but still close to a small boy. A wave knocked the child over, but as he began to cry I was close enough to see and hear the man say, "John, when we get knocked down, we never cry." With that, he picked the little boy up who immediately stopped crying.

Walking back to the game and thinking the boy looked familiar, I stopped short and realized it was little John-John Kennedy. As I approached the blankets, I looked up at the dunes behind us, saw a pair of oversized sunglasses looking down at us, and knew Jackie Kennedy was there watching. The gray haired man must have been secret service and just as I started telling the guys what was happening, he came up behind me asking our group to join him and circle around the boy while he changed his bathing suit into a dry diaper and clean pants.

At first I didn't understand why until he explained photographers were using zoom lenses to take pictures of young John any way they could. We did our job and to my knowledge, no pictures were taken that day. I know one thing; if any of us had spotted a photographer, things would not have gone well for him.

A dozen years later at a house party in Hyannis Port, I saw young John Kennedy again and this time we talked briefly. At that time, I owned a 1948 Dodge "Woody" and he asked if he could ride with me to another party on nearby Squaw Island. He was impressed that the car could fit seven passengers and during the drive I told him my Nauset Beach story. He was only two at that time so I knew he wouldn't remember. Still, he was very respectful, listened intently and said he vaguely remembered that particular secret service agent.

* * * *

There were several UMass girls I knew who worked on the Cape a couple of summers then became stewardesses for Eastern Airlines. Based in Boston, they lived in an apartment complex called Whittier Place at Charles River Park. A sign on their building proclaimed, "If you lived here, you would be home by now!" which must have irritated drivers stuck in Boston's famous traffic jams on Storrow Drive. They were great girls, very attractive and ready for fun. At the time I was teaching in Hingham and having enrolled in a Masters' Degree program at Boston University, they decided I should join their group.

When those girls threw a cocktail party, it wasn't just

a party. It was an event. Professional athletes, politicians, business men and women, up-and-coming lawyers, and most importantly, other beautiful "stews," were all there, each hoping to become part of Boston's "in" group. I was just a lowly school teacher and didn't fit the social profile. But since I could play the piano and drove a little white Mercedes 230SL, my image as a playboy was established.

After class one night, I called their pad, hoping to stop and visit on my way home. But they were away so I returned to the city to see Neil McInerney, another Cape friend who had just opened two adjoining bars on Huntington Avenue in Kenmore Square, called Mothers and Sloppy Joe's.

The head bartender was another Cape guy I knew called "Muzzi" and after the three of us chatted for a while they bought me a beer and offered me a job as a doorman. They had just received a license allowing bars to stay open until 2 a.m. and Neil needed someone to cover the last two or three hours. I had to teach in the morning but it was only two nights a week and the money was good. Besides, at that age, I thought I could handle anything. Boston University now owns the building but at that time, both bars eventually became popular hangouts for some of Boston's sports luminaries.

Joe Namath of the New York Jets was appearing at the annual Sportsman Show at Boston Garden and as I was standing at the bar one night, I heard a couple of Boston Patriots bad-mouthing him. Later that night, as I was checking the line coming up the stairs, I noticed a tall guy on the landing wearing a Sherlock Holmes cap with matching green and white tweed cape. I realized it was Joe Namath and motioned to him to come ahead, but he waved no and waited his turn. When he entered the bar, the Patriot blowhards were all over him, kissing his ass and playing buddy-buddy. I was dying to tell him how they'd been talking twenty minutes earlier. But Joe was grinning and ordered a drink for himself and one for each of the Patriots. Muzzi told him the drinks were on the house but Joe shook his head no, and asked for the check. Imagine! A legitimate celebrity not looking for special treatment and/or something for nothing.

There was a guy in army fatigues, sitting at the bar with a few under his belt, who yelled "Hey Namath! I played for South Boston High and I'll bet I was a better quarterback than you!" he shouted. I started over to throw the jerk out but Namath told me he'd take care of it. He went over to the guy, shook his hand, and said "You're probably right, I was just lucky," then bought him a drink. Now the guy loved Namath and in all my years of dealing with celebrities, and drunks, while working at and owning restaurants, I've never seen anything like that before or since. I knew a girl at UMass also from his home town, Beaver Falls, Pennsylvania, so we chatted about her for a while and after talking with a few customers at the bar, he had one more drink and left. Joe Namath was a real gentleman and a class act.

Years later I watched a female sportscaster

interviewing him during the Super Bowl when he had obviously been drinking. The sportscaster should have avoided or cancelled the interview but instead chose to let him babble on and embarrass himself. I'm sure it wasn't only her decision but when she later accused him of groping her, she attracted the national coverage her network wanted. If her report was true, Joe Namath was in the wrong, but whatever happened was handled poorly. Back in 1976 the movie Network illustrated that most television executives only cared about one thing: ratings. People couldn't have mattered less, except those who are usually members of a politically correct group

The passageway between "Mothers" and "Sloppy Joe's" was every doorman's job to police. Customers weren't allowed to take their drinks from one bar to the other but there was a table where they could leave their drinks and retrieve them when they returned.

Most people had no problem with the rule but one nasty- looking regular always gave me a hard time. Pushing his face into mine and with dead eyes, he'd claim, he wouldn't give up his drink. He'd always made me nervous but one night I finally said, "Listen, it's the rules. Why are you always giving me a hard time? I'm just doing my job. If you don't like it, take it up with Neil!"

As soon as I said that, I felt pressure on my stomach and looked down to see a handgun pressed into my stomach. There's no way to describe the feeling of having a Saturday night special stuck into your gut so after I turned white, I raised my hands in the air and said "Go ahead." And when I looked into those dead eyes again, I was sure he was going to pull the trigger.

I finished the night but then told Neil that was it for me. I was done. A week later or so, I was reading the Record-American in the teacher's room when a picture jumped out at me! It was that psycho being handcuffed by the Boston police! There were also pictures of his apartment in Chelsea showing a variety of guns and ammunition. It seems he'd been illegally supplying weapons to the criminal element in Boston for years. I wasn't surprised and must say that when he was found guilty and sentenced to twelve to fourteen years in a maximum security prison, I felt pretty damned lucky.

* * * *

The Pioneer Club was a popular speakeasy on Columbus Avenue in a tough part of Boston. Its owner, Lincoln Pope, was a handsome, classy man and one of the first black state representatives in Massachusetts. Sometimes I'd stop there after work to have a drink, listen to the music and say hello to Mr. Pope. The club opened at midnight and closed at four a.m. but to get in you had to be a member or someone's guest. A light over the front door illuminated a button which, when pushed, caused a black face to appear in a little round window asking for proper identification. Once inside, the door closed and was bolted behind you. If your ID checked out, another door opened to let you in.

After finishing their regular gig, entertainers from all over Boston arrived to sit in, sing or relax with friends and have a few drinks. A house band played every night and all drinks were a dollar. The only available food was fried chicken in a basket, also for a dollar. The tables were covered with white linen tablecloths upon which rested ashtrays and matches. The quality of music was terrific and sometimes the bandleader, George White, even asked me to sing! It took a couple of drinks to get up the courage, but I never got booed, so I must have sounded all right.

I was at the Pioneer one night during a so-called raid. A speakeasy was illegal of course because they stayed open until four in the morning. But to keep up appearances, officials in law enforcement would periodically stage a raid. Just before that happened, the waitresses appeared at the tables, asked what people were drinking and immediately cleared the tables. Ten minutes later, two detectives in suits and ties, accompanied by two smiling police officers, came through the now unbolted entrance door. We watched as they nodded, then beckoned the manager to join them. After standing around laughing and talking with each other for another ten minutes, they smiled at the customers and left. As soon as the cops left, the waitresses returned to the tables bringing everyone a fresh drink along with a basket of fried chicken, all on the house.

The Pioneer Club is long gone but for many years it was an important sanctuary for those in the entertainment community. After working all night at their regular jobs, musicians, bartenders, restaurant and hotel staff, black and white, had someplace special to go to where they could relax and unwind.

After the gun incident at the bar and long hours of studying for something I wasn't sure I wanted anymore, I decided to drop out of Boston University, even though I was just three credits short of my Master's degree.

One morning in the teachers' room, a fellow teacher, Leslie Gould, mentioned a ski club she'd just joined in North Conway, New Hampshire. She was heading there for the weekend and when I asked about it she invited me to come up some weekend. In fact, I could be her guest, stay at the lodge, and hopefully learn how to ski. I hadn't put on a pair of skies since I was a kid and was worried about looking foolish, breaking my neck, or both. But it was time for a change and I figured what the hell.

I was still working weekends for my father at Barker's then and when he asked what I'd like for Christmas, I mentioned the skiing invitation in New Hampshire. Dad thought that was a great idea and off we went to Brine's Sporting Goods store on Hancock Street in Quincy center. Thirty minutes later, I walked out with my Christmas present! A pair of black Head skis, a black parka, boots, poles and a red ski hat! I might not be able to ski very well but at least I'd look like I could. After school that Friday, Leslie and I hopped into her car and headed off to North Conway where my life entered one of its happiest and healthiest times. I swallowed my pride, learned to ski on the bunny slopes at Cranmore and Wildcat Mountain and joined the Ski-Bee Lodge. And to top it off, I even made money playing the piano in Jackson village at The Linderhof and The Jackson Tavern.

Once spring skiing was over however, back I went to the Cape. After five fun years at The Gay Nineties, during the summer of 1966, I decided to take a job at The Windjammer Lounge. Located behind the Hyannis rotary, it was a great local attraction but almost immediately, I realized I'd made a huge mistake. For the first time ever, I had to work during the day and that summer every day was hot and sunny. There I was inside making sandwiches and cooking hamburgers on a sweltering grille while everyone I lived with was at the beach. Lunch hours were busy but the afternoons were dead and I was bored. The nights were better because I was downstairs at the newly built Rathskellar style bar pounding on an old upright piano. Dave Crawford and Wayne Glover were the bartenders; Lee and Lucia, two beautiful girls from Ohio, were our waitresses.

The "Cellar Bar" didn't open until nine p.m. and soon, became a hangout for the college kids and wait staff from other restaurants who didn't get off work until at least ten o' clock. The sound system was lousy but no one seemed to care.

There was a very good piano player in the upstairs lounge but the college crowd seemed to like my laidback style and the fact I played '60s music. Apparently some of the upstairs regulars liked it too because some of them began showing up too. Plus, let's face it, it was cooler in the cellar!

Despite that, I still hated working days and wasting afternoons at The Windjammer. I missed the beach and all the fun I used to have hanging out with the guys and gals. One summer was enough and while Bud Maclean, the wonderful man who hired me and was always a gentleman, expressed his disappointment, he wished me luck and said he understood.

* * * *

My next stop was a place called The Mooring, an old fisherman's bar on Hyannis Harbor, then owned by Mike Mitchell, a burly, blustery Irishman from County Cork. Located next to the fishing boats, The Mooring had been serving food and drink for over fifty years to boat owners and other locals whose vessels were tied up along Ocean Street on Hyannis Harbor. Tourists staying in the hotels just across the street, also frequented the place, as did passengers booked on the adjacent Hy-Line Cruises waiting to sail to Nantucket and Martha's Vineyard.

Added to The Mooring's luster was its past association with President John Kennedy. In the early 1960s, the Secret Service and members of the press stayed at The Yachtsman Hotel, half a mile down the street. Both places were about the same distance from the Kennedy Compound so The Mooring became a convenient hangout for them when they were off-duty.

I'd first set foot in the Mooring with three friends from UMass in those years when we'd been house hunting on the Cape and needed a cold beer. The bar was so dark you couldn't see a thing, so we grabbed four stools and sat down while our eyes adjusted. "What can I get you?" the bartender yelled, busy filling up a beer cooler at the other end of the counter, to which we ordered, "Four cold Budweisers!"

The place was pretty seedy and smelled like stale beer, but as I looked around and saw the old fishing nets, lobster traps, anchors, sails and other nautical items hanging on the ceiling, scattered throughout the room, I liked it. It felt like a waterfront bar should. A white grand piano was just inside the door with an enlarged piano-shaped top and stools around it. Plastic upholstered sofas with cocktail tables were spread around in groupings around the walls.

The bartender was one strange-looking dude. Despite the darkness, he wore sunglasses. A bandana was wrapped around his head and he wore a tie-dyed shirt with something crude painted on it. He also had one dangling earring. After dropping off the beers, he headed back to the cash register with the money. It was then we noticed he wasn't wearing any pants. Other than the tee shirt and sandals, he was totally bare assed! We all cracked up, but that was that. We drank up and left.

At the beach the next day, we learned the dude owned the place. They called him Crazy Ronnie, for obvious reasons. I can only imagine what the Secret Service would have thought about that nut case two years later when JFK was President and lived less than a mile away.

Crazy Ronnie had been carted away in a straightjacket long before I visited the Mooring again, but I couldn't see where the most recent owner Mike Mitchell, had changed the place much. Although I presumed he wasn't tending the bar bare-assed, the same fish nets, lobster traps and piano bar were still there. When I was hired, I promised him I'd always wear pants when playing the piano.

Piano bars were my favorite places to play. I could talk to the people, tell jokes and encourage everyone to sing along with me. The piano bar at the Mooring was surrounded by ten stools which always filled up early. And for a change, there was a great sound system. My Gay Nineties singalong stuff went over well and brought people back every night. Some even believed "the more they sang and drank, the better the piano player sounded!"

In 1968 after Bobby Kennedy announced his candidacy for the U. S. Presidency, the Secret Service and members of the press began staying at The Yachtsman Hotel again, just as they had when his brother Jack was President. Excitement over the campaign was building slowly but no one could have imagined what lay ahead.

After my second summer at the Mooring, Mike Mitchell was so pleased with business he decided to build an addition to encourage more restaurant business and less of the bar. The place would be bigger but the piano bar would no longer be the main attraction. The atmosphere was going to change yet I knew I would still be expected to fill the house. To complicate matters, my friend, Barney Baxter, called me that February wanting to talk about a business possibility.

I was still teaching in Hingham, skiing and playing piano weekends in North Conway. But ironically, on the weekend Barney called, I was playing at the Linderhof Inn when, as the après-ski crowd danced and sang, the piano suddenly began sinking into the floor. Stunned, I stared at my bass player as the manager rushed up the stairs, his face ashen white, as he headed for the piano. He motioned for me to cover the microphone then whispered, "Act as if nothing has happened. We don't want a panic but get everyone off the dance floor!" Thinking fast, I quickly announced we were going to have a raffle and asked everyone to move to the sidewalls. Other than being a little loud from having a few drinks, the crowd obeyed. Then, somehow I explained there was a problem downstairs and asked everyone to leave by the outside deck staircases.

Then I hustled downstairs. The main beam and another one next to it had split length-wise from wall to wall beneath the floor of the piano. I was amazed the floor hadn't let go with all the people on it. I visualized the piano falling through the floor with me, crushing me, the bass player and the crowd. I realized that the scene could have been tragic.

At that time, building codes in New Hampshire were more lenient than they are today. But when the building inspector showed up and saw the damage, he realized what could have happened and closed the place down. That turned out to be for two weeks, but the hiatus gave me the chance to go to the Cape and meet with Barney Baxter.

CHAPTER 8

FOND TIMES AT BAXTERS

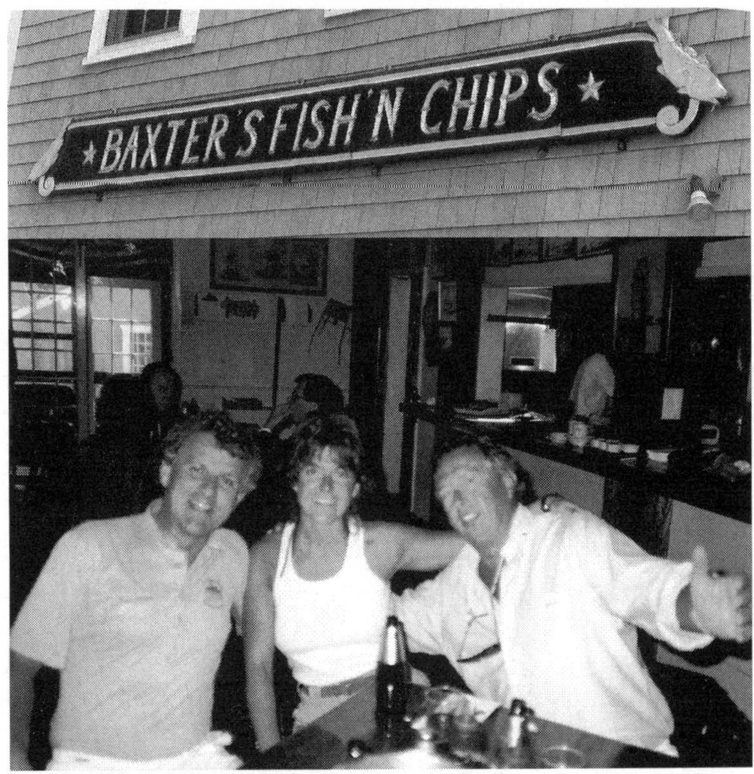

The author, pictured on the left, with sister-in-law Lisa Scoblick and Barney Baxter at Baxter's Fish & Chips, 1974.

The Baxter family had owned land on Pleasant Street on Hyannis harbor since the 1880s when Captain Benjamin D. Baxter sailed the seven seas. By the mid-twentieth century, his descendant, Warren T. Baxter, Sr. and his wife Florence had operated a fish market on that street for over thirty-five years. But after their son Barney returned from the Marines, he told his father he was going to do something else. Now that he was married and starting his own family, Barney felt it was too difficult to make a living just selling fish and proposed an idea to his father about building a seafood restaurant and lounge on the same site as the fish market.

After discussing it with his wife Florence, and other family members, Barney's dad, Warren Sr. decided to go ahead with the plan. Construction began the spring of 1966 and by the time Baxter's opened the following year, the site included a lounge as well as the fish and chips restaurant and the fish market. All were incorporated into the new building but there were two separate entrances outside which were also connected by an inside door.

The lounge part of the restaurant, The Boat House, was restricted to adults over twenty-one and served a fried seafood menu with cocktails, beer and wine. The other section, Fish 'n Chips had a separate entrance for casual family dining. The same menu was offered at both places but waitresses from the Boat House also had to serve the Fish n' Chips section. As business boomed, a small bar was eventually added.

It was always said that the Fish 'n Chips place was the only real deck anywhere on the Cape because the Governor Brann, an old fishing trawler permanently tied to the restaurant, actually had a real ship's deck where customers, with or without the kids, ate at picnic tables and in booths as they watched the harbor activity.

Baxter's lunch and dinner hours were busy right away, but as soon as the sun went down, business plummeted. Realizing that the only way the place could make money was through a strong bar business, Barney remembered The Mooring crowd when I played and where he often stopped for a drink on his way home. Barney's call to me was about asking if I would leave the Mooring and play piano at Baxter's.

During the 1960's, Mildred's, located at the Hyannis Airport Rotary was one of the few Cape restaurants that stayed open year-round. One Friday night after the sinking piano incident in New Hampshire, Barney and I made plans to meet there. After a drink or two with the locals, we headed for the Captain's Table, near the Mooring, where it was less crowded so we could talk. I didn't like the addition and changes Mike Mitchell was making to the Mooring that winter but felt uncomfortable about making another move. However, a few more gin and tonics changed my mind and ultimately Barney and I made the deal. I will always be proud to say, I was the first piano player or musician to ever appear at Baxter's Boat House. And I still think Baxter's is one of the best waterfront seafood restaurants and watering holes anywhere in the world.

The next morning, I showed up at the Mooring to give Mike Mitchell my notice and plenty of time for him to find a replacement. But when I told him I was leaving and explained why, his face turned beet red. "Get your f.k.ng ass out of here and don't ever come back," he snarled. I liked Mike Mitchell a lot and we'd always gotten along well but in retrospect, I've always felt bad about that. Mike lived for another twenty-five years, but that was the last time we spoke.

For years afterwards Mike accused me of taking away his summer business until he finally realized it was the lack of income during the winter months that was killing him, not me. He sold the Mooring and opened a steak-house on the Hyannis airport rotary, called, of course, Mitchell's Steak House. I was glad for him and must relate a story about Mike and the TV icon known in the advertising industry as "The Chicken Man," Mister Frank Perdue.

Since Perdue had a summer home in Chatham he often landed his Lear jet at Hyannis Airport. Company executives often met with him there onboard the plane and one night at six o'clock they decided to cross the street to try Mike's famous Mitchell's Roast Prime Rib of Beef. After they'd finished dinner and were having more drinks, Mike, clad in his Kelly green vest, headed over to their table in the middle of the room and loudly welcomed Mr. Perdue and his group in his thick Irish brogue. The other diners recognized "The Chicken Man" from his ads (he did look just like a chicken!) and listened carefully to every word Mike said. When he asked how he liked his prime rib, Perdue said, "Well, I thought it was rather tough." Not missing a beat, Mike replied, "Well so's your foooking chicken!" The dining room guests, those at the bar and even the employees, went wild. The Perdue party left quickly and the story was repeated across the Cape for weeks.

Baxter's was a great place to work and, fortunately, what Barney and I had hoped for soon became a reality. The bar crowd from the Mooring and other night spots began showing up there and by June the place was crowded and had a nightly waiting line

Believe me when I say that playing piano and singing four or five hours a night, six nights a week, is hard work. But it's even harder when you aren't that happy with how you play. I tried to compensate by playing long sets and using my voice more than the piano. But one night when my parents came to hear me, Dad gave me hell for playing too long and not taking enough breaks. As I attempted to sing over the noise, I strained my voice and it wasn't long before I was beginning to sound hoarse.

Fortunately, Eddie Watson, a piano and vocal teacher with whom I'd briefly studied, played every summer at The Colonial Lounge in Falmouth. During one of my nights off, he invited me to see The Jones Boys, a singing and dancing duo who performed in Las Vegas during the winter. They were appearing at The Casino in Falmouth and on one of their breaks Eddie introduced me. After we chatted for a while, Eddie told them about my hoarseness and they laughed. Then they said, "Man! You got to gargle with that sea water every day!"

Originally from Harlem, they told me that when they'd first started singing, many night clubs didn't have microphones. After finishing their regular gig, they'd go to a late night speakeasy and try to sing over the noisy, drunken crowd, often until three in the morning. Gargling with sea water, they confided, had cured their hoarseness and allowed them to keep working. The next morning I went to Craigville Beach and started gargling. Within three days, my hoarseness disappeared and once I started doing that I was never hoarse again. And I never again got a summer cold.

The perks at Baxter's were great but I was only making $75 a week for playing piano and singing six nights. I got a free meal and drinks but the cocktail waitresses were averaging over $100 a day, often for just one shift. Even though I knew I was part of the draw for the crowd, I didn't complain because I still had little confidence in my ability. I was glad to have the job but sometimes after closing, when a waitress would ask me to help count her tips, I'd feel a little resentful over how much money she'd made. The good news was that instead of spending, I was making money those nights and I loved working at the place. And as I told myself, I would have been hanging out there anyway.

When I purchased an electronic drum "sideman" to fill in behind me, some customers at my piano bar began calling it Sticks. The bartenders called me Stone Fingers and said the more drinks the customers sent me, the better Sticks sounded! Maybe so, but I still think the music got better the more everyone else drank.

Another perk during those crazy '60s was that bars stayed packed until one in the morning and after closing, there was usually a pretty girl waiting for me who was ready to party.

Barney always kept the lounge dark with just a few candles on the tables. During a break one night, I noticed a dark mass lying on the piano and when I went over to see what was up, I found a well-dressed guy with a crew cut passed out on the piano. No one knew how he got in but when I shook him, he started to babble and I recognized it was the comedian George Gobel, then appearing at the nearby Cape Melody Tent. After I called the bouncer over, we helped him out to the deck and pumped him with coffee. Once sobered up, the comedian explained friends had thrown a party for him in the hotel after the show with lots of booze but no food. After everyone left he felt hungry, called a cab and asked the driver to find a place with food and entertainment. The cabbie headed for Baxter's, let him off and somehow he walked in. Then, seeing the piano he climbed on it and passed out.

George was a kind and humble country boy from Nebraska. Once sobered up, he did a little routine on the deck that had everyone in stitches. I stopped playing to watch him and thoroughly enjoyed his act. Not long after that, I was sorry to read that George had died from complications during an operation for varicose veins. I was watching the Johnny Carson Show the night after George died when Johnny said wonderful things about him and had other comedians, Bob Hope, Jonathan Winters, and Jack Benny there also to pay him tribute. They even said, "You know, George may have been the funniest of us all."

When you worked for Warren Baxter, Senior, he had a strict rule: "No fighting!" If an employee got into a fight with anyone, no matter how justified, that employee would be fired.

The Golden Fleece, a fifty-five foot commercial fishing vessel, was tied up for three weeks at the dock next to the Boat House. Members of the crew often stopped in for a night cap before heading to their bunks and things always went well. But for some reason, one of the crew seemed to dislike the piano player. Every time he passed the piano on his way to the men's room, he'd make a snide remark which I tried to ignore. But one night, after we'd closed, I was heading to my car (then the only one left in the parking lot) when another car came screeching down the road headed straight at me.

Just as the driver slammed on his brakes, I jumped on the hood so that the car wouldn't hit me. When the driver got out and began attacking me. I recognized the hostile crewman. He threw a punch at me, which I ducked. Then I hit him harder than I'd ever hit anyone, before or since. Down he went. As he fell, he grabbed my legs tackling me to the ground. I fell on top of him and as my chin scraped on the pavement, I continued to pummel him.

Barney was inside counting the night's receipts, and heard the commotion. He came out yelling "Get outta here, Donny. I just called the cops!" With my chin dripping blood and my knuckles cracked and swollen, I left the guy on the ground, jumped into my car and headed for home. But I was in a panic and not over the fight. I was sure I had just lost my job.

First thing the next morning, I headed straight for Baxter's, hoping to see Warren Sr. and explain. As usual, he was in the parking lot wearing his crumpled hat and stoic frown. I asked if he'd heard what happened and he said "Of course." I explained that I'd just been defending myself and that the fight happened after we were closed.

"Go inside and take a look at the water glass sitting on the bar," he said, with a faint smile on his face. On the counter was a glass of water with a set of false teeth in the bottom. Puzzled, I went back outside where Warren solemnly told me, "When you punch a guy in the mouth Donny, at least let him have his teeth back." Then he chuckled, gave me one of his rare smiles, and I knew I still had my job.

The next day, two other crew members came to see Barney and apologize for the rest of the crew. They didn't like the guy either and were happy he'd had his ass kicked.

However, Warren was still so concerned he hired a police officer to show up every night at closing until the Golden Fleece pulled out to sea to make sure there were no reprisals on Barney or me.

Before and after I was playing at Baxter's, the vessel, Andrea Gail, out of Gloucester, was tied up at the dock next to the Boathouse and usually joined by her sister ship, the Hannah Bowden a swordfish seeker, also from Gloucester. Years later, and of course with a different crew, the Andrea Gail became famous in the movie *The Perfect Storm* starring George Clooney. Tragically, all of its crew had drowned during that notorious storm.

Baxter's is still a very busy and popular place but in those days, Warren Sr. paid the bills, did the ordering and ran the office with his daughter, Sally. My friend Barney handled the everyday demands both inside and out, and although he worked hard, he was a restless soul, and couldn't wait until Labor Day when the place closed for the winter. Shortly after high school, Barney married Brenda Wolfe, a wonderful girl from Yarmouth with whom he had three great kids, Ben, Amy, and Sam.

Like her mother-in-law, Florence, before her, Brenda took over the daily operation of the Fish 'n Chips side of the restaurant. Things were going well for them until the end of my second summer there when Brenda was diagnosed with cancer and died suddenly. She was only in her early thirties and it was a terrible loss for all of us, but especially Barney.

Life is filled with ironies and sadly, Brenda's mother and sisters would develop cancer as well; only one sister would survive. Yet, her father, Sears Wolfe, a hard living, hard drinking character who never took care of himself, defied nature and lived until just short of his one hundredth birthday.

I got a big kick out of Sears and really admired him. Even after losing his wife and all but one daughter to cancer, he kept his great sense of humor and remained upbeat. Barney had me keep my sailboat, The Shadow, in the yard next to the Boat House on the harbor and one day while I was painting the bottom, Sears came over to see how I was doing. His wife Betty had died some years earlier so we chatted for a while about women and life in general. His mother, Nina, was still going strong well into her eighties and he would last even longer.

CHAPTER 9

FOR BETTER OR WORSE

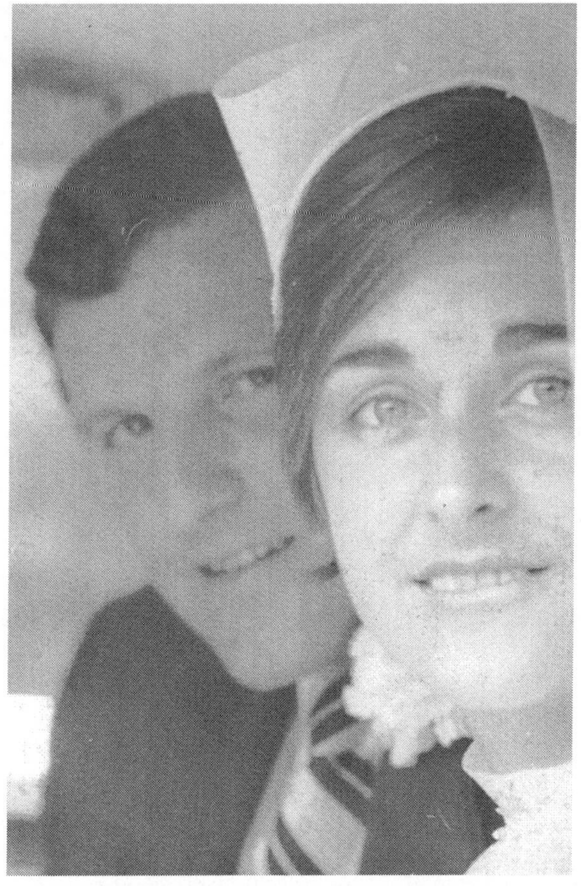

The author, pictured with his new bride, Donna Scoblick, on their wedding day, 1973.

After three winters in North Conway, skiing became such an important part of my life that I spent every winter weekend there. I continued to make new friends and was dating a great girl from Quincy. Playing piano at the Linderhof Lodge during the après ski hours gave me extra spending money and the lodge paid for my meals, drinks and even my lift tickets. I considered myself lucky because how many other school teachers spent their vacations skiing and partying then returned home with more money than when they arrived.

During my Christmas vacation that year, an unexpected gift arrived from Carbondale, Pennsylvania, a town just over the Pocono Mountains near Scranton. Her name was Donna Elizabeth Scoblick and she was an expert skier. I'd spotted her on the mountain several times but since I didn't ski as well as she did, I never could catch up to her to say hello. After two winters in France and Italy, skiing and working in small hotels, Donna had returned home to take a job teaching French and Spanish at Belmont High School, just outside of Boston. Like me, she'd come to North Conway as the guest of a fellow teacher who belonged to a ski club. One afternoon after skiing all day, Donna and her friends were headed back to their lodge, when someone suggested they stop for a drink at The Linderhof.

I was playing the piano when they arrived but during a break, a mutual friend introduced us. Donna was beautiful with long brown hair, brown eyes and a lovely athletic figure but I barely paid attention because I was dating someone else and caught up partying with my new skiing buddies. Besides, she lived in Boston and I lived on the South Shore which seemed much too far to go just for a date

However, that idea changed after I ran into her again on the mountain and at other après ski parties. There was something so appealing about her: she was quiet but personable, a classy woman whom everyone, including me, liked. Suddenly Boston no longer seemed that far away so I asked her for a date.

I was nearly thirty by then and after we dated for a while I was seriously in love. Several close friends were already married and I began thinking I, too, should settle down. I proposed to Donna and after one glitch, she said yes. By the time we were married, I owned an apartment house in Abington and the summer house on Cape Cod. I still taught and coached in Rockland near the apartment house and when Donna got a job teaching in Abington about the same distance away, we moved into one of the apartment units.

As newlyweds, we continued to ski in the winter and summer on Cape Cod. But once we were married, staying at the ski lodge and sleeping in bunk beds didn't suit us anymore so we bought a chalet in Birch Hill, a subdivision built by another skier from the Cape, Peter Shaeffer. By doing so we planned to rent the chalet out during the holiday vacations to help pay the mortgage and taxes. Since we still belonged to the ski club, we stayed there during the holidays until it was vacant again.

Unfortunately, there was so little snow for the next three winters most of our renters cancelled. The chalet was all-electric which seemed fine when we bought it, but after electric rates tripled nationally we were shocked. The Rockland apartment house was also all-electric. When I first owned it, the cost of electricity for the entire building was $4,000.00 a year or $1,000 per unit. After the rate hike however, it rose to $4,000.00 per unit. Electricity was included in the rent and with only one meter, I was in real trouble. Installing separate meters would cost over $10,000, an enormous sum of money for me at the time. Without the rental income, our teachers' salaries couldn't cover the mortgages and expenses as well as those for the Cape house. In a state of panic, I immediately put both properties on the market.

Doing so with the chalet turned out to be a mistake. Having spent almost all my summers on Cape Cod, I didn't realize that the summer rental market in North Conway was much stronger than the winter one. Renting out the chalet every summer would have solved our problems because it would have paid the mortgage and related expenses. We sold the chalet and still skied with friends on occasional weekends but snow conditions in New Hampshire were poor and the long drive back now seemed to take forever. Like the shadows that darken mountain slopes in late afternoon, our five year ski life in the White Mountains faded into the sunset.

Living in the apartment house during the school year was convenient but when summer ended Donna hated to leave the Cape. One day she asked if I'd consider living on the Cape year-round. We could rent the apartment until the building sold but this would mean commuting every day. I agreed but since I was coaching after school, I pointed out that we would have to take two cars on most days. Even so, the idea of living on Cape Cod year round was appealing.

During the summer, Donna often packed wine and cheese for our sailing ventures around the lake in the Shadow where we explored coves and gazed at the waterfront homes. We particularly admired an older home, with a glassed- in porch and boathouse located on a point of land shaped like Italy. One day we noticed a For Sale sign posted there and immediately Donna asked if we could look at it. I knew it was out of our price range but was curious to see at it as well. Taking a pen from her pocket book, Donna wrote down the phone number and as soon as we reached the mooring, hopped off the boat and hustled up to our house to call.

Less than an hour later, we were driving down a long bumpy dirt road to meet the owners, Tom and Laura Alexander, who couldn't have been nicer. Then in his sixties, Tom was a professor and director of student affairs at Cape Cod Community College. He sported a white pageboy hair style, a warm smile on his face, and was wearing a purple velour jump suit. Laura was a southern belle from Atlanta, Georgia whose father headed the IRS during the Eisenhower administration. She presented us with a bouquet from her garden and wore a wide brimmed hat sprinkled with the same flowers. Laura looked as if she'd just stepped out of the Gone with the Wind movie.

Back in the 1920s a Chicago investment banker built it as a hunting lodge and the Alexanders had done little to modernize it. But the huge fieldstone fireplace filling the living room and varnished flagstone floors in the living room and kitchen areas made a magnificent statement that needed no improvement.

As we toured the upstairs bedrooms, we noticed all the drapes had chairs backed up to them. Only later did we discover that the chairs' placement hid the fact that the drapes were three feet too long. Laura brought them from an earlier home in Georgia and rather than have them shortened, just rolled the surplus into a ball and tucked it under a chair.

Tom offered us a glass of wine after the tour but as he reached into the cabinet for glasses, I noticed a dead fly in two of them. He tipped the flies onto the floor, poured the wine and gave us each a glass. Donna had seen the fly and the look on her face had me biting my tongue again to keep from laughing. We both took a small sip, then made a polite excuse to exit and say goodbye.

We had both fallen for the place but the Alexanders' asking price was three times more than that of our house. That being said, all the way home I kept trying to figure a way for us to buy that house. It was crazy but when I finally worked through the figures, I felt with proper financing and the proceeds of the Cape and apartment houses, we could manage it.

Besides, Donna was so excited I couldn't say no. I wanted the house just as badly as she did so the next day I put the Cape house and Abington apartment building on the market. The apartment house sold the following month but our offer to the Alexanders was contingent upon the sale of our house. Fortunately, just in time, we sold it that month as well.

Moving into that wonderful old hunting lodge seemed like heaven. We felt as if we were living a dream. Although my father fumed when he found out how much we'd paid, we were determined to afford it. Donna consequently waitressed at the East Bay Lodge on weekends and full time during the summer while I worked as a landscaper during the day and played piano three nights a week. Two years later I decided it was worth taking a risk on renovating the boat house into a two bedroom cottage and then renting it out year round.

Looking back, living in that idyllic setting and being married to Donna was probably the happiest time of my life. We had a lively household with two dogs and a cat. Donna's brother and two sisters lived with us and I always sensed I'd married someone who brought out the best in me, complementing everything I did. But as crazy as it sounds, that wasn't enough. My system was uncomfortable being comfortable! Something else was driving me and I needed excitement, good or bad.

* * * *

After twelve years of being in the classroom and coaching kids on the playing fields, I still loved my job. But a new and more liberal movement was changing educational priorities. When administrators grow soft on discipline and judges force schools to accept constant troublemakers back into the classroom, it doesn't bode well as today's test scores reflect.

On our way to school one morning, I asked Donna how she'd feel if I left teaching. Surprised, she listened quietly as I described an incident that happened outside my classroom the day before. A student wandering the halls had walked up to the classroom across the hall from mine and began heckling the teacher and her student teacher. When I saw him make an obscene gesture, I shot out of my seat, intending to bring him to the principal's office. The student refused to move however, so after blasting him verbally I took his arm after which he tried to punch me. I then grabbed the back of his shirt and dragged him kicking and screaming down the halls to the assistant principal's office, fully expecting some disciplinary action.

But ideas about discipline were changing in the higher educational circles. Instead of supporting the teacher, the first words out of the assistant principal's mouth were to me, not to the troublemaker. When he said "You can't treat a student that way" followed by "And I want to see *you* later," I wanted to punch him instead of the kid! I retorted, "The day a student can get away with treating a teacher like he did you won't have to fire me, I'll quit." Incidentally, the student was roaming the halls because his teacher in the room next door never took attendance.

Storming back to my classroom, I ordered my class to "Get your books open! And where were we?" Then the bell rang and the class bolted out the door. Several teachers rushed into my room laughing because they said when I'd gone by their classroom, dragging that student, the class went quiet and paid attention the whole period. "You disciplined the whole hallway!" We all chuckled but the teacher who caused the problem by failing to take attendance was never disciplined. I, on the other hand, could have been fired and that was just the beginning.

Two weeks later, returning to my classroom after cafeteria duty, I found the principal standing at my door. He had a smug look on his face and couldn't wait to ask why I was late to class. But when I said, "Because I was breaking up a fight in the cafeteria and had to take the little angels to your office! Where were you?" it didn't go well. Although he was a good principal for the most part, he was still angry at the way I'd spoken to his assistant principal over the hallway incident and wanted to let me know it.

During the dozen years I taught, I watched as the

focus shifted from academic excellence to overwhelming concern for a students self-esteem and inner feelings. With few exceptions, every student graduated, whether they did their work or not. But most parents didn't seem to care. Some teachers kept trying but when administrators did nothing more than maintain the status quo, many gave up and took early retirement. When you can get eighty percent of your salary for the last three years you worked, while still in your fifties, why bother to fight it? For many teachers, it seemed the most practical and easiest solution.

Despite improved salaries and benefits, I believe teachers' unions have allowed too many administrators to lower academic expectations from when they were students themselves. Neither my wife Donna nor I went into teaching for the money. No one got rich teaching school but, like us, most teachers accepted that because they loved working with kids. Having a second job in the summer was part of the deal and I for one, enjoyed the change. I didn't need a union to get me more money for doing something I loved. Too many union reps couldn't handle the classroom anyway and were lousy teachers besides.

Several years ago, The Wall Street Journal reported a study done by Princeton University, I believe, stating they had found over 30% of teacher college graduates were incapable of handling a classroom. But I've yet to see a response or hear a solution from the National Education Association.

Of all God's many gifts to me, the one that allowed

me to be a teacher, a coach, and part of so many young people's lives, was one of the best. Watching a student grow is a powerful experience. There are still many excellent teachers today but too many in the profession don't seem to love teaching and are in it only for the money, benefits and the vacation time.

* * * *

At that point in my life, perhaps I'd been spoiled. Other than my baseball dream, everything that was initially important to me seemed to come fairly easily. Even so, I was frustrated and felt I needed something more to become a success. Neither Donna nor I realized it at the time, but that would soon be a curse. Instead of talking to her about it at length, I went ahead and resigned from teaching that summer, knowing she would support whatever I decided.

Having coffee with friends one morning, I heard them talking about a general store for sale in Marstons Mills called The Cash Market. It had been owned and operated by Loring Jones, Sr. then Loring "Junior" Jones and Frank McClusky, for over thirty-five years. A store had been in operation at that location since 1886 and it was only fifteen minutes from our house. Although the place needed a major facelift, I was psyched at the idea of owning my own business but unfortunately, being impulsive again, I hadn't thought about what such a lifestyle change would mean for me and more importantly, for Donna. The store was open long hours seven days a week so the vacation days and weeks off I had when teaching were no longer possible.

Initially I enjoyed meeting and chatting with the village residents, many of whom enjoyed watching the renovations. My father had owned a variety story in North Weymouth when I was ten and enjoyed helping me set up the place. One day my mother brought her eighty-two year old mother, Grandma Parker, over to see the place and when I came outside to greet her, wearing my butcher's apron, she said she thought she had been there before. I doubted that until she asked if there wasn't a little church up the street on a hill. There was and that inspired her to tell stories about her girlhood when she'd travel with my maternal great-grandfather and family, to pick cranberries for owners of the local bogs. As a child she'd slept on the floor of that church during the picking season along with other village children while the adults slept in the growers' houses until the harvest ended.

I was also amazed to hear her recall the elegant home just fifty yards down the street on the pond. Owned by a Doctor Higgins, it became a tourist attraction after he installed a flush toilet in the house. His elderly daughter, Pricilla, still lived there and told me that flush toilet was the first one on the Cape. People would arrive from all over the Cape just to get a look at it. Still sharp as a tack, my grandmother continued, "And you know Donald, we came here by horse and wagon, years before the Cape Cod Canal was built."

Route 149 was a well-traveled road all year but when I bought the general store, it only had a beer and wine license. The store was open year round but business slowed down during the winter. Donna missed our ski weekends and, having sold our chalet, our times in New Hampshire had ended. Years earlier, while still in college, Donna had skied in Aspen with her uncle and sisters. The first winter I owned the Cash Market, her sister Lisa had been living with us and worked for me that summer. As things slowed down, she decided to head for Aspen to ski and work there during the winter. It seemed natural for Donna to visit and spend her vacation skiing there as I planned to take time off in February to join them as well.

As soon as I returned from Aspen, I applied for and received a full liquor license which doubled sales. While I enjoyed the challenge of owning and running a business, lugging beer cases, stocking shelves, making sandwiches and cutting meat seven days a week soon lost its charm. I soon sensed that the store was not going to be my life's work. But another incident with a union provided the final straw.

During the second summer of my owning The Cash Market, the Teamsters Union went on strike and all the drivers for the liquor companies joined them. With no beer, wine, or liquor deliveries arriving at the package stores, our survival was in jeopardy. My best customers were tradesmen who stopped in almost every day at lunch time for sandwiches and a beer or another beverage. After five, some would return for a six pack and a couple of nips.

Many called their wives at home to see if they needed anything which also boosted sales.

The strike made my situation desperate and when our package store association learned there were distributors who couldn't deliver but would sell alcoholic beverages to licensed store owners who picked them up, we formed a transportation pool and rented a U-Haul truck. Foolishly, I volunteered to become the designated driver and even drove as far as Springfield to obtain stock at a wholesaler called Lion Distributors. That turned out to be one of the most frightening experiences of my life because rental trucks aren't designed to carry the heavy, condensed weight of cases of beer and liquor, especially when loaded beyond the suggested maximum weight. As I traveled the highway, heading home, the truck and cab swayed back and forth precariously which scared the hell out of me and the guy riding shotgun.

After one such trip, my nerves were still frazzled when I dropped off the truck at the Hyannis U-Haul terminal. All I wanted was to get back to the store, fill the empty shelves and beer coolers and go home. But as I was re-stocking, a driver from one of our liquor companies came in. We'd always gotten along well before so I wasn't prepared for what he said. "You know, you're crazy to be driving that truck. It's very dangerous."

I agreed but when I said I needed the stock to survive, he bellowed, "You guys are nothing but f--king scabs trying to bust my union!" Hearing that I snapped and said we'd better go outside.

Things began with a push but my manager and two customers broke us up before I could get at the guy. Now I was furious and shouted back, "You union guys never give a damn about the business owners! We're the reason you get a paycheck but without product we can't pay our employees or our bills! Get the hell out of my store and tell your boss if I see you driving a truck here again, I'm through doing business with him."

That was it for me and The Cash Market in Marston's Mills. I put the place up for sale the next day and three weeks later it was under agreement.

* * * *

After finishing college, my wife Donna had traveled to the mountain areas of France and Italy to work in hotels and restaurants in pursuit of her passion for skiing. Not only did she cover her expenses but she also developed into a fine skier and a first class traveler. Early in our marriage, she had mentioned how much she would like to take me on an extended trip out of the country, maybe even to Europe.

The sale of the Cash Market provided a perfect opportunity but even though I wanted to travel, I was deathly afraid of flying. And the thought of traveling or living in a foreign country gave me a lot of anxiety. But when Donna said, "Donald, if you want to see the world, you'll have to conquer those fears," I figured a few gin and tonics would help me overcome my fear of flying and told her to go ahead and make reservations.

Unlike most travelers, Donna always takes a minimal amount of luggage. She booked most of our lodgings in advance, handled all the money, and even reserved the rental cars. I drove the cars but she was the one who knew which towns and city attractions to visit. Fortunately, her prior experience and language skills helped us find the best restaurants and least expensive places to stay.

The flight was uneventful and the landing at London's Heathrow Airport was smooth, (I think I kissed the ground). We picked up our rental car, settled into a nice B&B and toured London for the next two days. Then we headed off to find my father's birthplace, the town of Blackpool in Lancashire, England.

April is a damp, cold month in England. Chilled to the bone we checked into a small hotel overlooking Blackpool Tower in the center of town. The hotel owner was a smiling Irishman with a heavy brogue, who greeted us at the desk with a snifter of warm brandy. Along with the brandy, he handed us a hot water bottle saying, "Take a good swig! You'll need the hot water bottle for the foot of your bed when you retire for the night." I hadn't seen a hot water bottle since I was a kid and as we sipped the brandy and warmed up, we had a good laugh about it.

My father was born in one of the many red brick

duplexes located downtown on Exchange Street. And after seeing it, I recalled stories my late grandmother Florence told about riding down the street in the Easter Parade, perched on a bale of hay on a horse drawn wagon turned into a float. While imagining her as a young woman walking down that sidewalk with my father and his sister, I felt her presence and began missing her again. Seeing my father's birthplace was a spiritual experience but remember, I still thought the McKeag family was Scottish. As we traveled to Scotland, hoping to find the family tartans and clan names, was I in for a surprise.

The Registry of Tartars building is located in the center of Edinburgh, next to Edinburgh Castle. Ancient bag pipes, swords, and famous warrior-kilts hang across its interior and as I admired them, a little ruddy-faced Scotswoman with a rolling brogue, came to the desk. I explained the limited information I had about the family and after she disappeared for about twenty minutes, she returned with a strange look on her face. Calling me over to the desk, she asked what I wanted first, the good news or the bad news.

Reminded of that old joke, I chuckled. But she was dead serious so I composed myself and asked for the good news first. Stretching as tall as she could and looking me straight in the eye, she said, "The good news is, I found your family name. It's ancient and tied to royalty." I smiled of course, but then a bit arrogantly, she added, "The bad news is, you're not Scottish. You're Irish! Knowing my father was told he wasn't Irish his entire life, I let out a howl. Immediately, the Scottish official frowned and told me to shush!

Ever since I was a small boy, many of my best friends were Irish. I'd always wanted to be Irish and let people believe I was when they assumed it because of my name. As soon as we returned to the Cape, I told Dad the story and he laughed. He said he'd always suspected that to be the case.

But Donna was a different story. When I told her she said, "Don't you dare tell that to anyone when we get home! You drink too much now!" I laughed but it really wasn't funny and she was right. I didn't know it at the time but another McKeag was coping with the demon that would ultimately control too many future decisions and have me baffled.

Paris impressed me more than I'd expected and I enjoyed watching my pretty wife approach police officers in a French or Italian city, asking for directions or for a good place to eat. With long brown hair down to her hips, her curvy figure and beautiful smile always got a positive reaction. And when she spoke their language, they were lost and couldn't do enough to help.

After renting a car, we visited the shops and cafes along the Champs D'Elysee and checked into a delightful inn on the outskirts of Paris. After walking around the city for a while, we returned to find the owner standing at the desk in full chef's attire. Greeting us warmly, he checked us in and minutes later served us our scrumptious fish dinner personally. It was then I learned what French service really meant.

Donna suggested we travel to Nice the next day but I never realized that besides palm trees, bouillabaisse, jet setters and the Riviera, that seaside resort was famous for its pizza. And although I'd never seen fruit on pizza before, I liked it. We also noticed that some of the outdoor cafés specialized in ice cream and sorbet desserts served on cut glass dishes and topped with fruits and liqueurs. My favorite was a lemon sorbet topped with kiwi slices covered with a lime green Sicilian liqueur with green leaves placed in a pale yellow dish shaped like a lemon.

Except for small tables for two, European couples rarely have a table all to themselves. We were joined at our table by a French couple who spoke perfect English. After chatting for a while the gentleman asked me how I liked Paris. I told him I thought France was a beautiful country but didn't think Parisians liked Americans very much. Impeccably dressed and sporting a thin, blond and lightly waxed mustache, the Frenchman's reply was classic.

"Donald, you must remember, Parisians don't like Americans, Oui? But they also don't like the English, the Germans, Swiss, Dutch, the Chinese, the Russians, the Danes and many other foreigners. They're not even very fond of other Parisians!" he explained. The ladies had been listening and after a good laugh, the couple invited us back to their home in Paris. We would have liked to do that but

I was anxious to visit Le Louvre and Donna wanted to do some shopping without time constraints so we thanked them and declined.

My idea of heaven would be to wander through a museum with classical music playing as waiters in tuxedoes served wine and cheese. Having spent time at the Le Louvre before, Donna left me to my reverie, set a time to meet at The Galleria next door, and went off to shop.

Mesmerized by the surroundings, I wandered through the bowels of the museum as time flew by. When I finally checked my watch, it was late. Donna would be wondering where I was, so I rushed up to one of the museum attendants and tried to remember the French word for exit. It was then that I first experienced the Parisian attitude toward foreigners. The guard kept shrugging his shoulders as if he couldn't understand me, while I attempted to use my limited French. Hundreds of English speaking visitors passed by him daily so I realized he was deliberately pretending ignorance. Finally, confronting his rudeness by grabbing his bow tie, I pulled him toward me, and said, "Listen you little prick, take me to the exit right now!"

That got his attention and he spewed, "Oh, Monsieur, pardon, pardon, C'est sortie, sortie!" then led me to the nearest exit. I'm not proud of that scene and never told Donna about it but I'm sure I was described as just another ugly American in the cafe discussions that night.

Even after five weeks of traveling I was still enjoying the sights, the food and most of the people in Europe. But eventually, driving on the wrong side of the road, checking in and out of lodgings, packing, unpacking, and trying to understand other languages got to me. I'd been out of my element for too long and was developing a bit of an attitude. Despite that, Donna remained calm and our trip continued.

Geographically, France is much like the United States, but certainly on a smaller scale. Many of the sights and much of the countryside remind one of some locations in the states. We began one morning, by sunning and swimming on the French Riviera at nine a.m. Then, at noon, hopped into the car heading for Val d'Isere, a resort she had skied at while managing a small hotel eight years before. Three hours after sunning on the Riviera, we were strapping on skis and shushing down the slopes, overlooking the Matterhorn, a spectacular sight despite the wild and boisterous Germans dominating the resort.

Unlike the Parisians, the French of the countryside were very friendly. I was awed by visiting the cathedrals and their exquisite stained glass windows, especially in Chartres.

French bread is everywhere. Baguettes are even strapped onto bicycles. During a break from one cathedral visit, Donna introduced me to chocolate sandwiches as we stopped by the side of the road. We were sipping some of the local red wine when she put two pieces of hard, dark chocolate inside the bread. The combination of wine, chocolate, and fresh baked bread was extraordinary as it whets your taste buds.

France is beautiful but I liked Italy even better. Its people, language, food, and colorful history create a relaxed life style that makes one never want to leave. When I told Donna I could live there, I meant every word. One of our first stops was at a quaint little hotel in a little fishing village on a beach, overlooking Naples Bay. We spent a week there but since there was no place to park, hotel guests had to back their cars down a goat path behind the hotel and park on the roof. It was a bit scary but once we were settled, we didn't need the car.

Thanks to Donna's knowledge of Italian, the staff got to know us better than other guests. The two waitresses, Rosetta "Piccola" and Rosetta "Grande," (one short and the other a rather large girl) waited on us each morning and since I'd studied Latin in high school and understood some Italian, I tried to speak a little. That had them laughing a lot but unlike the French, the Italians enjoy helping others with their language and before long, I could speak "tourist Italian."

Before our trip, a school teacher friend had suggested I read Irving Stone's The Agony and the Ecstasy about Michelangelo. He also mentioned that since the Italians loved President John Kennedy I should bring some Kennedy half-dollars with me. As it happened, I had at least thirty of them in a metal tin which I'd collected over the years from my businesses so I had plenty for the trip.

One morning, Rosetta Grande asked us to join her family for a communion celebration on the beach. Their homes were just a few steps from the hotel and they lived off the sea. They didn't have much materially and in many cases hadn't even been to Rome. But every day I'd watch the men pulling their boats up onto the beach, emptying their nets, laughing and smoking while waiting for the fish buyers. They were truly happy.

Even their church was on the beach and most would be baptized, married and buried without ever having left the village. Each of the three humble homes we visited had a picture of the Pope on one wall and across from him, a picture of President John F. Kennedy. Remembering the Kennedy half dollars in my luggage, I asked Donna if this might be a good time to give some of them to Rosetta and the other women. She thought it was a great idea so I trudged off through the sand back to the hotel.

Since I considered this a memento of our visit and nothing more I wasn't prepared for the people's reaction. At an appropriate time, I asked Donna to call Rosetta over to present her with a coin as well as one for each of the other women. The men gathered around as each woman hugged her coin as if it were a precious object. And when they burst into tears, I was speechless. At first, none of them wanted to keep the coin thinking it was too valuable. President John F. Kennedy had been dead for over fifteen years but like so many others, the Italian people hadn't forgotten him and still felt his loss.

CHAPTER 10

A CAPE COD RESTAURATEUR

YANKEE
NEW ENGLAND'S
MAGAZINE

The author's restaurant, The Asa Bearse House on Main Street in Hyannis, is featured in Yankee Magazine in September of 1982.

When we flew into Boston, my friend Kevin O'Neil and his wife Nancy picked us up at the airport and on the way home asked about my plans. When I explained I hadn't thought about it, Kevin offered me a job selling real estate. His family had been in the real estate and insurance business for generations and at the time he was managing the real estate sector located in their main office on Hyannis' Main Street. I told him I'd love the job and immediately started studying for my real estate license. I was excited at the thought of a new career and so was Donna since I would finally be working normal hours again.

One of my first listings, The Beachwood Inn and Tea Room, used to be run by five elderly women but its more recent owners, a couple from upstate New York, were tired of the business and wanted to return to the computer business they'd run before coming to the Cape. They also gave me the listing for their personal residence in West Hyannis Port, a lovely home overlooking the marsh and ocean.

As we toured the two properties, I was especially taken with the beauty of the Beachwood Inn. Built by Captain Asa Bearse in 1856, the inn was one of the last Victorian sea captains' homes remaining on Main Street and still had the original Sandwich cranberry glass side panels on the front door. Inside, black marble fireplaces, beautiful moldings and classic wood paneling added to its charm. Right away I envisioned its conversion into a restaurant and bar. Since it stood in the middle of one of the Cape's major shopping districts, the location was so perfect I wanted to own it. When I told Kevin what I had in mind, he thought it was a great idea and my real estate career ended before it had even begun.

Our European vacation had given me and Donna lots of experience with excellent service, fine food, and classic antique décor, which I hoped to recreate in a new Cape restaurant. But my wife was dead set against the idea, and for good reasons. She recalled the days when I would be working seven days a week in a stressful business that left little time for us. Donna did not want to see me returning to those kinds of hours. Moreover she remained worried about my drinking. Being a good wife and knowing I wouldn't change my mind, she finally agreed to help with the project if I promised to make time for us at least one day a week. Imagine the nerve of her!

I agreed, but it was an empty promise. My self-centered journey continued and one day in March 1979, as we sat with two lawyers and the head of the loan department, Donna handed me a note under the table. It said, *I don't approve of the restaurant project, but will support you as long as I can.* I kissed her and said thank you but deep down knew the drive and need to become somebody now possessed me. The restaurant would also enable me to rise above my father and achieve something he hadn't.

Our first priority was to change the name The Beechwood Inn to the Asa Bearse House, after the ship's captain who built it. One day a lawyer friend and bon vivant, Richard "Dick" Anderson, whose office was across the street, stopped by to say hello and told me he thought the new name was wrong. Believing, he was serious, I asked why. "Well Donald, it's like this. People always like the word 'Captain' in seaside restaurant names. There are three just in Hyannis. One is called The Captain's Chair, another, The Captain's Gig and of course, there's The Captain's Table. I think you should name your restaurant, "The Captain's Stool!" We both laughed but I obviously stayed with the name The Asa Bearse House.

After passing papers, we began extensive renovations to the building, inside and out. Donna handled the interior decorating while I worked with the carpenters, painters, and landscapers. Brian Olander, a Hyannis carpenter who had done work on our lake house, managed the construction along with Donna's brother, Tom Scoblick, who had left Pennsylvania to live with us and work on the project.

We converted the upstairs bedrooms into private dining rooms and young Bruce Besse was hired to do the landscaping. Since we planned to offer al fresco dining under bright pink and gray awnings with large matching umbrellas, I asked Bruce to build a new stone patio facing Main Street. Many of my friends, including Kevin O'Neil, took up a collection and donated the post lights to surround the patio.

Our goal was to bring a little slice of Europe to Hyannis but at the time, bylaws in the Town of Barnstable didn't allow outside dining. After attending the next meeting of the Board of Health, I stated and argued my case, without a lawyer or other restaurant owners to support me, and won the day. Today, when I travel down Main Street, Hyannis and see so many people eating outside, I feel a little proud knowing I'd been the one who fought to get those cafes.

* * * *

The Asa Bearse House opened in April of 1981 to a lot of fanfare. Several newspapers wrote articles about the event and people couldn't wait to see the results of all the work. Gerry Street, a fellow UMass friend and fraternity brother from Scituate, MA, had just finished his tour of duty as a navy pilot and stopped by one day to see how the project was going. Since he had restaurant experience, including menu planning and the hiring of staff, I asked if he'd consider becoming our manager. He took the job and the three of us, Gerry, Donna, and me, pulled everything together and hired a wonderful staff.

The Beachwood Inn had no liquor license and when we first opened, some of the elderly women who used to frequent the Tea Room, complained about liquor being served. One day while I was on the bar working the lunch shift, a waitress giggled as she gave me a cocktail order from a table of four well-dressed elderly ladies…one extra dry Beefeater martini straight up, two bourbon Manhattans on the rocks and finally, a Jack Daniels Old Fashioned. It was only 11:30 AM so I called Gerry over to share the order with him and said "I think we've just rounded the corner!" We both howled. The lunchtime clientele continued to grow from then on.

Operational duties were divided between the three of us. Donna ran the dining rooms, scheduled the waitresses and hosted most of the time. Gerry oversaw the operation, did the menus, pricing, cost analyses and even filled in when needed in the kitchen. I handled the office work, coordinated the sub-contractors, dealt with problems during the renovations, and most importantly, paid the bills.

There were only six bar stools in the original lounge area but some nights I'd tend bar, play the old upright piano, and wait on customers in the lounge at the same time. It was crazy stuff but we had fun and by winter, our business was growing so fast we needed to expand.

The easiest thing was to build an addition onto the rear of the building over to the existing garage. And best or all, it would be one more step towards my dream of creating a special space reminiscent of European charm.

When we purchased the Beachwood Inn, a three bedroom house behind it was part of the sale. Originally a barn for the main house, it had been renovated in the early 1940s and used as a summer rental. No one had lived there for years so I decided to gut the building and build an entertainment and unique bar attraction.

During our trip to Europe, the interiors of many restaurants and shops inspired me to create rooms like them; something that looked to the past as had the Gay Nineties Restaurant. Besides serving cocktails and food, I envisioned a place where customers could enjoy a classical ambiance that would become a showcase for fine musicians. In the summer of '82, I had the incredible luck of hiring two rugged football players from Cornell University as my night dishwashers. When I asked them if they'd be interested in a job during the day tearing a building apart, they agreed. Not only could they use the extra money but they also said they loved the idea of a job where they wouldn't have to think and could stay in shape by beating the shit out of something!

The contractor I chose for this project, Ernest "E. J." Jaxtimer, had worked for high quality Osterville builders Rogers and Marney as a kid, but now married and in his early thirties had decided to go out on his own. The Reading Room was one of his first commercial projects and today E. J. is one of Cape Cod's most successful builders. My brother-in-law, Tom Scoblick, did a lot of the finish work in the new room and once gutted, the building's interior had a cathedral ceiling and new walls. Some years earlier, I had purchased the interior parts of an old opera house, which we integrated into the Reading Room using its original brass rails, upscale moldings and carvings. Ironically, the opera house was located on Union Street in Rockland, Massachusetts where my family used to drive by every summer as we headed to my grandparents' camp for the weekend. During the 1970's, when I was teaching at Rockland High School, I would unknowingly be passing by its former location every morning again.

I also incorporated parts of other old buildings into the Reading Room. Among them were oak panels carved with white lilies and green leaves once part of St. Edward's Catholic Church in Boston's North End. Oak bookcases and shelves with matching drawers surrounding the bar area were from Hovey's Drug Store in Whitman, MA, home of the famous Toll House cookie. Church windows from Augusta, Maine allowed light to filter into the interior of the room. Old books from a Harwich library, purchased at twenty-five cents a pound, filled the book cases as well as others from different libraries. Altogether there were 1,612; I remember because I personally placed them on the shelves.

One of my favorite magazines, Architectural Digest, had a cover featuring a room in Chinese red upon which hung gold framed paintings and other artifacts. Impressed, I decided to copy the look. I would use that same color in the new room and surround the stained glass windows with paintings, and other artifacts as they had. I bought the paint but when I tried it on the walls, it seemed too loud and gaudy.

As I stood on a ladder with a roller wondering about the color, Howard Penn, my friend from across the street at Puritan Clothing, appeared and began evaluating our progress. When he saw the color, he yelled "Hey Pecker Head! What are you doing? Opening up a whore house?" I almost fell off the ladder as we both laughed. But that made me even more nervous. I finally said the hell with it and painted the wall red anyway. And once the paintings and other items were hung, it looked great. The red created a border that blended the items together which was why Architectural Digest had placed it on the cover in the first place.

While pleased with our progress I knew the room needed someone, preferably an artist, to do something unique and pull the colors and designs together. One day after the lunch hour, Donna and I took a walk down Main Street and found just the right man. Frank Balaam was running an antique shop just a block away and coincidentally, hailed from my father's birthplace, Blackpool, England, which we had visited just three months earlier. We talked about the town and its tower and soon learned he was much more than an antique dealer. Frank was not only a talented artist, but a sculptor as well. I hired him to do the painting, provide sculptures and apply his remarkable marbleizing – "trompe l'oeil" in French - onto the columns and fireplaces throughout the restaurant.

Shortly after The Reading Room opened, a photographer arrived unannounced from Yankee Magazine and wanted to take some pictures. At first, thinking it was someone's idea of a joke, I didn't pay any attention to him. But after lunch, I noticed a second man had joined him and was setting up the room with lighting equipment. I was interviewed by the photographer and Lo and behold, when the September of 1982 issue of Yankee Magazine appeared on the stands, there we were! Four beautiful pictures with a nice article and cover description, calling The Reading Room "The room that has everything," and "The most beautiful room on Cape Cod." The response was tremendous and for weeks, we received calls from throughout New England and even from New York City.

One Sunday morning, I even received a call from a couple flying their private plane from JFK in New York asking if we offered a Sunday brunch as well as valet service from the airport. I explained we didn't provide valet service but were only five minutes from the airport and that cabs were available. I also requested that when they arrived, they ask their server to let me know so that I could give them a tour. They arrived not long after that, enjoyed the food and raved about the place. Later that week two other couples also came by private plane from Portland and Hartford.

The Reading Room resonated with the beauty of the past along with comfortable surroundings, good service and fine food. For me it was a dream come true and undoubtedly the Yankee Magazine article had contributed to the room's success. But having jazz pianist, Dave McKenna playing there on a regular basis was probably my smartest move. Once he arrived, even our lunch business increased. We served more dinners and as business grew, other fine musicians and celebrities soon became regular customers.

A native of Woonsocket, Rhode Island, Dave's mother played piano and violin and his father played drums. By the time he was five, Dave enjoyed the piano so much, his mother began giving him lessons. After serving two years in the army, nineteen year old Dave toured with some of the biggest names in music. Initially he came to the Cape while playing in a group led by the great cornet player, Bobby Hackett. But by 1966, tired of living on the road and admiring the Cape's laid-back lifestyle, he moved his wife Frankie and sons, Doug and Steve, there permanently.

Years before my marriage I first heard Dave play when a girl I was dating worked at a Route 28 West Yarmouth bar called The Rooster. It was owned by "Crazy" Al Metz and although Dave was then appearing with a trio, right away I knew he was special.

A few years later I heard him again at The Columns Restaurant in Dennis Port owned by the talented singer Warren Maddows. Besides Dave, The Columns featured three other terrific musicians, all from Brockton: Lou Colombo, Dick Johnson and Tony DeFazio. Whenever I got out of work early, I'd rush down Route 28 hoping to catch their last set never dreaming those musicians would someday play for me. The only exception was Tony who sadly died young.

Now, with Dave McKenna appearing regularly in The Reading Room, the place was packed. During the summer, visiting performers from the nearby Melody Tent, among whom were Rosemary Clooney, Jack Jones, Tony Bennett, Shirley Jones, Diahann Carroll, Sergio Franchi, Rita Moreno, and Woody Herman, would rise from their tables to sing or play a song or two with Dave. I even kept someone in the kitchen late at night so that performers from the Tent could order something if they were hungry.

With no cover and no minimum, it was the best deal in town. A glass of wine was $1.95, a mixed drink was $2.50, and customers got to hear one of the world's great piano players. At those prices, no wonder I wasn't making any money.

* * * *

Being a fine musician himself, my father loved the Reading Room. Even though his eyesight was bad and his health poor, he enjoyed hearing Dave and others who played there, especially Lou Colombo. The musicians respected Dad's talent and always asked him to sit in and play with them for a while.

My father's birthday was in March and in 1983 I planned a party to celebrate his seventy-third birthday. Although he seemed weak and was actually far more ill than we suspected, he insisted on coming so my mother brought him, along with his trumpet.

It would be the last time Dad played and as Dave backed him up on piano along with fellow great, Lou Colombo on trumpet, other friends, relatives, and musicians came by to wish him a happy birthday. Even my new friend and former Red Sox star, Walt Dropo, came to congratulate him and shake his hand to remind him of the game he'd loved so much. Walter, a former first-baseman with the Red Sox and good friend of Ted Williams, used to visit my Hyannis restaurant where, to my wife's chagrin, we'd party a bit. Years earlier, while playing baseball for the University of Connecticut, Walter hit the longest ball ever seen hit from the UMass baseball stadium. Walt also went on to become the only player to hit more home runs than Ted Williams during a year when both were on the same team. Two years after being named Rookie of the Year however, teams learned he couldn't hit the curve ball and he was traded to Cleveland.

Dad really appreciated Walt's congratulations, loved playing with Dave and Louie, and seemed to enjoy the party. But, just two weeks later, loved and admired by his family and the many who remembered his musicianship and baseball achievements, he suffered a heart attack and died.

When my mother called I rushed to their house, knowing he was dying. Riding in the ambulance, watching as the EMT's worked on him, however, I was focused on regret much more than loss – regret for what we could have been as father and son. I guess we'd loved each other but having never done much together, there was always something missing. In the final analysis, I guess we all have to follow our own path.

Funeral services were held at the Downey Funeral Home in Hingham, a location far from public transportation, and Dave McKenna had never had a driver's license. He lived an hour away, on Cape Cod, but when we arrived in the limo, Dave was the first person I saw, standing alone in front of the funeral home. I never asked how he got there but that was the kind of friend he was. Lou Colombo and other musicians came later and we gave Louie Dad's trumpet to play at the end of the service which he then took home with him.

Tony Bennett had admired Dave McKenna for years and wanted to do a concert with him. But Dave always avoided it because he knew Tony expected him to read music and he hated doing that. Moreover, Dave claimed he was told that if Tony didn't get a standing ovation, he blamed the piano player. I'd always thought that was just a crazy musician's story until one night after Dave finished playing in the Reading Room and everyone had left. We were relaxing at the bar with Chick Chicchetti, musical director for singer Sergio Franchi, when Dave complained that he didn't want to go on the road again but his wife Frankie was pushing him to make more money. Once again, I opened my big mouth to say that even though I'd miss not having him playing for me, maybe he should. He would make more money doing concerts anyway. Maybe it was the drinks or the late hour, but Dave got mad at what I'd said.

As we argued the phone rang. I grabbed it and when the caller asked if I knew how to get in touch with Dave

McKenna, I replied that I'd take his number and see that Dave got it. As I was about to hang up however, he mentioned he was calling on behalf of Tony Bennett. Dave was still out of sorts and by the time I gave him the message Chick had left. Now it was time to drive him home and we didn't speak all the way to his house. I apologized as I dropped him off, but he just grunted and went inside.

The next morning in my office, when the phone rang and my secretary said Dave was on the phone, my heart went to my stomach and I felt sure he was going to quit. To my huge relief, he apologized and said he had just talked to Tony Bennett's agent about doing a concert at the Copley. Plans came together quickly and a date was set.

At that time, the Copley Plaza's manager was Alan Tremain who loved celebrities. Having managed hotels in Delhi, Palm Beach, and New Zealand, he was determined to make a name for himself in Boston and eventually wanted his own hotel. Once ensconced at the Copley, Alan contacted several Hollywood agents persuading them to have their movie star clients to stay at the hotel.

The Ritz Carleton was a chief competitor and had recently received international world-press coverage for refusing to allow Elizabeth Taylor and Richard Burton to stay there because they weren't married. After that, other celebrities began boycotting the Ritz and Alan stepped into the breach with The Copley Plaza.

Alan had successfully provided the hotel with a new image so when news of a Tony Bennett and Dave McKenna concert appeared in the press, Boston big shots began calling the Copley asking for tickets, even though most had never heard of Dave or heard him play. But Alan, bent upon catering to anyone who might provide big bucks down the road, started reclaiming comp tickets from Dave. He was shameless, even trying to retrieve tickets set aside for Dave's mother and other family members. My ticket was already taken which embarrassed David, but once again I opened my big mouth and said, "Don't worry about my ticket, Dave, just don't let that bastard take your family's tickets back!"

I missed the original broadcast but sometime later, while in Miami sitting on a yacht, someone turned on the TV and there they were, Dave and Tony in concert at The Copley! I could see Dave sweating and knew he wasn't enjoying it one bit. But Tony must have been overjoyed. His performance wasn't bad but Dave's piano renditions really carried the show.

When playing in New York, Dave would always be invited to parties, but usually wouldn't show up. A typical story of him goes like this: The phone in his room rings. The caller says, "I'm sitting with Frank Sinatra and Sammy Davis, Jr. They're in the same hotel you're in and they want you to join them. They'll take you to lunch where you'll have a few drinks, then hang out at the piano and they'll sing a few songs." Dave tells the guy "No thanks. I'm watching the ball game," and hangs up.

This was during the days of "The Rat Pack" when Frank Sinatra, Sammy Davis, Jr., Dean Martin and several others were the biggest names in show business. I was amazed he refused their invitation but when I asked why, he just said, "Because the Yankees were playing the Red Sox. Plus, I'd have to read music and I didn't want to listen to their bullshit anyway."

Dave was extraordinary and, as I've described previously, was the major draw and an integral part of the success of the Reading Room. But that modest, talented man was also the reason I was able to meet so many other great people who were well known in the entertainment field. Some of whom even became good friends.

When appearing at The Cape Cod Melody Tent – the Hyannis "theater in the round" – entertainers from all over the country, including Rosemary Clooney and Martha Raye, showed up after their show to hear Dave and often joined in to sing a few numbers. Rosemary embarrassed me one night when she dedicated the song "I've Got a Crush on You" to me then told the audience I looked like the actor, James Caan.

One night after closing, the four of us, Dave, Rosemary, Martha and myself, hung out in The Reading Room and talked candidly about several things. Rosie mentioned how proud she was of her nephew, George, and spoke a little about her husband actor Jose Ferrer, whom she had married twice, and was the father of her five children. She indicated he'd been abusive so they divorced in 1960.

I hadn't known she'd been a close friend of Bobby Kennedy and was at the Ambassador Hotel the night he was shot. Rosemary said she never got over that night and after suffering a nervous breakdown in 1969, her weight ballooned and her career disappeared. In the late 1970s, she began appearing in small night clubs and when Bing Crosby heard about it he got involved and helped her get back on track.

Martha was the daughter of Irish vaudevillians and began her career at the age of three. She started out as a big band singer but became a wacky comedienne appearing with W. C. Fields, the Marx Brothers and Bing Crosby in several films and on television. Despite her fear of flying, she became known as "Colonel Maggie" for her tireless work entertaining the troops from WWII through the Vietnam War where, she told us, she lost her only son.

That night, she got lost trying to find the ladies room and when she finally came out had toilet paper all over her face as if to mimic whiteface. Then, she started singing Swanee like Al Jolson and we all cracked up. Around 2 a.m. when I dropped the two women off at the hotel, Martha even tried to get me into her room! They were great people and during the Christmas season, I always watch the movie White Christmas, starring Rosemary Clooney and Bing Crosby, and think of that night Rosy Clooney, Martha Raye, Dave McKenna, and I spent goofing off at The Reading Room in Hyannis.

CHAPTER 11

STARDUST ON MAIN STREET

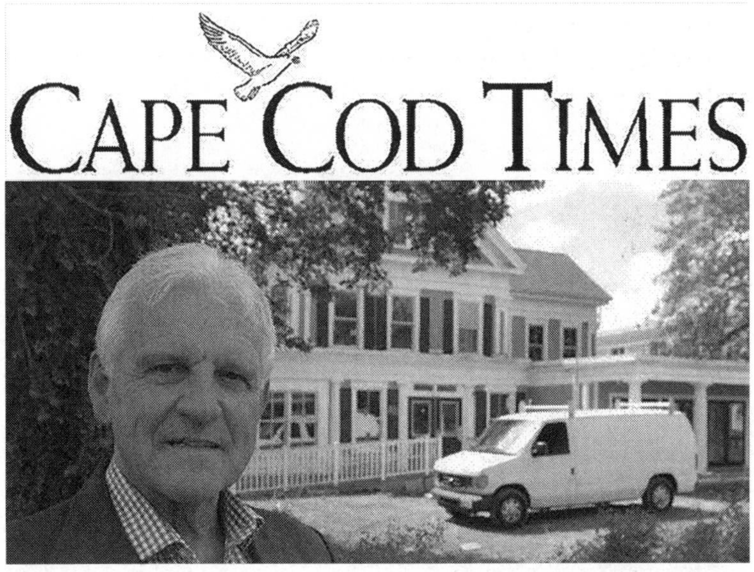

In 2011, The Cape Cod Times recalled the golden days of the Asa Bearse House when it was owned by McKeag and attracted celebrity patrons.

By the time I purchased the old Beachwood Inn, Walter Beineke, Jr. had become the most well-known person on Nantucket. Walter had spent many happy summers on that island with his family but by the late 50s and into the 60's, Nantucket had been in decline; property values were low and the tourist industry was flagging. Walter was the heir to the S&H Green stamp fortune and in 1957, determined to revive its economy, dipped into his trust fund to buy up much of Nantucket's commercial waterfront. Unapologetically, he told The New York Times he intended it as an "elitist project" meant to draw wealthy people to Nantucket to spend money and invest in summer homes. It would also encourage more tourism on the mainland, he said, especially in Hyannis where the ferry was located.

His project was enormously successful by the 1980s and one day while visiting Hyannis for a dental appointment, he stopped for lunch at the Asa Bearse House.

During the meal, Walter asked his waitress if the owner was around, he'd like to speak to him. I knew about Mr. Beineke and was eager to meet him. Our relatively small success with the Asa Bearse House had already inspired me to think about improving downtown Hyannis. (Auto dealer Ken Shaunessey had purchased Kevin O'Neill's family store across the street and had been restoring it and other property in the east end of town along with fellow restauranteur, Charley Leonard.) After Walter congratulated me on what we had done, I asked his opinion about the idea of upgrading Main Street. His response took me aback however when he said "Well don't count on your fellow merchants for any real help. It won't work. I tried that first but eventually had to buy the properties I wanted by myself. Most merchants have no vision. They'll never admit it, but most are looking out for themselves and want someone else to do the work and provide the money."

I should have listened because many of our Downtown Hyannis Association talked a lot but rarely did anything to effect change, especially if it was going to cost them money. Town authorities weren't much help either. One of my ideas was to increase the number of downtown residents by allowing apartments over the shops as they do in Provincetown and other seasonal communities. It would encourage small grocery and other domestically-oriented stores to locate there year-round. But the fire department opposed the idea believing second floor apartments posed a danger and would be prone to fires. I guess the department all had their bedrooms on the first floor at home.

During the short time I headed the downtown business owners' association, some of our group made several positive changes. Mr. Beineke was correct however because other members were still thinking of themselves first, rather than looking at the big picture and working as a group.

Undeterred, I turned my attention to encouraging

more rooming houses and small inns in the downtown area. My electrician and surrogate kid brother, Scott Condinho and I purchased another former captain's house just a stone's throw from the restaurant on Pearl Street. Ironically, it had once been owned by Captain Asa Bearse's son, Asa Jr., which led us to name it The Captain Bearse Lodge. Donna decorated it beautifully in late nineteenth-century style, and it seemed to be a beginning. But with town officials allowing several residents to keep making money illegally by using their yards for parking lots, owners had little interest in selling or upgrading their properties. So the rooming house idea also failed.

After traveling to other resort areas, including Newport, Rhode Island where I spoke with the town manager about signage improvement, Hyannis' lack of understanding about how the town's appearance could be improved, ultimately discouraged my efforts. Back in the late 1960s when most of the Navy personnel left Newport, the panicked town fathers went to resident multi-millionaire heiress Doris Duke asking for help. Ultimately she gave them two million dollars, which the town had to match, but she also demanded full control on all major decisions. Like Nantucket, Newport was revived with seed money from the very wealthy but that would not be the case in Hyannis. I soon learned that, with few exceptions, I would have to be satisfied with the classical aura that Donna, I and my friends had created at the Asa Bearse House, The Reading Room, and The Captain Bearse Lodge.

Fortunately, business remained strong as our regulars and other visitors continued to seek us out. Among the visitors was comedian George Carlin who arrived for lunch at the bar just after being released from Stamford Connecticut's Edge Hill Rehab Center. He wasn't drinking but my kitchen crew went wild with excitement when they heard of his arrival. After the meal, he graciously appeared in the kitchen, got their names and addresses and sent signed pictures and a note to each of them. I'm far from a prude but to me he seemed a quiet man with a natural knack for humor and I could never understand why he needed to use so much foul language in his act.

* * * *

The same year I bought the Cash Market, the talented and beautiful actress Lee Remick, along with her husband, British director Kip Gowans, purchased a nearby waterfront home in a small section of Osterville called Seapuit. The sellers were the Mathesons, who had long summered in Sepuit and were one of my customers to whom I once delivered food and liquor in my prized black and green, 1938 Dodge market truck. I never got a chance to meet Lee or deliver groceries to her at that time because I sold the store. My opportunity would have to wait three years when we met on the patio of The Asa Bearse House.

In 1945, the war was over and I was six. My father was still pitching for the Boston Braves' minor league team in Hartford, Connecticut when ballplayers didn't make much money. Most of the players had to work off- season at another job and games were mostly played on week-ends or at night so players could work a day job. Mr. Frank A. Remick, the owner of Remick's, a classy department store in Quincy, was a huge baseball fan. After watching my father pitch several times over the years, he offered him a job in the men's department when the Braves' season ended.

A shrewd business man, Mr. Remick was one of the first to host style shows, now known as fashion shows, in his store during the Christmas seasons As he planned to display high quality clothing and other merchandise, especially during December, he asked employees if any of their children would like to model in his shows. Volunteered by my mother, I was presented as the young son in a family group and my older sister was played by Frank's daughter, Lee, the future movie actress. Even now, I remember hating the whole affair. The weather was bad, the car was freezing, and I had to wear short checkered pants, high socks, a hat, bow tie and saddle shoes. A large crowd attended and as a further enticement, Mr. Remick was one of the first to serve wine and cheese during the shows.

From that time on, whenever Lee Remick appeared in a movie or on television, my mother always reminded me about the time I modeled with her. That didn't mean much at the time but later on I hoped to meet her so I could tell her my story. Fast-forward to the day that my hostess at the Asa Bearse House rushed inside from the patio to say, "Don! Lee Remick is sitting outside with her husband!" My heart began pumping like a race horse and as I headed over to her table, hoping she hadn't become a snob, there she was. After all these years, Lee Remick having lunch at my restaurant!

Approaching the table, I apologized for the intrusion, introduced myself and said something stupid like "Rumor has it you are a famous person." She looked up at me with a dazzling smile and brilliant blue eyes surrounded by strawberry blonde hair and said "Well, maybe to some." and I knew she was no snob. After exchanging pleasantries, I told her the reason I was especially glad to meet her. When I got to the part about Remick's and modeling in the style shows, she gasped, stood up, and gave me a hug in front of everyone. Her parents had divorced when Lee was in high school and she had moved to New York with her mother who was also an actress. Lee said her now eighty-year old mother, Pat, was living on an island - its name escapes me - but still had pictures of those shows which brought back memories of the father she had adored. After that, Lee and Kip were regular customers and we became good friends.

Lee liked auctions but Kip didn't so one night at the restaurant, she asked if I'd mind joining her at a Dick Bourne auction in Hyannis. Watching people's reactions when they saw her sitting in the audience was quite interesting. Whenever she bid on something, people would seem to be intimidated and were often hesitant to bid against her.

Another time, several women who worked at Puritan Clothing across the street, were having lunch at the bar as they did almost every day. Our bartender, Judy Teixera, in addition to being gorgeous, had that rare quality of disarming any resentment women might have toward her looks and making them like her. As I walked by them one noontime, one of the group said, "Hey Don, you guys are in Cosmopolitan Magazine! There's a picture and article on Lee Remick and she mentioned your place." Lee had been to some of the finest restaurants in the world, but when the reporter asked her to name her favorite, she said "The Asa Bearse House in Hyannis on Cape Cod." How's that for a loyal friend!

Still another day while I was bartending, Lee and Kip joined me there for a snack of chips and salsa and Bloody Marys. I mentioned that Shirley Jones, the award-winning singer-actress of Oklahoma!, Carousel and other musicals had been in the Reading Room the night before and after singing with Dave, sat and talked with me for a while. Shirley had also won an Academy Award for Elmer Gantry with Burt Lancaster but when we met the previous summer, she couldn't have been more down to earth. Somehow the conversation turned to skiing and when Shirley heard Donna and I had been going to Aspen for years, she invited us to stay with her at her lodge in Lake Tahoe. I didn't think anything of it but when Lee heard this, she gave me one of those looks and said, "Well, you had better stay with us first!" I laughed but realized then that even famous people can get territorial when it comes to friends.

Three years later, Lee was diagnosed with lung cancer and it was devastating to so many. Whenever I knew she was on the Cape, I'd call to see if she'd like some company and I could usually make her laugh. Often we'd tell stories about our past and one of Lee's tales involved her lead role in the Broadway hit, A Little Night Music, written by her friend Stephen Sondheim. The cast was invited to perform at Windsor Castle and after the show, were to have dinner with Prince Phillip. After dessert, the Prince gave a tour of the palace grounds where he began by pointing to a fourteenth century well located in the center of the cobblestone courtyard used for obtaining water whenever the castle was under siege. The group walked over for a closer look and when Lee bent down to peer into the well, she felt a hand grab her rump. She quickly looked up to find Prince Phillip standing there with a big grin on his face. We both laughed like hell.

Another story involved the newly-elected President John Kennedy who was recuperating from the campaign by staying in Hollywood with his sister Pat and her husband, actor Peter Lawford, for several days. Lee was having lunch with friends at the Brown Derby when the subject of the President being in town was just casually mentioned. The next morning however, Lee was awakened by frantic calls from the same friends saying her name was splashed all over the newspaper naming her as the mysterious blonde seen having a secret meeting with the President at The Brown Derby. Later the press learned it was Marilyn Monroe but having seen Lee there first, they'd assumed she was the blonde and it was not a pleasant experience for her.

Lee also said she'd met the President, briefly, during a White House performance of the same Broadway show A Little Night Music. But this time Jackie was with him and they were seated separately at the end of two long tables with a large space between them. After finishing her dance, Lee left the stage and when walking by the President's table, heard that unmistakable voice leaning over to say "Wonderful job Miss Remick. We Massachusetts people have to stick together and I'll be by your dressing room later, just to say hello." When I asked what happened she laughed and said "I got dressed as fast as I could and got the hell out of there!"

Lee was a fighter but that time together was one of the last days she would spend on the Cape she loved so much. After returning to California her health deteriorated quickly and on July 2, 1991, that classy and beautiful lady left the stage of life. Her husband Kip sold their California home and lived in the Cape house year round from then on. I bumped into him once and a while but his life was a lonely one without Lee.

Another celebrity who usually dined on the patio at the Asa Bearse, was known mostly in the sports world. Bob Wolfe was a successful Boston lawyer but would become famous, or infamous, depending on your perspective, as the first high-powered sports agent.

Approached by a Red Sox pitcher for help with his contract, Bob did such a great job that other athletes began calling and eventually he gave up his practice to help other sports figures. As it happened, I had hired his daughter Stacie and son Gary to work as bus kids and got to know Bob and his wife Anne when they came for lunch to check out the food and see how their youngsters were doing. Anne also came in several times with Carol Yastrzemski, wife of Red Sox star Carl Yastrzemski.

Unlike some other agents who came after him, Bob sincerely cared about his players and the sports world in general. His client list read like a Who's Who. Among them were Carl Yastrzemski, Larry Bird, John Havlicek, Doug Flutie, Julius Irving, Derek Sanderson, Mark Fidrych, Jim Plunkett and Thurmon Munson.

Bob bought a condominium in South Yarmouth, as did his client Celtics star Larry Bird, and when I was tending bar one afternoon, Larry arrived with Bob for lunch. I knew pro basketball players were tall but I had no idea Larry was over six foot ten! Our restaurant had high ceilings but he still had to crouch on his bar stool just to fit inside the room. Another time he came with a friend, but wisely sat outside where there was no ceiling.

Bob Wolfe always stayed in great shape playing tennis and walking. He never drank to excess or abused his body in any way. But while watching a football game one night, he fell asleep and never woke up. I liked him. He was a good guy and only sixty-five years old.

* * * *

When I first opened The Asa Bearse, and if the weather was good, I'd be out on the patio, like Warren T. Baxter Sr. picking up debris outside his restaurant from the night before. Then I'd sit with my coffee for a while and watch the town come to life which was when I met Sidney "Sid" Chase, a Hyannis native and a descendant of the original Captain Bearse family.

A diminutive accountant with piercing blue eyes, Sid had a million dollar smile that could win anyone over and he soon became one of my favorite people.

Mornings, Sid parked his baby blue Lincoln Continental in front of the Hyannis Post Office where he'd read the paper, do the crossword puzzle, and watch the girls go by and not necessarily in that order. The restaurant was next to the post office so after he got his mail, he'd often join me for coffee on the patio where we'd reminisce about the building before it was a restaurant and when it was a private home, then several businesses.

Sid was one of those people who seem to have tough luck during their life. In his early twenties, an automobile accident shattered both hips leaving him partially crippled and unable to play sports or participate in many physical activities. But that didn't stop him from fathering four beautiful children.

Sid and his cousin Sauni Chase Tiknis also told me a story about their relative, Captain Asa Bearse, who built the house in 1840 and went on to marry three times. That wasn't uncommon in those days but in his case, all three wives were sisters! Captain Bearse sailed regularly to Halifax, Nova Scotia where he first married Sarah who died in childbirth. Returning to tell her family the sad news, the Captain returned to Hyannis with her sister Caroline who died three years later. He married the third sister Hannah after another visit to Halifax and she outlived him by twenty years. All are buried behind the First Baptist Church just down the street from the restaurant and I've re-visited their graves and that strange story several times over the years.

After telling me stories of his younger days when he was a serious drinker. "Donny, I believe I'm still the only man in the town of Barnstable who was arrested for public intoxication three times in the same day!" he once said. The cops knew him so well they always left the cell door unlocked so that when he woke up, he simply left. The story was over thirty years old and he'd been sober longer than that, but the way Sid told it was still a riot. We both laughed but I'm sure his drinking contributed to the breakup of his marriage.

Even in his late sixties, Sid's bad luck continued. His office was in South Yarmouth on busy Route 28, but that didn't stop two druggies, looking for money, from breaking in and beating him up in broad daylight. Sometime later he contracted food poisoning at one of the area's finest restaurants. Still later, diagnosed with throat cancer, he had to have his voice box removed. But Sid never quit and always kept that wonderful smile and great sense of humor.

One day, as he was having lunch on the porch with his lady friend, I was griping about entertainers and entertainment in general. I'd always hired jazz musicians but some customers asked me to try hiring other types of musicians as well. Finally we hired a rock group but all they did was take long breaks and go outside to smoke marijuana. One weekend of that was all I could take so we fired them. When I told Sid about it he grinned, widened his baby blue eyes and, speaking into his throat mike, said "Sit down my friend. Have I got a story for you!"

In the 1950s Sid had owned The Captain Gray Inn in West Barnstable where they served breakfast and dinner to the public as well as their guests. During the summer, the inn also featured a small bar area with several tables which Sid saw as an opportunity for someone to play the piano at night to attract liquor business after the dinner hour. After hiring a young piano player and listening to him for two nights, he fired him. I didn't know where the story was going until he adjusted his throat mike, leaned over to me and said, "You know who that piano player was Donny?"

"Of course not, how would I?" I replied. "It was Burt Bacharach! That's how much I know about entertainers!" Sid grinned. Moreover, he had signed a contract agreeing to pay the musician for the entire summer. At that time, Bert Bacharach was one of the most successful songwriters in the country and as usual we both had a great laugh over it.

Sid wrote his own obituary where, despite his trials

and tribulations, he stated how grateful he was to God for the life he'd been given and for his family and many friends.

Since appearing at the Melody Tent for several summers, singing star Rita Moreno would often have lunch on the inside porch at the restaurant.. A small and unassuming woman, Rita always smiled at Donna when she was at the hostess station but my wife didn't know who she was until a customer told her. When Donna mentioned it to me, I asked her to introduce me the next time she arrived and Rita was there the next day. When Donna brought me to her table, the star seemed happy to talk with us and said she was bringing her husband for dinner that night. Seeing the glossy photo posted in the hallway, Rita soon began coming to the Reading Room to hear Dave McKenna.

We went to see her show one evening and she looked stunning. Returning to the Reading Room afterwards, Rita and her husband were just arriving and joined us. But it was late and Donna was tired so she chatted for a while but then went home. I had to close up so I suggested the couple join me for breakfast at the all-night restaurant across the street. But no sooner were we seated when two policemen arrived looking for Rita with terrible news that her brother had been killed in a motorcycle accident in California. Obviously distraught, Rita and her husband rushed back to the hotel and sadly, I never got a chance to see them again.

Rita Moreno is one of only eleven actresses to win an Oscar, Emmy, Tony and Grammy Award. Her husband Leonard died in 2010 at age ninety, but Rita is still appearing in movies at the age of eighty and still looks darned good.

Another showstopper who arrived for dinner one night was comedian Red Skelton who happened to be in Hyannis selling his paintings at the nearby Kennedy Gallery (no relation to the famous family.) He was alone so when I went over to greet him, he invited me to join him. As we talked and drank wine, he began telling stories and joking with the customers. Not only was the whole place in stitches but he didn't need foul language or off color jokes to convey humor or his genuine love of people. Besides being a great comedian and actor, Red was a fine artist who specialized in self-portraits of clown figures. Allegedly Frank Sinatra paid $400,000 for one of his originals. I bought one of his "transfer" paintings for a lot less money but that didn't matter to Red. He autographed it and wrote a nice note on the back of the frame.

Comedians seem to be prone to having deep sorrows in their lives and Red was no exception. His only son died of leukemia at age fourteen but Red continued to bring laughter and joy to others for the rest of his life.

We always knew when comedian, Henny Youngman, was in town because he simply showed up and provided the place with free entertainment all night. Known as the "King of the one- liner," Henny always stayed late because

I'd always give him a meal and let him use my phone to call his wife, which always cost me money because it was long distance.

Henny was the first comedian to use a violin prop in his comic routine, even before Jack Benny, and even at eighty years of age, he still appeared regularly on the Tonight Show with Johnny Carson. At the Asa Bearse House, his routine was always the same. First, he'd compliment his waitress on the service then tell her how lovely she was. Next, he'd say he wanted to give her something special, "a diamond pin." The waitress would reply, "Oh, Mr. Youngman, you shouldn't, that's too much!" Then when she brought him his check, he'd grab her hand and hand her a business card with his name, a dime and a common pin attached to it. Get it? "A dime and pin!" He always made a big production out of it, which may seem corny to some, but no matter how many times he did it, the waitress, me, and the staff, got a big kick out of it.

* * * *

In the fall of 1983, not long after winning their third consecutive U. S. pairs title, ice skaters, Kitty and Peter Carruthers, showed up at the Reading Room during Sunday brunch. Accompanied by their internationally known coaches, Evy and Mary Scovold, who were then living in Mashpee, they were training for the 1984 Winter Olympics in Sarajevo, Yugoslavia. Kitty and Peter were adopted as infants by Charley and Maureen Caruthers and grew up in

Burlington, Mass. Although not biological siblings, they skated as a brother and sister team all over the world and in addition to their U.S. titles, won the bronze medal at the 1982 World Skating Championships.

On Sundays, the Scovolds gave the couple a break from their grueling schedule to bring them to the Reading Room because they said the people there always made them feel so special. Besides being modest and native to Massachusetts, they were great kids and very special to us as well. I remember a crowd gathering in the bar that year of 1984, to watch them skate and win the very first medal, a silver, for the U.S. at the Winter Olympics in Sarajevo. We sent flowers to Sarajevo with a card signed by the whole staff but unfortunately, never saw or heard from them again. We never even knew if they'd received the flowers.

After four consecutive U.S. national figure skating titles, the pair toured with the Ice Capades for five years, then retired. Peter became a well- known figure skating commentator and has worked for ABC Sports, ESPN and Universal Sports ever since.

I know the place was unique but for some reason, celebrities, actors and actresses, even a few superstar athletes always seemed to find their way to the Asa Bearse. One of them, Academy Award winner Harold Russell, had traveled the country on behalf of American Veterans for many years. His first wife had died and when he re-married, he and his new wife, Betty, moved to Cape Cod.

Born in Nova Scotia, Harold moved to Cambridge, Mass after his father's death and the day after Pearl Harbor, joined the army. But while training paratroopers, some TNT exploded as he was unloading a truck and he lost both his hands. Since he refused to quit the service, the U.S. government asked him to appear in a training film called "Diary of a Sergeant" about wounded servicemen. Director William Wyler was making a post-war film called The Best Years of Our Lives, and after seeing Harold in the training film, decided to use him in his movie. Harold won a special Academy Award for "contribution to the morale of our troops during the war effort" and another for Best Supporting Actor and is still the only actor to win two Oscars for the same role.

He and Betty became regulars for lunch but sometimes he'd show up alone and sit on the patio with a glass of wine just to people-watch. If he asked the waitress to find me and join him, as I came over to his table, Harold would break into his big grin and say, "Remember Donnie, it's not what you have lost that matters. It's what you do with what you have left that counts." He'd become famous for saying that in the movie and we'd chuckle then talk about Hollywood and the movie business.

I will always cherish those afternoons on the patio but after I sold the restaurant and moved to Falmouth, I lost track of them until 1992 when I read that Harold had sold one of his Oscars because Betty was ill and he needed money to pay her bills. He was roundly criticized by the Hollywood elite for doing that and consequently, all Oscar winners must now sign an agreement not to ever sell the statue.

Harold published his autobiography The Best Years of My Life back in 1981 but until recently, I'd never read it. When I did, his big grin came back to me and I thought of what a great difference his life had made to so many veterans who had lost limbs and suffered terrible injuries fighting for their country. Harold practiced what he preached and his philosophy of "It's not what you've lost, but what you do with what's left that counts," resonates with me even more today.

Television producer Alfred DiScippio was another notable visitor to the Asa Bearse House who admired pianist Dave McKenna. Al grew up in Everett and practiced law in Boston before moving to New York to take a job with The Singer Corporation of sewing machine fame. While hired as a lawyer, Al proved so knowledgeable in other areas that the Singer executives soon put him in charge of their entertainment division where he directed and produced several of their national television specials. One evening in The Reading Room, Al was reminiscing and mentioned he had directed Elvis in "The '68 Comeback Show starring Elvis Presley" which aired on December 3, 1968. But then Dave started playing and we both stopped talking.

The first time I'd ever heard the name Elvis Presley, I was home from junior high school, lying in bed with a severe case of athlete's foot. The radio was on and when the disc jockey mentioned the singer's name, I remember thinking the name was odd and pretty funny. Rock'n Roll was just beginning, but it wasn't long before Elvis became The King. Years later on August 16, 1977, I was sadly on my way to Trans-Atlantic Motors in Hyannis to trade in my pride and joy, a 1963 Mercedes Benz 230SL coupe I'd owned for nine happy years. That little car had seen me through so many wonderful times but it needed serious repairs and by then I was married and living permanently on the Cape. It was time for a change. But when the DJ interrupted the music to say that Elvis Presley had died, everything stopped. I somehow felt older and my mind flashed back in time to that day in junior high when I'd first heard his name.

Not long after that, Al and I were having lunch when I mentioned we hadn't finished our conversation about the Elvis Special. I told him that story and my reaction the first time I'd heard his name. Then asked what the famous singer was really like and Al replied, "During all my years in the business, Elvis Presley was the nicest, most cooperative person I ever worked with. After every take, he would come up to me and ask if I was happy with what he'd done." Then he'd say, "Would you like me to do it again, Mr. DiScippio?" Al then shook his head and said, "Nobody ever did that."

After I sold the restaurant I lost track of Al as well but whenever I see an Elvis movie or a re-run of one of his concerts on television, I think of him and how much he had admired Elvis, the person as well as the entertainer.

CHAPTER 12

FALMOUTH & THE FLYING BRIDGE

The Flying Bridge of Falmouth, 1959.

It was still 1983 and at the age of forty-three I was supposedly a success. I had the houses, boats and sports cars to prove it….as well as the pretty wife who had worked just as hard as I had. Articles had been written and my picture had been in newspapers and even Yankee magazine. But that winter, with my father's health failing, I felt I had nothing left to prove. Business was booming but my wife Donna was tired of never seeing me or having any time together. That winter, I found myself sitting on the porch of our lake house, watching the ducks splashing around and wondering what was missing. Donna was in Aspen with her sisters where I was to join them for two weeks in February but I'd already made up my mind. Although I hadn't yet talked to her about it and had no idea what I would do next, I decided to put the restaurant on the market.

Before going out west, I decided to discuss the idea with my accountant as well as take care of my taxes. It was already snowing when I met him in his office and the roads were getting bad, so our conversation was brief. After reviewing tax forms and ensuring everything was in order, we discussed the potential sale and the papers that would be needed when the time came. I intended to go straight home when I left his office but the snowfall had created such a quiet and beautiful scene, I decided to drive around the harbor for a while.

Just around the corner from my accountant's office, with everything seeming mystical and frozen in time, the first place I focused on was The Flying Bridge Restaurant overlooking Falmouth harbor and the docks. They were closed for the winter but seeing a solitary car in the parking lot, I thought the owner, Phil Wormelle, might be inside. Phil had become a Reading Room regular during our Friday cocktail hours so I knocked on the door which he immediately opened and was glad for the break.

I hadn't been to The Bridge since the late 1960's and other than the upstairs bar area, had never seen the inside of the place. Phil gave me a tour but when I saw how big and beautiful the place was, I was amazed. When he said the place was on the market and had been under agreement for the last three months until the deal fell through, I was stunned again.

"You should buy the place, Donald?" he suggested. Cringing, I replied, "No way Phil, I'm already trying to sell my own restaurant. My wife never sees me and buying this place would be the last straw!"

But now he had my heart pounding. His price was about the same as I was asking for the Asa Bearse House but The Flying Bridge had so much more to offer. Taking one last look, I said goodbye and headed out the door, convinced the price was a steal. But then Phil yelled, "You know the slips and the gas docks are part of the sale" and I was stunned once more! I'd presumed the docks and slips were owned by the Falmouth Marine boatyard next door.

I went back inside and asked, "How many slips are there Phil?" and when he said "Eighteen!" I could feel the color draining from my face and left. All the way home I couldn't stop thinking about owning that magnificent place and almost went off the road twice. No matter the consequences, I knew

I was going to buy The Flying Bridge.

For over a hundred and fifty years, Wood's Hole was Falmouth's only harbor. But since it mainly serviced Martha's Vineyard and Nantucket, many residents wanted a harbor closer to the center of the town. In 1906, a town meeting voted to purchase the Davis property near Main Street, which included Deacon's Pond, a saline pond near the beachfront that could provide access to the sea. The name reflected its current owner, Joseph Davis, Jr., deacon of the Falmouth Congregational Church, who purchased it in 1804 from the Bowerman family, owners of the property since 1767 when the pond was called Bowerman's Pond.

To finalize the purchase and create a new harbor, the town raised $75,000 by selling municipal bonds. The state matched that figure and soon after the dredging and creation of a basin with stone jetties began. For over a year residents watched as exhausted workers, many from the Army Corps of Engineers finally smashed through a temporary dam to let the roaring sea crash into the newly man-made Falmouth Harbor.

Initially the harbor was frequented mostly by commercial fishermen, recreational sailors and ferries that brought locals to the Islands. Before long however, maritime businesses and rooming houses sprang up around the perimeter of the harbor. With Falmouth Heights and the nearby beach the area became a popular summer retreat for politicians and tourists anxious to spend money, see a ballgame, and be entertained. It was a wonderful, lively place that delighted Falmouth residents and visitors alike.

Following the last years of the Great Depression, during the 1930's, Henry F. Phillips, a businessman from Portland, Oregon, made a fortune developing and marketing the Phillips Head screw and screwdriver. Later in 1946, he also developed the first screw-in spikes for golf shoes. Mr. Phillips had spent summers on Cape Cod for years and during that time purchased the Falmouth Marine Company and several other pieces of property along the town's inner harbor. By 1948 his health had begun to fail so he retired and put his son-in-law, Fred Wormelle, Phil's father, in charge of the entire operation.

In keeping with his failing father-in-law's wishes to provide work for his boat builders during the winter months, Fred began construction of the Flying Bridge in the fall of 1956. Adjacent to the Falmouth Marine, the restaurant was completed in 1958. Unfortunately, Mr. Phillips' health declined so rapidly he never got the chance to enjoy the place and died soon after it opened.

When I first decided to buy the property, it consisted of two hundred and eighty feet of harbor frontage, three piers, sixteen boat slips, a gas dock and a large parking lot. There were two separate restaurants, each with its own kitchen, dining room, and bar. The one upstairs had white linen tablecloths, finer décor and a more expensive menu. Downstairs, the restaurant was more casual with an open kitchen, a view of the customers and a less expensive menu with lighter fare. Excluding the outside decks, the total seating capacity was five hundred and fifty.

Since the purchase of The Flying Bridge marked the first

time anyone had paid a million dollars for a restaurant on Cape Cod, several friends and other restaurant owners predicted I'd go broke. Fortunately, that didn't happen and in fact, my first restaurant, the Asa Bearse House sold for more than a million just a year later.

It was exciting to be involved in buying and selling such unique properties, but when I told my wife Donna that instead of getting out of the business, I was buying another restaurant, I could see the hurt in her eyes. She didn't say anything but I knew she had been looking forward to having me home again. Now she realized I was to be consumed again by the renovation of yet another restaurant.

Had I been willing to talk about it and include her in the project, we might have worked things out and stayed together. But, as sad as it is to admit, once I'd thought about buying The Flying Bridge, we both knew my marriage was no longer a priority. Donna just wanted a normal life with a normal husband but I needed more. Now that I was in the "Big Leagues," at least in the restaurant world, owning such a place would give me the opportunity to do what I really wanted to do: relive my youth and escape personal responsibility. So, without thinking of my wife or anyone else, I went ahead and did just that.

If a divorce can be amenable, I guess ours was. But after Donna packed and I drove her to the airport, the enormity of what I'd done hit me. She had been the perfect wife for me. We never argued or had cross words and she had always supported me in everything I'd wanted to do. I never expected to be divorced and was ashamed and angry at myself. But I didn't realize I was now powerless over something else; the need to be a big success. It controlled me and I was off again.

As I returned from the airport, our dog, a German shorthair pointer named Cocoa, was the only one to greet me. I hadn't been drinking alcohol for quite some time but now, sitting alone in my dream house on the water, I grabbed an expensive bottle of wine usually saved for special occasions, took a glass out of the cabinet, popped the cork and went upstairs to the porch. Looking across the water and knowing perhaps the happiest part of my life was over, I toasted the setting sun. And when it disappeared, I did the only thing I could. I sat and cried.

But a driven life is a powerful force and can be an addiction as well. After several sleepless nights, the excitement of a new project and living on the edge returned and I was back in the game. Off I went in my battered 1953 Ford 100 pickup, determined to make The Flying Bridge the same success in Falmouth that the Asa Bearse House had been in Hyannis.

* * * *

Having a big mortgage payment is bad enough, but when it's on a seasonal business it's scary. I would need almost $100,000 in the bank when we closed in October just to get through the winter. But knowing that Falmouth Marine's rent for the slips and the office income together would total more than half the annual mortgage amount, I felt confident my analysis was correct and that everything would work out.

The upstairs restaurant would continue to offer fine dining but downstairs would become a casual bistro called McKeague's - I was too uncomfortable to use the real spelling.

Falmouth residents were excited about the new look and we were mobbed right from the start. But I soon learned what a huge endeavor I had assumed. Many days in July and August, we served over a thousand meals. Ordering food and liquor was a constant as was dealing with dozens of salesmen, deliveries, and the unloading, storing and stocking of supplies.

The place was so large we needed three managers, two secretaries, eight bartenders, twenty-five to thirty servers, ten bar backs and bus people, and at least twenty people manning the two kitchens. Since many of the help were college students, they needed training so the hiring process took longer than usual. In addition, we needed valets, boat boys, and eight door men on the alert.

Some people would drink all day on their boats or at the beach then show up after our entertainment started, carrying what we call in the business, a "foreign package," i.e., their drunkenness had been acquired somewhere else. One of the major dangers facing any large and busy establishment serving alcohol is that your license is always in jeopardy. Liability and insurance premiums swell in proportion to the number of customers served and their behavior can get you shut down fast.

Since disco was still in vogue I built an elevated dance floor with strobe lighting on the ceilings. Disc jockeys supplied the music and since a line formed outside every night, our doormen had to keep an eye on them as well. Sixty-five employees can give you plenty to worry about but I loved having most of them around. Besides, this was the Major Leagues! Time for Don McKeag to play ball!

May 12, 1984 was the grand opening of the new Flying Bridge Restaurant. But on the morning of the second day we opened, my young chef, Roland, had a meltdown. Bursting into my office, he broke down in tears, said he couldn't take it and wanted to quit. With my heart pounding, I tried to stay calm. Sitting him down, I got him a cold beer and said, "Roland, give it time. It's only been two days! You'll be fine." He went back to work and lasted the season. But there was never a day when I didn't worry about whether he'd show up or not. Any owner of a large restaurant, unless he's a chef himself, lives with the knowledge that the chef and kitchen crew have the power to make or break you. Unless you put that thought out of your mind, it will drive you nuts and you will never last.

* * * *

After going through a divorce and struggling to renovate and get The Flying Bridge open on time, I was exhausted. But living alone can get to you too. I needed something else in my life and having young attractive women around was an obvious temptation. Being single again presented plenty of opportunities, especially since owning a restaurant and night club is like being in a candy store. You want to try everything but in my case I was out of practice and my moral upbringing got in the way. Unfortunately, I chose to ignore my past problem and found that having a few drinks helped me rationalize doing it.

I've been told that beautiful women were my downfall. But I make no apologies for that. I enjoyed the chase and had fun being chased. I guess I'm a romantic who can't stand the romance for very long. Besides, at that time, I wasn't looking for a serious relationship anyway. I needed to feel better about myself and being with lovelies of the opposite sex was my best solution.

The trouble was the solution came with a double-edged sword. One edge restored my confidence, allowing me to relax and enjoy the experience. But the other edge allowed me to override my value system and could put me in shaky situations. I knew it was a trade-off but my new and exciting life style seemed worth the risk. That was until Fate, that nasty lady who had knocked me down during high school, arrived on the harbor one beautiful day still wielding her cruel wand.

Business was booming, both inside and out, and there was a line waiting to be seated. I was circulating around, bussing tables and chatting with people when I noticed two attractive women having cocktails at a table in the sun. As I headed over intending to say hello, one of the women beat me to it. When she smiled and said, "Hello Don, how've you been?" she looked a little familiar but when she said her name

I was speechless.

It had been twenty-five years since my high school sweetheart got pregnant by another guy. But here she was, my first love, sitting at a table with her girlfriend. At my restaurant!

My initial discomfort quickly passed so I ordered them another drink along with a strong one for myself, then sat down to catch up on the past. Both women were living in Miami where my former girlfriend was a partner in a hotel. After a week in Martha's Vineyard they had taken the ferry to Falmouth harbor and eventually planned to head back to Boston. During our conversation, I suddenly felt the need for closure on my past and asked about their plans for the rest of the day. They were open to anything and since I had to check on my Hyannis restaurant anyway, I asked if they'd like to join me there for dinner.

We met in the Reading Room for more wine and dinner as Dave McKenna played in the background. They'd seen Dave at the Copley Plaza and hearing him play at my restaurant made quite an impression. But it was late and after a long day with numerous cocktails, we were all tired. Since they didn't have reservations anywhere I insisted they stay with me at the lake house. And after a brief tour, I showed them their bedrooms, laid out towels, turned on the lights and went downstairs where we had a nightcap (which we certainly didn't need). The girlfriend asked to use the ladies room and when she left the room, my former heartthrob told me her friend wanted to sleep with me.

Lady Fate was listening I'm sure, but this time I said "Sorry, I'm not interested. After waiting all these years, I'm sleeping with you!" The other gal got the message and went upstairs. We made love, but what I remember most about the act was still feeling angry about being cheated on all those years ago. The next morning I felt ashamed and when I brought her coffee into the bedroom she started to cry. She apologized for how she had hurt me but I guess at the time she had no choice. I'd taken my pound of flesh but unlike Shakespeare, I found no revenge and there was nothing sweet about it.

* * * *

The Flying Bridge continued doing well and like the Hyannis restaurant, celebrities began stopping in after performing at The Falmouth Playhouse two miles up the street. Madeline Kahn, of Mel Brooks movie fame and a favorite of mine, stopped in one night and others, like the singer Stevie Nicks from the band Fleetwood Mac, even came by boat after sailing from Martha's Vineyard or Nantucket.

I was having lunch at the bar one day, watching a sailboat tie up at the dock, when someone onboard got off and came up the hill to talk to the waiter, Ricky Starr. The two talked for a moment before Ricky came over to tell me the boat belonged to Stevie Nicks. Her group wanted to come for lunch but insisted it be in a private setting. Since just eight people were dining inside the casual restaurant and only two tables were occupied on the deck, I told Rick the band could have the upstairs all to themselves. However, Stevie insisted that the entire restaurant be emptied and expected us to ask our other patrons to leave.

Hearing that, I lost it and stormed outside. The messenger happened to be Stevie's manager so I asked who they thought they were and said "There's no way anyone is leaving! And get that boat off my dock before I have it towed!" As the manager scurried down the hill, I yelled for good measure, "And tell 'Stevie' if it weren't for electronics, she couldn't even get a job waitressing at this restaurant!" Three adults and two small children were sitting at one of the outdoor tables and as I turned to go back inside, I saw them laughing and smiling at me so I smiled, waved back and returned to my lunch.

I felt sorry knowing that Ricky had been dying to wait on the rockers but when he came in a few moments later, he, too, was laughing. When I asked why, he wanted to know if I recognized the balding guy sitting outside at the table for four. When I said no he grinned and announced, "That's James Taylor!" James and his family were having lunch while waiting for the ferry back to Martha's Vineyard and wanted Ricky to make sure he congratulated me on my interesting observation of today's musical talent!

Even though the restaurant was open seven days a week for lunch and dinner, we still catered functions and booked weddings upstairs between normal restaurant hours. Whenever I think of functions however, one that took place in the fall of 1985 will always stand out in my mind. Normally we closed in early October, but made an exception for a couple from Woods Hole who wanted to get married on Halloween. The groom was Catholic, the bride-to-be Jewish. All four parents disapproved of the marriage but even so, the couple persisted with their plans and told their parents. "We don't care anymore! We're getting married, period. Come or don't come!"

On the Friday night before the wedding, the couple threw a costume party and several members of the wedding party arrived early to decorate. The bride was dressed as Elvira of television fame and the groom as a WWII pilot, complete with leather jacket, scarf, helmet, goggles and a parachute! Everyone had a great time and some of the guests even helped clean up afterwards. I couldn't believe it but then they asked to come in early the next morning to put up an altar for the wedding. Sure enough, at seven a.m. there they were building a rose arbor on the stage, covering the dance floor with flowers and even arranging folding chairs for the ceremony.

The bride and groom soon arrived on a sailboat from Woods Hole and planned to sail to Martha's Vineyard after the wedding, unless the weather was bad or they'd had too much champagne. The bride still wore her purple Elvira dress but had added a veil and tiara to the costume. She looked beautiful. The groom still had the helmet and goggles on but was wearing a white shirt with a pumpkin tie and no parachute. A Justice of the Peace conducted a short but sweet ceremony that was lovely, despite the rather bizarre celebration.

That afternoon, when I heard the band playing The Monster Mash, it sounded just like the record. Sure enough, the singer was Bobby "Boris" Pickett who had written and recorded the song in 1962. A friend of the groom, he was so down to earth guy when we met, I had the nerve to ask if his royalties from the song were still as good as they once were. "They are and they're giving me an excellent living!" he said. The song is so popular radio stations play it year round so I'm sure his royalties are still giving him a good living even today.

When the group sat down for dinner I went downstairs to McKeagues to see how things were going and became so busy I forgot about the wedding....until I heard the roar of a motor that sounded like a chain saw! Fearing the worst, I rushed upstairs to find the groom, revving up a small chain saw, without the chain on the blade, carefully cutting the wedding cake. The room was loud and smoky but it was a hilarious scene. Everyone got a piece of cake and then waited for the newlyweds to board the boat. Before they sailed out of the harbor towards their future, I handed them two bottles of champagne for the trip and wished them luck.

The sail was full and the sun was setting on Martha's Vineyard, but I couldn't help thinking of the day I'd watched that same sun sitting on my porch after my divorce. I hope that couple is still together and whenever I hear The Monster Mash on the radio I remember them, Bobby Pickett, and that crazy wedding party on Halloween.

* * * *

Terry Lyons, a very large and wonderful man from Brockton, loved cars, trucks and boats. While running the family business, Quinn Freight Company, he had become a member in high standing with the Teamsters' Union and was searching for an antique classic yacht to restore. He had several reasons to do so....first to entertain friends and the union boys and secondly, because the vessel had to be large enough to accommodate his three-hundred pound body.

Wandering around a boat yard in Quincy one day, he spotted an abandoned relic that had been washed ashore during a storm and left to rot in the yard. She had the size, style and class he wanted and when he inquired the owner said, "You can have her. Just get her outta here!" Terry consequently called the Russian boat builder he'd used on another job and asked him to come over and look at it. The next day, after hearing the carpenter's opinion, Terry had the boat hauled away.

After some research he learned the boat was a thirty-eight foot Elco Cruisette built in 1941 by the Elco Boat Company in Bayonne, New Jersey for Mr. Dexter Coffin of the Jared Coffin House family in Nantucket. Christened *Speakeasy*, it was one of the last yachts to come off the assembly line before the government commissioned Elco to build wooden hulled PT boats used during WWII.

For five years after her 1979 restoration, Terry enjoyed cruising around the Cape and Islands. But then, tired of paying the high maintenance costs of a wooden boat he decided to buy a fiberglass sport fisher and knowing how much I loved the *Speakeasy*, he offered her to me at such a reasonable price I bought her.

The *Speakeasy* was a classic mini-yacht powered with twin Chrysler 285 HP engines. She had a spacious cabin with a mahogany interior and classic 1940's brass and chrome fittings. A comfortable galley and head provided the necessities along with plenty of standing room. After converting the "V" berths into a king sized bed with a TV and built-in sound system, I lived on her for three seasons. The kitchen crew kept her brass and bright work polished and made sure there was always a good supply of iced Crystal champagne onboard.

Still trying to recapture my youth, I partied, drank wine, felt great and pushed aside the demons which is probably what led me to break the first rule of any business owner: "Don't mess with employees!" and "Don't dip the company pen in the company ink well!" I should mention one other. "And don't be a Damned Fool!" But of course I didn't think any of that applied to me, especially since I was single again and no one was getting hurt.

I paid for that flawed thinking one night on the *Speakeasy* when something happened that, but for the grace of God and the fact I hadn't been drinking, would have changed two lives perhaps forever.

Ignoring those cardinal rules, I began cavorting with one of my lovely employees who was in an unhappy relationship. We began meeting on the *Speakeasy* after the other restaurant employees left and it certainly wasn't my finest hour. On this particular night, the wind was blowing so hard the lines from the boat to the dock were stretched to the limit. I'd fallen asleep just before my partner in crime was leaving for home and as she held her pocketbook in one hand, her car keys in the other, she tried to grab the line and jump onto the dock. But the line was so taut that when the wind gusted, she lost her grip and fell overboard.

The wind was howling so loudly no one on the nearby boats could hear her cries for help. I was sound asleep as she was going under for the last time when something startled me awake. Rushing to the stern, I heard a moan and saw a hand in the air. A sudden surge of strength filled my chest and arms enabling me to pull her back on board with one yank.

Choking and sobbing as I held her close, she kept saying I'd saved her life. That wasn't so and I knew I was the cause of a very nice girl almost drowning. But for some reason, an angel or some other benevolent spirit, had used me to rescue her. Although she was chilled and trembling as I comforted her, I felt gratitude knowing it wasn't her time and also marveled at the odd tricks the mind can play on someone when under stress. When I pulled her out of the water, I saw that she was still holding her car keys. Even when drowning, she was worried about what her boyfriend would say if she came home without the car and her keys.

After I covered her with a blanket, she calmed down and soon afterwards we walked through the parking lot and up to my office. I put her under a warm shower and dried her off but she was anxious to get home. Her clothes were soaked so I found a waitress shirt and a pair of Bermuda shorts for her to wear then followed her to the car. I said, "Please drive carefully, we don't need another accident!" and watched as she drove away.

As I walked back to the *Speakeasy* the moon was especially bright and I wondered why neither of us had been drinking that night as we often did. What had awakened me out of a sound sleep and pushed me to the stern of the boat just in time to rescue a drowning girl? And what accounted for that surge of strength that enabled me to pull her out of the water so easily? When back on board the boat, I thanked God she was all right and realized I'd been very lucky.

That night should have been an important lesson for me but it wasn't. Like so many other things, excitement can also be addictive. After a night of tossing and turning, I was back at my desk early the next morning. Admittedly though, when the phone rang, I jumped. Danny, a dockworker at MacDougall's Boatyard across the harbor, was on their dock checking the gas tanks when he spotted a small basket floating near the pilings. When he pulled it out and realized it was a pocketbook, he checked for identification. Within it was a wallet with a girl's license and picture on it. She looked familiar and since he thought he'd seen the girl working at the Bridge, he called me.

A wave of relief swept over me as he spoke and I asked him to bring me the pocketbook right away. He was there in fifteen minutes and I gave him fifty bucks which he didn't want to take. He didn't realize I was so grateful to have it back I would have given him much more. By now it was ten a.m. and knowing her boyfriend was at work, I called my friend with the good news. She began thanking me again, which I asked her to stop, but then her voice changed into a hushed tone and she asked. "What are the chances of that happening?"

We both knew what a narrow escape we'd had but after another pause we laughed quietly, mostly in relief, until she added, "Well, I guess we got away with another one!"

CHAPTER 13

MORE STORIES FROM THE FLYING BRIDGE

The author's 1941 Elco Cruisette, named *Speakeasy*, was often docked at the Flying Bridge. It is pictured here cruising the waters of Martha's Vineyard in 1985.

When the eighty-three foot cruise ship Monkey Business began tying up at our long dock for extended periods of time between charter dates, stories and events on the dock of the Flying Bridge became more prevalent. The vessel was out of Miami, Florida and its captain was a handsome young Swede known as Captain Lars, or something like that. He was personable and efficient and his crew, consisting of five cute little blondes with great figures and bubbly personalities, was a welcome addition to the scene. On most nights, they'd hang out at the downstairs bar so we got to know them pretty well and always included them in the conversation. They were fun to have around and we were always interested in where they were cruising to next.

However, as I was having lunch at the bar one day, I noticed there was a long waiting line and tables weren't turning over as they usually did. I asked our pretty blue-eyed hostess, Katherine, a Tar Heel from the University of North Carolina, the cause. Smiling and batting her eyes she replied in her lovely southern drawl, "Don, you'll have to talk to Captain Lars about that. If those girls keep washing the decks during lunch wearing those tight, white, shorts, the customers, especially the guys, are never going to leave. They're staying longer at their tables just to watch them!"

We both laughed and I spoke to Captain Lars that night. The girls still wore their white shorts but the decks of the Monkey Business were washed at three p.m. instead of noon and the problem was solved.

Unfortunately, the fortunes of the Monkey Business took an unfortunate turn that summer when she became indirectly involved in a major scandal that altered the 1987 presidential campaign. Early on the campaign, Gary Hart, a senator from Colorado, was the Democratic front runner and many thought he would win the nomination. Perhaps overconfident, and certainly naïve, he thought chartering a high- profile ship with pretty girls on board was a good idea and would be ignored by the press. His campaign had been touting the high moral ground but when pretty model, Donna Rice, was photographed sitting on his lap, the picture appeared in newspapers across the country and he was considered a hypocrite.

After that, his campaign and ultimately his entire career, was over. Five months later, the cruise company had so many cancellations they decided to change the name Monkey Business because of its association with the scandal. But as they say, "Time wounds all heels and heals all wounds." Today there is a Monkey Business II sailing out of Miami to major ports across the world and business is booming. People always love a scandal.

Oddly enough, the winter before the scandal I had met up with the yacht by accident when I was looking for something to do in Florida and found a cheap flight from Puerto Rico to St. Martin's Island. I'd never been to St. Martin's before and had no reservations but that didn't stop me. When I landed, an attractive local tour director was standing in the terminal looking for her group and asked if I was with them. When I said no and explained I had no place to stay, she gasped and started cracking up. "You're crazy! It's February and everything on the island is booked,'" she said. Then I guess she took pity on me. Heading over to the travel counter, she made a couple of quick calls and came back smiling. She'd found me a wonderful cottage on stilts, right on the beach, for two nights.

As I was jogging by the water the next morning, I saw a boat in the distance that reminded me of the Monkey Business so I headed for the marina to get a closer look. Sure enough, there she was. But no one was on deck so I shouted, "Anyone home?" until heads popped out of the portholes and two of the crew finally recognized me. Once on board they seemed happy to see me and after drinking wine and reminiscing for a while, insisted I stay for lunch. I took them out for dinner that night, which was a lot of fun, but my stay was up at the hotel and I had to leave the next day to fly back to Florida. I never saw them or the ship again but always hoped they hadn't lost their jobs because of the scandal.

* * * *

Another familiar yacht on our dock was called the Miss Gretchen, a 48 foot Broward owned by Edward Fish, president and CEO of Peabody Construction in Boston. Ed was a quiet guy who rented a slip for the season but appeared only on weekends. He seemed to enjoy being alone relaxing in the sun, having a few drinks and letting the world go by. Early in the morning, I'd see him sitting on his deck reading the paper and in afternoons he'd be there again, sitting in the same seat watching the harbor and restaurant activity. Years later, I read Ed's obituary in the Boston Globe and learned he had been one of Boston's most generous philanthropists. But this story isn't about Ed Fish. It's about his captain, Jack McKittrick, a native son of Belfast, Northern Ireland, who lived on the boat full-time with his girlfriend and shipmate, Mary.

Since the owner only used the boat on weekends, the couple had a lot of free time so we usually got together at the end of the day to talk and have a drink or two. Jack had great stories and never bragged about himself but my favorite tale concerned the four years he'd lived in London as captain of a unique craft owned by Richard Burton and Elizabeth Taylor. I couldn't imagine them owning a boat but they were so popular in England the British government had awarded them a de-commissioned navy vessel which they'd converted into a floating celebrity retreat. The boat was tied up at a dock on the Thames River and Jack said in four years, it never went anywhere. During his time as captain, he'd moved the boat only four times, twice to turn her around to clean the hull and twice to check out the equipment and give the engines a workout.

Imagine how screwed up the world is having wealthy people from all over the world flying into London just to join two actors for dinner and cocktails. Kings, queens, business barons, politicians and others, all fawning over two movie stars famous for having high-profile extra marital affairs -- then acting on a movie screen in roles about the same people having dinner with them. I asked Jack what it had been like to work for the Burtons and he said most of the time was boring. But whenever Richard was around, it was usually great fun.

He said the actor was often alone when Elizabeth was away making a movie. But if his actor friend, Richard Harris, was anywhere near London, Burton would invite him on the boat. Both of them were fine soccer players before their movie careers and Harris was supposedly good enough to have played professionally. One night, after Jack drove them to various pubs, they were soused by the time he got them home. The dining room on the boat seated over a hundred people and was always set for dinner. Fine china, Bacharach stemware, and linen tablecloths with silk napkins were the order of the day and huge cut glass chandeliers on the ceilings provided the lighting. Burton told Jack to go to bed but that he and Harris were going to continue imbibing. Jack nodded and headed for his room. But after being asleep for what seemed only a minute or two, he was awakened by shouting, yelling and the sound of glass being shattered. Certain the two men were having a fight he jumped up, put his pants on and rushed into the dining room where he was greeted with a scene of total devastation.

Somewhere Burton had found a soccer ball which the two were kicking from one side of the room to the other, smashing plates, stemware and furniture, even the chandeliers. Shouting, jumping, and laughing uproariously,

Burton finally spotted Jack and said, "Go back to bed, Jackie! Everything here is just smashing! HaHa! We'll see you in the morning!"

Both actors were pretty quiet at breakfast but when the harbor launch came to pick up Harris, the two of them hugged and laughed again over what a "smashing" time they'd had. Waving to Harris as he sailed away, Burton turned to Jack and said, "Jackie! That's what one does when one has the money to do it! Now call someone to get this mess cleaned up before Elizabeth gets back." In October of 1988, shortly after we closed for the season, Jack and Mary took the Miss Gretchen to Florida and unfortunately, I never heard from them again.

* * * *

Earlier that fall I received a call from a regular customer and former lawyer of retired boxing champ Marvin Hagler. Both men were from Brockton and Marvin was then hosting a grand opening for his sporting goods store near the Hanover Mall. The lawyer, something of a celebrity wannabe who even shaved his head and wore an earring to look like Marvin, asked me for a private room for some celebs who were coming for dinner that night.

No sooner did I agree, hung up the phone and handed it back to the hostess than it rang again. The lawyer wanted to talk to me again and I was annoyed. When he said, "Why didn't you ask who the celebs were?" I told him I figured he wanted to keep that information to himself.

But when he said, "John and Bo Derek are coming for dinner at seven-thirty with four other guests," my mood brightened. Handing the phone to my hostess, I rushed upstairs, jumped into the shower, shaved (again) and put on a fresh white shirt with a different tie, figuring it was the least I could do for a "10"!

After following his career and attending all his fights, John and Bo Derek became close friends with Marvin. When they heard about the grand opening of his new sporting goods store near the Hanover Mall, they flew from Los Angeles to Boston to surprise him.

John had been a successful actor in his own right but was best known for his choice of beautiful wives. There were three of them. His first was Ursula Andress, who had starred in several movies, became the first James Bond girl and was one of the first women to appear on the cover of the new Playboy magazine. His second wife, Linda Evans, was the young actress on the TV western Rawhide. She had launched her career on the same show as Clint Eastwood and later earned fame playing Crystal on the hit show Dynasty with co-star Joan Collins.

Bo Derek became famous for her figure and sexy role in the movie *10* with British actor Dudley Moore. She may not have been as good an actress as the others but for me, John's third wife was really Number One. But Bo Derek wasn't just any old "10." Believe me, she was really a "12!" Standing about five foot six, she had pale blue eyes with beautiful skin and wore very little make-up, just a little pale pink lip-gloss. She was very soft spoken but also quietly funny with a pleasing personality.

John asked me to join them for a drink on that cool autumn day and as we talked, I asked how he liked the Cape to which he said he visited Provincetown a few years earlier and enjoyed it. When he noticed my raised eyebrow and faint smile, he said “Hey! It wasn’t what you’re thinking!” then laughed and added, “But to tell you the truth Don that was in the summer. This time, I’m freezing my balls off!” We laughed again, had a great time telling stories that night, and needless to say, when they left my opinion of that lawyer who brought them in and introduced us, rose considerably.

The Flying Bridge also had its share of customers who were politicians. Edward “Eddy” McCormack, a graduate of the U.S. Naval Academy and nephew of John McCormack, former Speaker of The House, went on to become the Attorney General of Massachusetts. Back in 1962, when John F. Kennedy was President and Bobby served as Attorney General, Ed wanted to run for Jack’s vacant senate seat, even though “Teddy”, the youngest Kennedy, had just turned thirty and was eligible to run for the position. Ed received requests to drop out but refused. Unfortunately, he went on to become known for a comment he made to Ted during their debate criticizing his qualifications.

Ed and his wife Emily owned a summer home in Falmouth Heights for years and kept their beautiful blue schooner, Emily, in a slip right in front of the restaurant. As they had lunch on the deck one day we discussed his political career; never dreaming that a few years later I would have a close friendship with Ted.

Boston's mayor during that time, and later Ambassador to the Vatican under President Bill Clinton, was Raymond Flynn. He and his police commissioner Mickey Roach would stop at the Flying Bridge after running the Falmouth Road Race, have a few drinks and circulate through the crowd shaking hands. Both were personable guys who enjoyed relaxing and listening to the music. The mayor knew I'd been a teacher and coach so we would talk about sports and his athletic days as a star basketball player at Providence College. Ray was also that rare politician who seemed sincerely interested in how my business was doing.

But former Governor Edward King will always be my favorite. Ed was born in Chelsea, Mass. and went to Boston College where he studied hard and played football. After a stellar career at B.C. he played professionally for the Buffalo Bills and the Baltimore Colts. Subsequent to his football days, Ed joined a large accounting firm where he gained something few politicians ever have; a firsthand knowledge of financing and fiscal responsibility. The state was floundering badly under liberal Democrat, Michael Dukakis, so Ed challenged him in the Democratic primary and won by more than 100,000 votes. He not only won the election, but as governor, he also had the guts to use his knowledge of accounting to enforce the will of the people in contrast to most politicians who promise to represent the taxpayer but never do.

However, when he started to follow up on his campaign promises: freezing property taxes, cutting spending on inefficient social programs and helping the business community widen the tax base, he offended the same liberals who'd created the mess in the first place. The Taylor family, owners of the liberally biased Boston Globe, shocked that a governor might help the private sector and think about the taxpayer for a change, launched a smear campaign that even ridiculed Governor King for having lobster rolls for lunch at the Parker House Restaurant. One failure wasn't enough for liberal Democrats however. They brought back the same man who failed miserably the first time! In their minds, performance didn't matter and Dukakis should be given another chance. Edward King was defeated by Michael Dukakis and it wasn't long before Massachusetts, once again, had an economy in the tank and a zero bond rating. Even so, the Globe still loved him and in keeping with the liberal Democrat playbook, failure doesn't matter. Now they insisted that Dukakis should be President. And in 1988, he became their candidate.

Although a lifelong Democrat, Ed finally couldn't take it anymore and in 1987, became a Republican; telling the press, "The Dems have ceased to be the party of the sensible center," I met Ed and his beloved wife Josie after he'd been governor and when they, like the McCormacks, arrived at the Flying Bridge for lunch one day. They returned several other times but usually came for an early dinner before I returned to the restaurant for the night. I always wished I'd had a chance to know them better. Ed King died in 1995 at the age of eighty-one and was still one of my heroes, that rare politician who does what he believes is right and refuses to follow the party line just to win an election.

* * * *

In late fall 1989, after closing the restaurant and docks for the season, I was preparing to spend the winter in Florida when a real estate broker from Osterville called to say he had someone anxious to buy the property. I told him it wasn't for sale but he said the buyer was willing to pay far more than the property was worth and was determined to buy the place. I really didn't want to sell but along with other issues, I'd been having serious problems with the septic system that summer. Despite the fact that the restaurant was the major pollutant in the harbor and the town was installing a major sewer system upgrade down the street, the Flying Bridge had been excluded from those plans. Later, I learned it was politics as usual. Someone in Town Hall had decided to allow the pollution rather than have the restaurant be connected to the new system which would entitle the property to eventually be converted into condominiums. I could have fought that in court and probably would have won, but I was tired and didn't need an expensive court case.

A more serious concern was the fact that with the real estate market in the Northeast still in free fall, banks were failing and I had other properties to worry about. I decided it wouldn't do any harm to hear what the man had to say. The broker called the next day and I said he could bring his clients to meet me at the restaurant at noon. Exactly at noon, like a scene from The Godfather, two black Lincolns pulled into the parking lot and three large men in leather jackets, got out. The broker joined them as they approached the entrance so I left my sandwich and cranberry juice, went downstairs and opened the door, still uncertain as to what I would say.

As the broker introduced me to the group, the exuberant buyer, Ralph Bruno, smiled a lot and I immediately liked him. But the conversation was brief. Ralph owned a successful Italian restaurant off Neponset Circle near Boston called The Venezia but after telling him three times the place wasn't for sale I realized he wasn't going to take no for an answer.

Again my mind was reminded of something from The Godfather, but it really wasn't like that. I was just uncomfortable about selling. Finally, Ralph handed me a pen and piece of paper and said, "Don, why don't you just put down a figure you'd be comfortable selling the place for. Then let's see what happens."

Tired of all the talk, I took his pen, wrote a crazy figure on the paper and handed it back to him. Then I said. "That's the price Ralph. I told you I didn't want to sell anyway. I'll guarantee the liquor license at time of sale, and everything else you see around you. But nothing else; no small print items and no lawyers' games! When I get back from Florida, if there's a signed offer at that price with a certified, non-refundable check for $100,000 and no other stipulations, we might have a deal." We shook hands, Ralph grinned again and they left.

When I went back inside to look around at all I had done to the place, I began sweating profusely. I should have been proud and happy over the chance to make a lot of money. But as I walked along the docks, in the cold, crisp harbor air, I felt I'd somehow failed again. I didn't really want to sell and wondered if I was actually going crazy.

Early the next morning, I left for Florida but kept thinking about that potential sale. No one, I told myself, would pay the price I had demanded. But two weeks later, my secretary called me at the Palm Beach Hotel to say a large manila envelope had arrived from UPS with Ralph's lawyer's return address on it. I was so shocked I couldn't book a flight home for several days.

As soon as I arrived home, I called my lawyer, Steve Jones, and headed for the office to open the package. Everything I'd asked for was there; the certified check for $100,000 along with a letter and the agreement which, although somewhat long, was relatively simple. Still in a daze, I didn't sleep all night and couldn't believe anyone would pay that price. It was much too high and didn't make any sense.

I had a genuine concern for Ralph's being able to make a go of it but I dropped the package off at my lawyer's office anyway and prepared to do the deal. As usual when working with lawyers, there were some glitches, the biggest being over a second mortgage. But fortunately, as it turned out, they withdrew the second mortgage contingency and within two months, things ironed out and the sale took place.

Everything went well on the surface but not so well with me. I pick up guilt like lint and believe it or not, when I left the closing, instead of being excited about having just become a millionaire, I felt guilty and unprepared. That Irish expression of, "If things are going too well, there must be something wrong." had kicked in again. But the odd thing about this case was I hadn't wanted to sell. For years, I told myself (and others) I'd done it for the money but the truth was my personal life was in turmoil again and I needed a change to make me feel better.

In retrospect, selling the Flying Bridge was positively the worst business decision I've ever made. It has haunted me ever since and always reminds me of the college athlete who was given the chance to make it into the big time only to ruin everything by quitting or doing something equally foolish. Just like that high school athlete who did something stupid just as he was about to pitch an important game.

Ralph Bruno and I have remained friends even though we don't get to see each other very often. But his timing wasn't much better than mine. In addition to paying too much for my restaurant, Ralph also purchased the Shawmut Inn in Kennebunkport, Maine, near the George H. W. Bush residence. After the wrecking ball destroyed half the rooms in preparation for renovations, the bank reneged on his loan. Ralph was renovating the Flying Bridge at the same time and as savings and loan institutions began to fail, the business environment was grim.

Fortunately for Ralph, George Bush became President and the three major networks gave him over a million dollars to take over and equip a large part of that Maine hotel for television coverage. The hotel was saved but that didn't help him with the Flying Bridge. After several attempts to re-organize and form partnerships, the property went to auction.

CHAPTER 14
HIGH PLACES

The author's beloved Hyannisport home on Sunset Hill in 1989.

After our divorce, my ex-wife Donna moved to Aspen to live there permanently. I still had friends and other connections there so it wasn't long after I sold the Flying Bridge when I found living solo in the lake house lonely and decided to visit that mountain resort. Some friends from the Cape were renting a place in the center of town for two weeks that had an extra room so they asked if I'd like to join them. That worked out well and before the group returned to the Cape I found a place to stay for another week.

Aspen has been a skiing mecca for the rich and famous since the 1930's and during the 1950's, the world's top skiers were Stein Erickson, Tony Seiler and Andrel Moulterer, "The Blitz from Kitz"- short for his hometown Kitzbuhl, Austria. Andrel won a silver medal at the 1956 Winter Olympics and remained a dominant force in Aspen and the skiing world well into his 60's when he opened a ski shop in the center of Aspen frequented by celebrities and prominent skiers. Donna had worked for Andrel at one time and after she and I married, he did me a huge favor by letting me keep my skies at his shop. After a long day on the slopes, lugging your skies back to the car or a hotel room is a gigantic pain in the ass.

After I finished skiing, we'd relax with a beer, laugh and tell each other stories, mostly mine. He loved to laugh and liked Michelob beer so on my way back from the slopes I'd always stop to pick up a couple of six-packs at the "Packy."

Before joining friends on the slopes, I usually took a run myself. One morning the tennis great, Martina Navratilova, was standing behind me in the triple chair line. I recognized her from the matches on TV and soon realized the woman with her was her significant other. As the three of us got on the lift, I said hello and how nice it was to meet them. But they weren't the slightest bit friendly so I shut up, sat back in my seat and enjoyed the ride.

Because western ski areas have higher elevations than the northeast, it generally takes longer to get to the top. The two women spoke only to each other and ignored me the entire trip, but as we prepared to get off the lift, I had to open my big mouth again saying "Nice to meet you but I hope you'll be careful. I wouldn't want you to get hurt and lose your tennis career." At that moment I was thinking of a former star pitcher for the Red Sox, Jim Lonborg, whose baseball career had been shortened after blowing out his knee skiing in Sun Valley. I was just trying to be nice but Martina sneered at me and said "Only bad skiers get hurt! People only get hurt when they try to be careful!"

I was pissed about that but then I watched her ski. Swinging her poles in the air, she skirted over to the tree line then swooped down the slope like she'd been shot out of a cannon. Never mind her tennis skills, that woman was a great skier as well!

At the end of the day, I picked up the Michelob as usual and as we relaxed at the shop, Andrel sipped a beer and sharpened some skies. I told him my Martina story and at first he just grinned. Then he burst out laughing. "Donald, don't you realize? If Martina hadn't become tennis champion, she would have become almost as famous skiing on the women's tour! She was the national champion of Czechoslovakia!"

Maybe the joke was on me, but I still thought she had behaved like a nasty witch.

* * * *

When I visited Aspen the following year, I stayed with my sister-in-law Lisa who was living in the employee condos and working at the Top of the Mountain restaurant. After breakfast there one morning, I was walking toward the lift with my skis when I noticed a tall guy slightly bent over and slowly wide-tracking down the bunny slope. He looked familiar and I soon realized it was Clint Eastwood. He was working with an instructor and obviously hadn't skied much.

At that time the Dirty Harry movies were smash hits at the box office and here was their star, the ultimate macho man, snowplowing on the beginners' slope in snooty Aspen. I was impressed to see him willing to try something new even though he was looking clumsy in public, and knew he had to be a good guy. Obviously he didn't give a damn what people thought and I wished I'd met him in the lift line instead of that arrogant tennis diva, Martina Navratilova.

Another morning when I was on the double chair lift, it was unusually cold and the guy riding with me had a scarf covering much of his face along with a two-day beard. I can't stay quiet for long so after a minute or so I began talking which got him laughing at something just as we reached the top. Recognizing the laugh and the partially covered face, I said "Is that you, Jack?" and indeed, it was Jack Nicholson, although during the ride I hadn't had a clue. He was quite cordial and said he'd take a run with me but had to meet his daughter at a pre-arranged spot half way down the mountain. I saw him another time at a bar downtown but didn't want to bother him.

Somewhat later after moving to Hyannis Port, I was again in Aspen at The Top of the Mountain restaurant when I heard someone calling my name as I picked up my tray. Teddy Kennedy, Jr. was at a table with a pretty girl, waving for me to join them. The girl happened to be the actress Brooke Shields and Teddy had a big smile on his face as he introduced me and saw my reaction. After breakfast they asked me to take a run with them. Brooke is a tall girl and was still a beginner but willing to learn. Teddy, on the other hand, was a bear on the slopes and even with his artificial leg, attacked the moguls (bumps), with a vengeance. I had to hustle just to keep up with him.

That night I told Lisa and her girlfriend about seeing Teddy K., Jr. and Brooke Shields and two days later, when I took them to brunch at Andre's, a posh restaurant in the center of town, there was Brooke, sitting across the dining room with her mother. I never expected her to remember me but she came right over and greeted us with a dazzling smile. Even more amazing was when she said "Hi, Donny. How are you?" I introduced her to the girls and she was so gracious. But after chatting for a while, she gave me a hug and rejoined her mother.

During that winter, one of the oldest buildings in Aspen, the Hotel Jerome, became one of my favorite haunts. The place was a throwback to the old wild-west days and when I stopped there to have a drink with friends or talk with the locals, every now and then, when there wasn't a band, they'd ask me to do my thing on the old upright piano in the corner. Nothing fancy, just my kind of place.

John Denver was riding high at that time and I really liked his songs and the movie he did with George Burns called *Oh, God!* He used to stop at the Jerome every now and then but I was disappointed to hear my bartender and waitress friends say they didn't like him and he wasn't a good tipper. No excuses, but I think that might have been when his personal life was falling apart.

The Tippler at the base of Aspen Mountain was another place where everyone who was anyone gathered after a day on the slopes. In those days, you didn't see many black skiers but I met two at the Tippler and both were professional football players. The Pittsburg Steelers had just won the Super Bowl and their star receiver, Lynn Swann, was standing at the bar with a friend of mine who then introduced us. He was a great guy and although I never spent any time with him after that, whenever we bumped into each other somewhere, we'd say hello and stop to shoot the breeze. Years later, I read where he'd gone into politics and not long ago, ran for governor of Pennsylvania, as a Republican.

The other guy, called "O.J." as in O.J. Simpson, may have been a Heisman Trophy winner, a star running back for the Buffalo Bills, and the face of the Avis car rental ads on TV, but the day I met him, first on the slopes then in the Tippler, he was just rude. He'd been dating a girl who was part of our group and even she was embarrassed by his attitude and arrogance. This was years before his murder trial but having witnessed his behavior in Aspen, I wasn't surprised when I heard what happened.

During my time in Aspen, I'd toyed with the idea of investing in property there. One possibility was a boarded-up saloon and former whorehouse located smack in the center of town. Prices were already high by then and with my former wife living in the town, I no longer felt comfortable there. I was also having trouble with my chronic shoulder, which now ached every time I skied. But when I also injured my right knee and started skiing defensively, skiing wasn't fun anymore. I had plenty of money so I told myself it was probably time to quit and spend the winter in warmer climates.

Of course, less than three years later, the value of that saloon and former house of ill repute, now restored, had quadrupled. Without knowing it, I was on my way to perfecting a skill for buying high and selling low.

Hyannis Port is one of the "quaint little villages" Patti Paige sang about during the late 1950s in her popular hit song "Old Cape Cod." The Hyannis Port Golf Club is located at the top of Sunset Hill and one sunny day I met friends there for a day of golfing. Just to the left of the club entrance, I noticed a For Sale sign stuck inside a tall hedge and wondered what was behind it. Having sold the restaurant and lake house, I was looking for a fresh start and a new place to live so I pulled the car over, got out and walked down the driveway. Behind the hedge I found a little jewel of a house that overlooked Martha's Vineyard, Hyannis Harbor, and even the Kennedy Compound.

The house was once the laundry cottage and maid's quarters for the former James Prendergast estate next door and since it had only one bedroom and needed major renovations, the asking price was really too high. But the place was just what I was looking for and I knew the location, panoramic views and spectacular sunsets would more than offset the price.

Money wasn't the problem. But while I loved the idea of owning the house, moving into such a prestigious neighborhood as Hyannis Port was challenging for a blue-collar kid with middle class values and working habits. Besides, at forty-six, I wasn't sure I was ready to be just a single and retired playboy.

My little laundry cottage was surrounded by large,

rambling homes, many of them owned by people whose families lived on trust funds and had spent summers in Hyannis Port for generations. They were always very pleasant to me but even though I'd worked hard to afford that little house, I sometimes felt like the proverbial fish out of water living there. One morning, as I was having coffee on my deck looking over at Martha's Vineyard, I asked myself, "What the hell are you doing living in Hyannis Port?" Growing up with that mentality of knowing your place, at times I could feel out of place no matter how my neighbors treated me.

I had unknowingly acquired the guilt of the Irish even though no one admitted to being Irish. I'd heard relatives faulting people who had risen above their station – unless, of course, that person happened to be one of their sons, daughters or someone related to them.

I mention this because when my parents bought a place in Florida and started driving there in winter, Dad would sometimes complain about how much money they spent on gas. My business was doing well so as a surprise one year, I bought them a beautiful chocolate brown Mercedes Benz diesel sedan with tan leather interior. It was only a year old, had low mileage and got thirty-six miles to the gallon when diesel fuel was thirty cents cheaper than regular gas.

At first my parents seemed thrilled with the gift. But after several months, my father called from Florida one morning to thank me again for the car but then announced he intended to trade it in. Stunned, I asked him why and Dad replied that as soon as people saw him driving a Mercedes, they raised their prices in motels, hotels and shops. That was ridiculous of course, but I guess having lived through the Depression and growing up poor made him uncomfortable with having people think he was rich or putting on airs by driving an expensive car. After that, I even felt a little guilty having an expensive car myself!

However, once he was gone and I was living in Hyannis Port, I plunged into the renovations on the house and as soon as I began entertaining and having friends over, that foolish guilty mindset disappeared.

Like most areas with wealthy seasonal residents, Hyannis Port has a golf, yacht and beach club. There was also a Civic Association which allowed dues paying seasonal members to have a voice in village affairs. I wanted to be part of the community so I immediately joined the Civic Association. But no one told me that their dues were exclusive of the yacht club, which controlled the docks and the launch that ferried boat owners to their moorings.

My boat, the Speakeasy, was on a mooring next to Ted Kennedy's Mya, and after donating money to the club for the rebuilding of the pier and dock house, I'd presumed I was a member in good standing. A lovely high school girl named Tracy was running the launch during that summer. But after ferrying me to my boat for three weeks, she was instructed to let me know that since I wasn't a member, she could no longer take me to my boat. That was bad enough but her father happened to be President of the Hyannis Port Club. Her father had nothing to do with it but the idea that anyone wouldn't realize how inappropriate it was to have a young girl telling someone they didn't belong infuriated me. Members of the yacht club chatted with me at the post office almost every day yet no one thought about telling me the rules. A couple of phone calls straightened everything out but after that I had no interest in being a part of any Hyannis Port club. Just having my own circle of friends was fine with me.

During one of my many years working amongst the middle class, I had composed a list of what I would do if I ever made some real money. Golf lessons, traveling, especially to the Olympics, writing a book, studying piano seriously, attending a tennis camp, the Kentucky Derby and buying a small horse farm in Vermont were on that list. However, once I owned my little house on the hill, as well as the boats, cars, and heady times with friends in high places, I put that list aside.

Ironically, when my mother stopped by with a friend one day after one of my parties, she gazed around the room and saw remnants from the previous night. She said, "Donald, it is obvious you do not do well with too much free time!" and I laughed. But although she didn't discuss my drinking, I'm sure it was on her mind. However, she not only remembered my "what I'd do list" but then asked if I planned on doing any of those things now that I had money. I lied and said I was going to start soon but had no intention of doing anything that required self-discipline.

Still regretting the sale of the Flying Bridge, I was determined to live life with abandon and as little responsibility as possible. I filled my days with lunches at waterfront restaurants, boating, hanging out at local gin mills and partying at my little house with friends, neighbors and several guests.

Earlier, I mentioned that when John F. Kennedy ran for President in 1960, I was a student at the University of Massachusetts in Amherst and could remember seeing him coming out of St. Francis Xavier Church in Hyannis with Jackie one summer while he was still a Senator. Three years later, I was back in Amherst practice teaching in Greenfield, MA on the day he was killed.

Well, just five years later, in the summer of 1968, Bobby Kennedy had also been killed just three weeks earlier and I was heading for my job playing piano at Baxter's Boat House in Hyannis. My friend, Joe Hassett, a law student at the time, was running the launch at the Hyannis Port Yacht Club and on my way to work, I stopped by to see him. His wife Susan, also a friend and pregnant with their first child, had come by to bring him lunch. Both Susan and Joe were native Cape Codders and Joe's father had been a former police chief of Barnstable. Susan's dad, Jack Crawford, was a former Boston Bruins and a great guy.

As we sat in the launch talking about Bobby, we saw

Ted Kennedy walking down Irving Avenue, the street on which I would someday live, and I will never forget his eyes….dull and vacant, staring straight ahead as he passed us on the pier. The grief was etched on his face and while he nodded politely, he said nothing. I had never seen such grief and the three of us were so choked up we couldn't even speak to each other. It was so very sad that we said nothing more and I left.

Ted continued spending summers on the Cape with his family after his brothers were gone and I'd always hoped to meet him. The first time we met was July 4, 1975. We were both aboard a 48-foot pleasure craft, The Silver Fox, owned by my friend, the silver-haired bon vivant, Howard Penn. The party vessel was sitting on a mooring in front of the Hyannis Yacht Club among a fleet of others which were packed with groups enjoying cocktails and waiting for the fireworks to begin.

Howard's father, Abraham "Abe" Penn, founded the Puritan Clothing Company in 1911 and over the years had expanded to several locations on and off the Cape. Sixty years later, Howard and his brother Milton ran the company. The Kennedy family often shopped at the Penn's Hyannis Main Street store. Staunch Democrats, the Penn family had supported every Kennedy campaign and that day Howard even provided his boat for some Kennedys to watch the fireworks.

Knowing of my interest in meeting him, Howard brought Ted through the crowd to introduce us. But with the party in full swing, our meeting was cordial but brief. It would be fourteen years after that Fourth of July, when I was living in Hyannis Port, before we met again.

While attending a fund raising dinner at the State House in Boston, Dickie Gallagher, a friend and former aide to the Senator, brought Ted over to re-introduce us. Dickie's family had spent summers in Hyannis Port for many years and his father, "Big Ed" Gallagher, had been a fine athlete at Boston College. He had also pitched for the Red Sox before going into the insurance business and becoming one of Joseph P. Kennedy's main golfing partners.

Ted came over to say hello with a big grin on his face and after shaking my hand, surprised me by telling some stories about my little house on the hill. After he asked how I liked living in Hyannis Port and I said I did but wasn't sure the feeling was mutual, he laughed and said "Well now you know how the Kennedys felt!" We bumped into each other several times that night and got along so well he invited me to a cocktail party at the Compound the following weekend. The Irish poet, Oscar Wilde once wrote, "Laughter is not at all a bad beginning for a friendship and it is far the best ending for one." Unfortunately, in my case, only half of that would be true.

Not long after moving to Hyannis Port, I began hosting Bloody Mary parties on Sunday afternoons. After doing so for several weeks, Dick Gallagher showed up after

Mass one day, with the Senator in tow. Ted said he'd heard the Sunday brunch party at Donny McKeag's was the toughest ticket in town and when I said, "That's right! And where's yours?" everyone, especially Ted, had a big laugh.

One Sunday when I had a particularly lovely date, I'd run out of two key ingredients for my Bloody Marys, (V-8 and Clamato juice) and Ted began teasing me. In his loud stage voice he said, "Donny, why don't you plan these things properly! You people should boycott this place!" That got a lot of laughs but then he nudged me onto the deck and invited me and my date to stop by his house after everyone left.

Excited about seeing the Compound and having a chance to talk with Ted, my date quickly helped me clean up after everyone left and we headed down the hill. My car's top was down so along the way I pointed out some of the houses, their owners and their background. But I wasn't paying attention when we arrived at Bobby's house, next to Ted's driveway, and as I turned into the parking area, I spotted something and barely had time to slam on the brakes.

Standing in the middle of the driveway, a pyramid of tomato juice cans, three feet high, was topped off with a shaker glass filled with limes and celery stalks. A bottle of Absolute Vodka sat on the lawn next to the pyramid, sitting in a bucket of ice with three glasses around it. It was a hilarious scene and as we were cracking up, a voice came from behind the shrubs, saying "The bar is open but I certainly hope you brought some V-8 juice?" It was Ted of course and my date never forgot that fun afternoon with a great guy. That would be me, right?

From then on when a group was invited to the house for lunch and a sail, especially if a celebrity was involved, and if Ted thought my funky piano playing might be useful, I'd get the command call informing me I was needed at the house to "crew for the good ship Mya." I was also expected to stay for lunch afterwards.

One St. Patrick's Day party at the house, I was exhausted from playing piano and singing for too long. I'd stopped and was getting ready to leave when Ted saw me and bellowed from the other room, "Donny, where do you think you're going?" Kiddingly, I yelled back "I quit! You're not the only 'world leader' I play for you know!" Not missing a beat, Teddy said "Yeah, but I'm the only one who would listen to you!" Everybody howled but then some poured themselves another drink and I ended up playing for another hour.

One morning when Ted's secretary, Dolores Stevens, called, I begged off saying I was too busy doing yard work. Five minutes later, Ted called back to say, "Okay Donny. I'll just have to tell Jimmy Buffett and his band that you were too busy to meet them." Suddenly willing to handle boat duties or anything else, I dropped everything and said "I'll see you in ten minutes!"

Unfortunately Jimmy Buffet's pregnant wife wasn't

feeling well so they decided to return to Boston. The rest of the band stayed on though and despite a huge black cloud hovering over the breakwater at the entrance to the harbor (thunder and lightning storms were predicted) when I mentioned it to Ted as we left the pier, nothing was going to change his plans. Finally, a half hour out to sea, it became obvious the weather was turning nasty so we came about and scurried back to the mooring. The launch driver was waiting, decidedly unhappy about his impending soaking and a van was sitting at the dock and everyone fit in to except Ted and me.

Making a beeline up the hill on foot, we arrived at the house just as the skies opened up. While watching the deluge from the side of the porch, Ted joked, "I told you we shouldn't have gone out. But that return was perfect timing Donny, nice job!"

During lunch, I watched as Ted regaled the band with stories about the house and memories of the family. The musicians were awed and after dessert he asked if they'd mind playing something for us in the living room, to which they happily complied. I was especially taken with one of their members, a young girl from North Adams, Massachusetts who was only about five feet tall but could play the fiddle, trumpet, flute and even the trombone. What a talent!

The leader of the group played piano and keyboard. He had co-written some of their songs so when he and the band played, it was a real treat. After they finished however, Ted announced, "Thank you. That was terrific. But now Donny and I are going to do a tune for you!" I couldn't believe my ears and for the only time, refused to play.

The other guests laughed when I said "You've got to be crazy! There's no way!" except Ted who gave me "The Look" and motioned for me to follow him into the kitchen. I knew I was in trouble and pleaded, "There's no way I'm going to embarrass the two of us in front of that talented bunch! We don't even have a song! I don't know what key to play in when you're singing! It'll be a disaster!" As usual, he wouldn't take no for an answer and hauling me out of the kitchen over to the piano, he smiled at the group and announced, "Aah, since it's raining out, aah, I thought we'd do, aah, We'll Sing In The Sunshine." The group laughed and applauded. Lucky for me I knew the song and Ted sang it in the key of C.

As we performed, the band got up to join us and I must have been playing alright because after that song, we did two more. The thing I'll remember most about that day is knowing that I would be the only one who ever played the piano for Ted Kennedy when he was singing with the Jimmy Buffet Band.

Heading down the driveway on their way back to Boston, the group waved to Ted and to me as we stood on the porch. Watching the van disappear around the corner, Ted said, "You know Donny, you should start listening to me. When you just go for it things usually work out and everyone has a good time." I made my usual smart-assed reply but that was the Teddy we all loved. Not the famous Senator, just a regular good guy trying to make sure the people around him had a good time.

Two signs at the entrance to Marchant Ave and the Compound read Private Property and, No Admittance Please. But some people don't obey signs and could care less.

One day after a nice sail, Ted and I were in the house having lunch, and watching a beautiful sailboat pushing past the breakwater. A car came down the driveway and stopped in front of the house which was bad enough, but when four people got out and started walking around, I got angry.

Ted was still eating but said, "Donny, if it bothers you that much, go out and say something!" I went out on the porch and yelled, "What's the matter with you people? "Can't you read?" which didn't disturb them in the slightest. They just smiled and said, "Oh, we love the Kennedys! We just wanted to take some pictures." To them this made everything all right. Their invasion of private property meant no more to them than the signs. Completely oblivious to the situation, they took their pictures waved then got back into the car and left.

When I returned to the house, muttering "You should have a monitored gate to stop this bullshit," Ted frowned. "Dammit Donny, I'm not going to live in a stockade and be held hostage in my own home!" he said gritting his teeth. And that was the end of it.

Ted lived his life the way he wanted, unprotected and vulnerable, which took courage. But, given the tragedies he and his family had endured, I wondered if there wasn't a fatalistic side to him that sometimes just didn't give a damn what happened.

If Ted took a break from Washington during the week, I'd sometimes get a call to join him for lunch and a sail which usually meant just the two of us. Once aboard the Mya, he was a different man. The sea was his sanctuary and one of the few places where no one could get at him. After passing the breakwater, we'd often sipped on a glass of Louis LaȚour-Pouilly Fuisse wine, and talked about the Cape and our mutual friends. If he needed anything done on the house or the boat, he'd ask for suggestions. Even though he had several people who'd done work for him in the past Ted wasn't above looking for a bargain. There were also times when I'd go forward, lean against the mast and let him be alone with just his thoughts and some peace and quiet.

Although always interested in others, he rarely talked about people or Senate business. One exception was during a sail when he mentioned the actor Rod Steiger who had recently testified before a sub-committee on Health, Education and Welfare which Ted chaired. Steiger had struggled with mental illness himself and when Ted said he'd been deeply moved by what the actor said, I wondered if he'd also been thinking of his sister Rosemary.

Jack Fallon was a close friend of Ted's who lived in Weston, Mass. but spent the summer and fall on the Cape in his gorgeous home overlooking Seapuit Bay where he moored his sail boat. Jack, who had helped develop the Prudential Building and other large Boston real estate projects, also oversaw funding for the JFK Library and other Kennedy family investments. I knew him as a customer at my restaurants and at other sailing and social events, including Ted's Thanksgiving parties where they obsessively chatted about sailing.

Towards the end of a party one February night, the two of them cornered me and said I was expected to meet them at Ted's house at nine o' clock the next morning to go sailing. Since snow was forecast for later that night and the next day, I thought it was just the wine talking. Early the next morning, heading for the john and seeing the heavy snowfall on my deck, I went back to bed, convinced I could sleep in. But at nine o'clock sharp the phone awakened me with Ted's sarcastic, "Where are you? Jack's here. What? Are you chickening out?" Knowing how I would respond, he hung up. I grabbed my ski clothes and rushed over to meet those two crazy men of the sea. Sailing in a heavy snowfall? I must have been crazy too!

There was plenty of snow but as it turned out, very little wind so we ended up sitting in the middle of the channel with only a raised mainsail. I finally asked if anyone knew what the schedule was for the steamship ferry Eagle, which provided passenger service to the Islands even in winter. I had asked for a specific reason knowing the ferry wouldn't be able to see us through the snow, but Teddy just winked at Jack. "We don't know Donny. The Mya is a wooden boat so their radar won't pick us up. Haha!" I didn't find that very funny and suggested we should at least keep the motor running to which both he and Jack agreed.

Finally, after sitting in the snowstorm for another half an hour, Ted said, "Well, we might as well head back in. There's not going to be any sailing today." Once we secured the boat we got into the car and were heading back to the house when Ted asked, "Donny, do you know someplace where we can stop for an Irish coffee?"

"Sure," I said, "The Captain's Table is on the way home and they're open year round. Why not stop there?" But when we arrived Ted and Jack continued talking about sailing in the parking lot and told me to go inside and order the coffees. I entered, looking like the Abominable Snowman and my friend Al, the bartender, asked where I'd been. Before I answered, I noticed some of the people at the bar were looking out at the harbor. When I asked why, he said they'd been watching a large sailboat sitting in the snow, in the middle of the channel, for almost an hour. They couldn't see it anymore and were wondering what happened to the boat and the idiots on board.

"Al, make me three Irish coffees will you? And by the way, I'm one of those idiots and the other two are coming in right behind me!" Al was laughing as Teddy and Jack arrived just then and although there were some strange looks, nobody said anything. After we finished our drinks and were heading home, I told them the story. Jack got a big kick out of it but for some reason Teddy didn't think it was funny at all.

As he was with nearly everyone he knew and respected, Ted was a caring friend. Jack's health had been failing for quite some time but when he ended up in Cape Cod Hospital, Ted brought me with him one day when Jack was nearly comatose. Despite Jack's condition, when Teddy leaned over him and said "Jack, the wind is up, let's go sailing," the monitors went wild. Ted was holding his hand and when I saw Jack open his eyes and smile, it was hard for me to control my emotions. Most people have no idea of just how many times my friend Teddy did that and even less about how much it meant to so many people and their families over the many years he served the public, his family, and so many, many friends.

CHAPTER 15

CAPERS, CHARACTERS & CARS IN PALM BEACH

The author became friends with Hollywood actors, including Andrea Dromm (*The Russians Are Coming! The Russian's Are Coming*! and *Star Trek*) and Arthur William Carter (actor, diplomat, and Bon vivant). They are pictured here in 1999.

After renovating my little jewel on the hill, it wasn't long before I needed another project.

Every morning when I headed off to meet the guys for coffee in Hyannis, I would pass a For Sale sign on a property at 326 Scudder Ave. There was an interesting but dilapidated French-style house with a carriage house next to it that always caught my interest. The sign had a real estate number on it and with the Flying Bridge money burning a hole in my pocket, I called.

Like the Asa Bearse House, the early 19th century house had been owned by another seafaring man, a Captain Simmons. At one time the captain owned over six hundred acres stretching all the way to Craigville Beach on a road frequented by stagecoaches. I toured the place and after hearing its history, couldn't resist buying it.

At that time, the property was part of the estate of another captain, Captain John "Jack" Frost, whose granddaughter Ethel Frost, had inherited it in the 1950's. She was a real character who liked to tell a story about when President John Kennedy came to the Cape and the motorcade would pass by the house heading to the Compound. A little bathroom on the end of her house, just five feet from the road, was once the outhouse; Ethel loved to tell people that she was the only person who ever watched a President of the United States go by while sitting on a toilet!

As he had with my lake house in Centerville, Brian

Olander did another terrific job with the carpentry work. But by the time it was finished, the economy and real estate market had gone sour. The bills kept pouring in and when I was offered a lot of money to rent my little house on the hill, I decided to do it and move into my newly finished Scudder Ave home. I'd already rented it out to friends on the condition that I could stay there too if need be. But once again my timing was terrible thanks to Hurricane Bob who arrived on August 18th 1991 and reminded me of my father and those days at The Skipper Restaurant during Hurricane Carol in the summer of 1954.

As its name suggests, Hyannis Port sits at the entrance to Hyannis harbor where storms usually hit hard and do serious damage, depending on the tide. That night as the wind howled and trees crashed down around us, six of us sat around the fireplace with candles in the windows when I heard a knock on the door and opened it to find Ted standing there with his son Teddy Jr. Both were soaked to the skin and, naturally, I invited them. But almost immediately Ted indicated he needed to talk to me in private. We had been together earlier that day when I barely got the Speakeasy out of the water before the heaviest surge. Ted, on the other hand, opted to leave the Mya on her mooring and after checking the chain on the mooring line, jumped in and swam to shore where I was waiting for him.

Now though, he was visibly upset. It seems that Teddy Jr. had drilled two holes in their Wianno Senior sailboat because he'd heard sinking it was the best way to protect a smaller boat during a hurricane. Ted was beside himself and wanted to know if I knew anyone who could go down and raise the boat. There was nothing to be done at that moment of course, but I got him calmed down and said I knew someone who could take care of it in the morning. He finally relaxed, had a drink with the group and left with his by then chastened son.

* * * *

Like most college party-lovers during the 1960's, my fraternity buddies and I spent our spring breaks in Fort Lauderdale, Florida having great times in the sun. But after I started working at a real job, I began spending my winters skiing in New Hampshire. I no longer went to Florida, and certainly not to Palm Beach, Florida! That place was out of my league. Now that I was wealthy and living in Hyannis Port though, I thought it might be time to spend the winters in a more posh setting.

When I heard that some friends from the Cape were selling condominium units in the old Palm Beach Hotel, I booked a flight and went to see what they were like.

Located on Sunrise Avenue in the center of town, the Palm Beach Hotel dated from the 1920's. But after its once elegant history, later owners had failed to keep up with the times and allowed the hotel to fall into disrepair. Several investors finally purchased the property and in the 1990s, converted the rooms into condominium units. Among them was Cape Cod native and realtor, Paul Drouin, who purchased several units from the investors, hoping to make money on their resale. When I arrived in Palm Beach, Paul invited me to stay in one of his units but of course, still charged me for the privilege.

Most of the condos were small but you couldn't beat the price or the location. Efficiencies started at $30,000 but larger ones sold for as much as $60,000. Conveniences abounded. Not only did the building have a heated pool and a beautiful beach just a block away, St. Edwards Catholic Church was next door and across the street on South County Road, Green's Pharmacy served breakfast and lunch daily. In addition, a Publix supermarket stood across from the building's front door.

Sauni Chase Riley (one of my pal Sid Chase's beautiful daughters) sold real estate for Paul on the Cape but he also asked her to come to Palm Beach for the winter to promote the sale of his hotel units. I'd known Sauni since the 1960's when we met at the Vet's Club, a popular Cape college hangout across from the Hyannis Airport. At that time she was dating Marshall Riley, a football player at Notre Dame who came from Attleboro, Massachusetts and we were all good friends. Sauni helped with the negotiations and paper work and even did most of the decorating.

For me, the condo was meant to be an investment where I would live during the winter and rent it out during the offseason. Given the nearby stores, supermarket and watering holes I didn't need a car. I enjoyed several winters there until I sold the Flying Bridge, until my outsized ego, convinced me, once again, that I needed something bigger.

I'd noticed a for sale sign on a cute little Spanish-style house, built by the Arnold Bread family in the 1930s, which was just around the corner from the hotel on Sea Spray Avenue. It had three bedrooms, a separate guest house and a large pool with two grapefruit trees behind it. The grapefruit trees were important because the most popular libation of the day was called either a Sea Dog or a Greyhound. A cocktail made with freshly squeezed grapefruit juice and vodka, preferably Absolute. My second little house was still within walking distance to everything and Worth Avenue, where I rarely shopped, was only two streets away. If I needed to travel beyond Palm Beach, I could call a cab.

Comedian Stephen Wright once said, "A fool and his money are soon partying" and as it turned out, I was on my way toward proving him right.

* * * *

During the 1920's, Joseph P. Kennedy purchased a waterfront estate in North Palm Beach designed by Addison Mizner, the most famous architect of the Roaring Twenties and from then on the Kennedys spent winters in Palm Beach. So it was hardly a surprise when Ted called one day to invite me over for a drink and a tour of that home. While decorated in the Spanish style the house, like the one in Hyannis Port, was charming and comfortable.

Neither home tried to impress and both were meant for the family to relax, play tennis, swim in the pool or ocean, or simply sit in the sun and tan.

Another day we'd just finished playing tennis when Ted decided to charter a boat for lunch and a cruise on the Inter Coastal Waterway, known to locals as the Lake. The ocean was too rough for sailing that day so Ted chartered a power boat. At that time Miami Vice was a popular television show whose plots often concerned the heavy drug trafficking between Miami, Mexico and Columbia. Drug cartels were making millions through sea and air transportation of cocaine and often used cigarette boats as nocturnal getaways on Florida's waterways. As the illicit traffic increased, drug enforcement agents were pressured to search any craft that seemed at all suspicious.

By the time we headed out the water was so choppy Ted told the captain to avoid entering the channel that led into the ocean. Mischievously though, in hopes of getting a rise out of the female guests, he asked the captain to speed toward the opening then peel back into the calm water. After several unsuccessful attempts, Ted gave up the idea and we simply cruised around the waterway. However our antics must have aroused suspicion with the shore patrol because they soon roared up with loud speakers blaring, "Attention! Shut off your engines and drop your anchor. Prepare to be boarded!"

As they came aboard, the Drug Enforcement Administration officers seemed a bit arrogant. But once they realized Ted Kennedy was one of the passengers, they grew increasingly uncomfortable. To their credit, however, they asked Ted a few questions, scrutinized the rest of us and conducted a thorough search. When they finished, the officer in charge apologized for the inconvenience, saluted and left. We laughed about it afterwards but it was unsettling. Nothing illegal was found but we had no way of knowing who had chartered the boat before Ted. Someone could have left contraband on board by mistake or perhaps the wrong person, hearing that Ted Kennedy was chartering the vessel, would purposely hide something on board to create trouble for him. It turned out fine but was really no laughing matter.

Another day when I was still based at the Palm Beach Hotel, I arrived at Ted's house with my car's top down and seeing that, he wanted to take a ride. We cruised around the island and over the bridge to West Palm but on the way back he said to take the road behind the Palm Beach Golf Club. As we passed the course, he pointed to a flag on one of the greens and shared with me that years earlier when he was young and had a date, he decided to borrow his father's car without his permission and while he was playing golf.

Knowing where his car was parked and where the keys were, Ted managed to get it out of the parking lot without being seen. As it happened though, "Dad was standing right where that flag is and saw his car go by with the top down, me at the wheel and a pretty girl sitting next to me!" We both laughed; but I detected an air of sadness when he said, "He wasn't that upset when he got home. He just said 'Teddy, I guess you're just going to be one of those fellows who always gets caught.'"

Later on we were sitting in the living room when I commented on the ornate ceiling beams painted with different shapes and designs which I thought interesting. To that, Ted just laughed saying, "You know, when I was a boy and my father wanted to discipline me he'd make me count the dots on those beams and there were hundreds of them!" Again we laughed but the feeling of loss and the love he still had for his father was there.

The next day when I returned to the hotel from the beach, I found a message in my box from Ted asking me to meet him and his date at the cinema in the West Palm Beach Mall. The note read, "Donny, there's a Woody Allen movie playing and I need a chaperone!" Presuming my presence was needed to dispel any press attention or gossip about him, or his date, I quickly dressed and headed out only to hit heavy local traffic. I was a little late but after buying a ticket and dashing into the theater, I breathed a sigh of relief. It was the early show and only six or eight other people were seated in the entire theater.

Despite the darkness, I could see the silhouette of Ted's big head down front with his date so I shuffled down the aisle to join them. Because of the thick carpeting and dim lighting he couldn't hear or see me coming so when I came up behind him and put my hand on his shoulders, his bulky body burst out of the seat like a rocket and scared the hell out of me. Realizing what I'd done I tried to apologize. But after quickly regaining his composure, Ted said "That's okay Donny, don't worry about it."

The movie was pretty bad so we left early and nothing more was said. But I couldn't forget what I'd just experienced. I now understood what it was to be Ted Kennedy, a prisoner of the past, always on guard and never knowing if someone, no matter where you were, might be planning to harm you.

* * * *

Every now and then, some of life's happiest times come when least expected. One wild and rainy Palm Beach day, I was having lunch with friends at Chuck and Harold's on Royal Palm Drive when a guy came in to have a few drinks and tell someone his tale of woe. After splattering me with water from his rain coat, he sat down next to me and I became his victim. Explaining he was a dentist from Minnesota who had just gone through a nasty divorce, he said the IRS was after him and he was in Palm Beach to sell a car he'd kept stored in West Palm. After buying my little house on Sea Spray, I now had an empty garage so I asked about the car. When he said it was a 1959 Rolls Royce I became curious but that really wasn't the car I had in mind. However, when I heard the selling price was only $35,000 I suddenly became intrigued.

The dentist offered to pay the cab fare if I would just take a look at it so we headed out into the monsoon, hailed a cab, and arrived at a West Palm Beach garage called Ragtops. Even on blocks and covered with dust the car was so beautiful I fell in love with her. After talking to the mechanic and bartering with the dentist, I offered the man $29,500 if he would put new tires on her and, just like pulling teeth, he took it! Suddenly I was the owner of a Rolls Royce and began having some wonderfully unique times and a lot of fun driving that car. Especially when watching the reactions of people as I handed the keys to a valet at a restaurant or club. After driving it around town for a while, however, I decided it would be nice to have a chauffeur for special occasions, special dates, or just for the hell of it.

Not long after that thought I met a little French girl named Noelle who was serving drinks at a cocktail party. She was a lovely Parisian girl who had overheard me talking and wanted to be my driver. She thought driving a Rolls Royce would be a blast so I bought her a chauffeur's outfit, which she loved wearing, and as we cruised around town, Noelle also loved watching me and my date sipping Cristal champagne in the backseat, looking like big shots. Sometimes, while driving along the beach, she'd crank up the music as we headed over the bridges to a restaurant somewhere, and would be having as much fun as we were.

I'd promised my realtor friend Sauni that as soon we closed on the condo, I'd take her out on the town to celebrate. Once I owned it, we met for drinks in Chesterfield's Lounge at the Brazilian Court Hotel and stayed for dinner. Afterwards we visited an old Palm Beach haunt called O'Hara's for a coffee and Sambuca where Sauni knew just about everyone in the room. She immediately brought me over to meet Richard "Dutch" Wagner who owned and operated the family business, Wagner Bird Seed Company with his brother Bill. Like me, Dutch was living a tough life; divorced, single, and driving a Rolls Royce! After Sauni explained our coincidental situations, we became instant friends.

The next day I showed up at Nando's Restaurant with my white 1959 Silver Cloud and Dutch was there as well. After seeing and admiring my Rolls, he asked me to follow him out to the parking lot to look at his 1978 cream-colored Corniche "Rolls." Although expensive-looking and with a fine tan leather interior, to me his car lacked the classic lines and appeal of mine. To me, there was no comparison.

Although nineteen years older, my beautiful Rolls had a regal presence, that wonderful smell of old leather, and a bar! Walnut trays with chrome edges were attached behind the front seats and folded out to provide a resting place for the passengers' drinks. Above the trays push buttons on silver nameplates labeled Bourbon, Gin, Scotch, Rum and Rye waited to fill the sterling silver cups located on the rear doors along with a seltzer bottle. Each button had a tube running under the seat into the trunk where shiny aluminum tanks could be refilled when empty. The bar had no place for vodka thanks to the Cold War of the 1950's. Great Britain, the United States and other countries had

had banned all Russian products. Today, however, vodka sales total more than all the other liquors offered in the Rolls combined.

Nevertheless, Dutch had a surprise for me when he opened the passenger door and the glove compartment of his Rolls. Pointing inside he said, "Read that!" I peered in to see a little brass plate proclaiming, "In 1978, this Rolls Royce was custom made for Mr. Reginald Leach." The name was familiar but I could not place it. Grinning, Dutch asked, "How do you like that? Know who that is?" I didn't until he told me that Reginald Leach was the real name of actor Cary Grant who owned the car until 1980. Dutch bought it a couple of years before Grant died, but I said he'd have to do better than that if he wanted to be a "star" around me! We laughed, headed back for more drinks and had the best shrimp scampi I've ever eaten.

Nando's had been in business for more than forty years and was a wonderful restaurant. But in 1994, changing times and too much competition meant they finally had to close. I missed the nice people I met there and of course, that wonderful shrimp scampi.

* * * *

One Sunday, Dan Burns, a friend and neighbor from Hyannis Port who was staying at Sunnyside, his brother's Palm Beach home once owned by actor Douglas Fairbanks, Jr., stopped by my house to have a Bloody Mary. As we sat by the pool, he complained that he had never ridden in the Rolls. Happy to oblige, I took him for a spin and then to brunch at Chuck and Harold's. When we pulled up to the valet next to the hostess station, the café tables were filled and people didn't seem to notice the Rolls. However since I knew the hostess, I leaned out the window and asked in a loud stage voice, "Excuse me! Would you have any Grey Poupon?" The crowd, especially the hostess and staff, had a good laugh as we got out.

Another memorable Rolls Royce caper took place on a day when I'd just had the car's oil changed at Ragtops and was heading home along A1A in West Palm. I spotted a girl in a pink string bikini selling hot dogs under a lime green umbrella in a parking lot and since I hadn't had lunch, I pulled the Rolls in to get a couple of dogs. Waiting in a line of mostly working men and trying not to be distracted by the bikini, I began talking to the others when a TV station's van appeared. I figured they were just getting a hot dog like the rest of us until a female reporter and a cameraman got out and asked who owned the Rolls.

I identified myself and they asked if they could do an interview with me and the hot dog girl. When I asked why, one of them said, "Well people don't see a guy in a classic old Rolls Royce, buying hot dogs from a pretty girl in a pink bikini very often!" The interview went well, bikini girl and I had some laughs and the reporter said we'd be on the six o'clock news. Hopefully bikini girl got to see it because I was tied up that day and forgot to watch. I've always thought if that TV station is still there, I'd stop in to see if they had kept a tape of that interview.

No less memorable was an introduction Sauni gave me at Chesterfield's Lounge in the Brazilian Court Hotel. The moment I walked in, she took me over to meet two friends she had mentioned before, Bill Carter and Andrea Dromm. A famous author or movie director should write about the life of Arthur William Carter. But since that hasn't happened yet, I've appointed myself to mention a few things about the most fascinating man I've ever met, and also one of the kindest and most generous.

Bill was in his early seventies when we were introduced and will always be my shining example of Rudyard Kipling's definition of "The Successful Person." The real person who "treated those two imposters, success and failure, just the same." Born aboard a cargo ship in Liverpool, England, Bill and his family emigrated to New York in the early 1920's. Before the United States entered WWII, Bill enlisted in the British Army and participated in the battle of Tobruk facing General Erwin Rommel's tanks. British forces suffered vast casualties but Bill saved the lives of several soldiers by hiding them under the hot sand as the German Luftwaffe strafed the airfield.

After returning to New York City as a war hero, handsome Bill became re-acquainted with Nancy "Trink" Wiman, daughter of Dwight Deere Wiman, heir to the John Deere fortune. Before long, a Hollywood talent scout approached him to become an actor. Trink's father Dwight had rescued Broadway during the 1929 stock market crash so his power in the entertainment community enabled Bill to sign a movie contract and eventually star in two movies,

I've Always Loved You with Claude Raines, and My Kingdom for a Cook with Charles Coburn.

But acting bored him --"too much standing around" – as Bill put it, so he went to New York, married "Trink," and returned to Los Angeles to go into the real estate business. Among his many friends, Frank Sinatra, actor Clifton Webb and crooner Bing Crosby, all bought homes from him. Ten years and two children later, Bill's marriage to Trink ended. Their divorce was the first ever reported on the front page of The New York Times and as we were cruising in the Rolls one afternoon, Bill recalled that event, accompanied with that wonderful grin, saying, "Donald, I believe I'm still the only man who ever got a John Deere letter!" I almost went off the road.

It had been over forty years since that divorce when I met Trink at a party in Palm Beach and found her quite pleasant. Then I heard rumors that she had killed her second husband and got away with it. I drove Bill home after the party that night and casually said "You know Bill, divorcing her was probably a good idea," which gave both of us a good laugh.

My favorite Bill story coincidentally, concerns one of my favorite movies,The Quiet Man starring John Wayne and Maureen O'Hara. The director, John Ford, was a friend of Bill's and we were having lunch at the bar of another defunct restaurant called Le Petite Marmete, when the movie appeared on their television. I asked if Ford was really a friend and Bill said yes. "And I've got a story about that too."

It seems that Ford had just purchased a script about an Irish ex-fighter returning to Ireland and wanted to make the movie there. But the studio refused, claiming it would cost too much money. They were insisting he'd have to film it in Utah but Ford, recalling their past connection, remembered that Bill had a farm in County Mayo. He called to ask if Bill could suggest any locations in Ireland that would be inexpensive to rent but Bill said "Why not use my farm. I won't charge you anything!"

Never a bragger, Bill enjoyed telling a story then watching the person's reaction. Hearing what he'd said, I gazed dubiously at him. "Are you telling me they made The Quiet Man on your farm?" As usual, it was true but his reply was just a smile.

Then I learned from a mutual friend just how modest Bill Carter really was. During the Eisenhower Administration, Bill was appointed Assistant Ambassador to the Vatican in Rome, became a member of The Knights of Malta, was accepted into the Order of Cypress and appointed the Catholic representative to the United Nations.

Frank Sinatra and Peter Lawford were part of the Hollywood group he socialized with but he hadn't been very fond of either one. However, he did tell me that one night at a cocktail party, they introduced him to Peter's brother-in-law, Senator Jack Kennedy, and told him he had just met the next President of the United States. Bill said the man was personable but at that time, he hadn't been overly impressed.

Having met and sailed against Ted Kennedy at the New York Yacht Club and knowing of my friendship with him, led Bill to tell me what it had been like at the Vatican in Rome on the day President Kennedy was assassinated. The entire community shut down and he said that walking back to his hotel most people he passed were weeping and some held candles. Bill said he'd been in war where death was always close by. Tragedy and anguish were common. But this was different. A President from another country had been killed yet the people of Rome and throughout Italy mourned him as if he had been their own.

* * * *

Unable to forgive him for their embarrassing divorce, Bill's former wife Trink used the John Deere clout and her high priced New York lawyers to prevent Bill from ever making any money, either from the family or from any project of his own. When their son Dwight died from a drug overdose, he left his father several million dollars. Bill and his son had been very close so the young man's death left Bill devastated. Despite that, Trink made sure the money stayed tied up in court and Bill never got a penny of his son's gift. Later, when he had some serious financial troubles, his daughter, worth millions in her own right, was afraid to pay the rent for Bill's apartment for fear that her mother would find out.

In addition to acting, Bill received awards for boxing and swimming and became a lifelong friend of former boxing champions, Jack Dempsey and Rocky Graziano. Another friend was the beautiful actress-swimmer Esther Williams, who had Bill appear as a swimmer in two of her movies. When I asked if they were something more than friends, Bill simply smiled again and mentioned that she used to be married to actor Jeff Chandler, a grey-haired leading man I'd remembered as a kid. He said that Esther came home one afternoon unexpectedly, to find him trying on her bra and panties and that ended their marriage.

During his halcyon days in New York City, Bill became a close friend and bodyguard of Broadway song writer Lorenz Hart, co-writer with Richard Rodgers of The Great American Song Book. Hart even used Bill as the model for some of his song lines. A second songwriter, Vernon Duke, wrote the popular song I Can't Get Started with You using Bill's experience for the line, "I've flown around the world in a plane, settled Revolutions in Spain" etc.

I once asked Bill why he didn't write a book which I believe would have been a best seller and rescued him from debt. His answer described the kind of man he was. "Donald. I could never use my friends to make money. I've had too great a life to spoil it by saying things in print that might be embarrassing or hurtful to the people I've loved and cared so much about."

And perhaps he was right. Maybe some of the things

I've written here, and not just about Bill, shouldn't be in print. But I'm comfortable with it and can still see that incredible man heading down the street in his rusted-out Toyota Corolla he called his Japanese Rolls with a yellow tennis ball on top of the aerial so he could find it in the Mall parking lot.

Despite having lived such an extraordinary life, when Bill went broke I never heard him complain. The laughter and friendship he shared with those of us lucky to have known him, was priceless. Bill kept his priorities straight and stayed grateful for the life he'd been given. I now see him as a model and hope to handle my situation half as well as he did.

* * * *

Andrea Dromm was the other half of Sauni Riley's introduction that day at Chesterfield's with Bill. Andrea and Bill met during the summer of 1977 when both were hanging out at P.J. Clarke's, a popular Manhattan celebrity bar. A former model and actress, Andrea began modeling in New York at the age of six but later studied drama and acted in student productions at the University of Connecticut. Her background as a child model won her a job with the Eileen Ford Agency but by 1963, she'd become famous as the beguiling stewardess in the National Airlines commercial who asked "Is this any way to run an airline? You bet it is!"

Her career took off, prompting friends to urge her to

head for Hollywood where she landed her first role, playing Yeoman Smith in Where No Man Has Gone Before, the second pilot for Star Trek: The Original Series.

Had she kept that role, she would have been set for life but she gave it up for a role in The Russians Are Coming, The Russians Are Coming starring Alan Arkin, Carl Reiner and Eva Marie Saint and that changed everything. After playing the part of a pretty blonde, blue eyed teen-aged baby sitter in love with a Soviet submarine sailor, Andrea hoped her movie career would blossom. But that didn't happen and after hosting a television special on surfing, she returned to New York to resume modeling. She became the Clairol "Summer Blonde" girl on television for a while but her career soon ended.

Andrea and Bill lived together in Palm Beach for the last seventeen years of his life and during that time would sometimes stay at my little Palm Beach house on Sea Spray Avenue. Andrea now lives on Long Island and still misses Bill deeply. But knowing what good times they had enables her to feel grateful and philosophical about how their careers ended. At this writing Andrea and I still stay in touch and always talk about Bill. He wouldn't have it any other way.

CHAPTER 16

HYANNIS VENTURES, REDUX

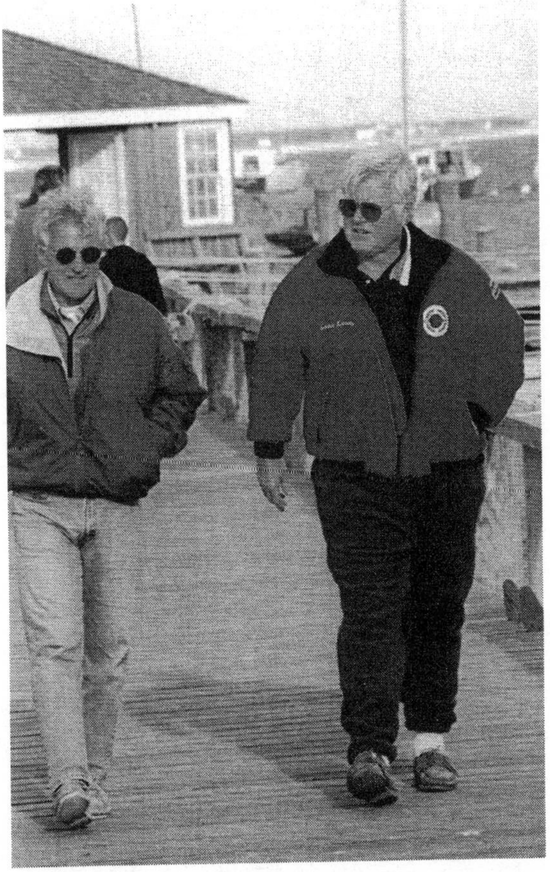

The author became close friends with Ted Kennedy over the years. He is shown here, walking with the late Senator at the Hyannisport Yacht Club in 1996.

Even in the late 1980s, despite being fairly wealthy and having all the things that went with that, I couldn't stop competing in that crazy marathon of trying to prove myself. After months of driving past an abandoned candle factory on Scudder Avenue with a For Sale sign on it, I called the number and bought the place. Once the Old Harbor Candle Company, the property consisted of a large concrete building which served as the retail gift store upstairs with a production unit for the making of candles and other related merchandise, downstairs in the basement. Three other wooden structures on the property were used for storage and one had a colorful history.

During the mid-1800s, it had been the village's one-room schoolhouse, then later a temporary house of worship during construction of St. Andrews Episcopal Church at the top of Sunset Hill across the street from my house. During the '30s and '40s, it became a service station where Joseph P. Kennedy and other wealthy Hyannis Port residents bought their gas, had their cars serviced and even stored some of their cars there for the winter.

The station closed in the late 1950s and the Marvin Blank family built the factory as a second location hoping to profit from the thousands of tourists flocking to Hyannis Port during the John Kennedy Presidential campaign and subsequent election in 1960. Since most everyone who wanted to see the president's summer residence had to pass by the candle store, business was booming during those heady years. After the President's death, Mr. Blank and Eunice Kennedy Shriver produced a model of the eternal candle burning at his grave with the profits going to the Special Olympics. But soon after, the crowds diminished, business floundered, and they had to close.

Initially I hoped to build condominiums there but the real estate market was so bad that just the word "condo" was poison.

Instead of loaning money, banks were going out of business. I had paid cash for the property and now felt stupid for that. No banks were investing in construction so I left the concrete building vacant for the time being and used the outbuildings for auto and boat storage. Ted K used one of the buildings to store the light fixtures and other parts of the aluminum dome that once covered the family pool but was dismantled after his father died.

The heavy machinery used to make candles still remained in the basement but since there was then no E-Bay I couldn't find a buyer for it. I finally called a scrap metal dealer and let him take it away for nothing. However, I kept the more than one hundred cases of candles left in the basement which were still usable. During September of 1989, Hurricane Hugo pummeled the nation's Southeastern coast, wreaking havoc, especially in the Carolinas where the devastation was still being felt months after the storm. Thousands of people remained without power and as I watched the news one night, many residents were still asking for help.

Remembering those cases of candles at the candle factory and wondering how I might get them to the Carolinas, I called Ted. After meeting me and seeing the cases of candles at the factory, he moved quickly. "C'mon Donny, let's go back to the house. I'm calling Thurmond and Hollings right now." (Strom Thurmond and Earl Hollings were the two South Carolina senators.) The fact that it was Sunday didn't matter to Ted, he just grabbed the phone in the kitchen and while covering the mouthpiece, whispered, "This is great. UPS is shipping stuff like that to the Carolinas for nothing. No charge."

As I sat in the kitchen, I couldn't help thinking of all that had gone on there over the years and it felt strange to be watching the youngest Kennedy son laughing and talking about candles with two other U. S. Senators just trying to relax at home on a Sunday morning. No matter the situation, Ted was a guy who got things done.

After the calls, we had coffee out on the porch and as I was about to leave, Ted moaned, "Well! What about *me*? Don't I get any candles for doing all this work? The Kennedys lose power too you know!" We both laughed but early the next morning a UPS driver was knocking on my door looking for the cases of candles. A week later, I received a letter from each of the Senators thanking me for the candles and for remembering the people of South Carolina. I appreciated that but it was Ted who made it happen.

Several weeks after the delivery of the candles, Ted stopped by to see if I might be interested in selling the candle factory property. He said the family had plans for the future that might require space for parking and storage facilities. With the economy still weak and the nation's banks in crisis, I had no chance of building condominiums, so I said I'd consider selling the property. He assured me there was no rush but asked me to keep quiet about it until or if there was a sale. He also wanted me to continue overseeing the property. The next day I received a call from the New York office to discuss the price and see if a sale was possible. I was also told I would be paid for the period of time I was overseeing the property

The real estate market in the Northeast was in a free-fall and none of my properties were selling so that phone call had me walking on air. I'd been carrying mortgages and expenses for far too long and with the exception of rentals, had no other income. The sale would not only lift a huge weight off my shoulders but I would also be helping Ted to facilitate the family's plans for the future.

The closing was set for two weeks after Easter and I felt relief was on the way. That is, until I read the local papers and saw that my former lawyer was going to jail for embezzlement, my dentist was closing his practice and entering a rehab and my payroll provider was being indicted for income tax fraud. When I watched the 11:00 o'clock news, it didn't get any better. Executive Life, my life insurance company, had filed for bankruptcy; I wouldn't be worth anything dead either. But the knockout punch came when I saw William Kennedy Smith, Jean Kennedy's son, being arraigned in the Palm Beach County Court House and charged with rape.

Previously the New York lawyers working on the candle factory deal had told me that unless all the siblings, Jean, Pat, Eunice, and Ted, signed the purchase and sales agreement, the sale couldn't go through. Now, just two days before our lawyers were to meet, a national and international press blitz came to Palm Beach over the impending William Kennedy Smith rape trial.

The day before the closing, I received a call from one of the lawyers in New York. He apologized for the unfortunate situation but also informed me that the closing was off.

I had understood that, but was still devastated. What, after all, are the chances of a simple real estate deal on Cape Cod being cancelled because of a rape charge fifteen hundred miles away?

After dealing with the upsetting family situation and the press, Ted flew back to Hyannis Port and called to say he'd be over in the morning. His voice sounded terrible and when he arrived I'd never seen him so shaken other than that time on the dock after Bobby's death. The Candle Factory was forgotten as I listened to him describe the scene in Florida which was quite different from the one I'd seen on television and read in the papers.

The "Au Bar" where it all began, was a restaurant/bar around the corner from my Palm Beach house that I often frequented. It was a supper club mostly for people over forty, not the young people's hangout described in the media. It seems that after the dinner crowd arrived and the music began, Patrick Kennedy and Wiliam Kennedy Smith, two of the youngest men in the place, met Ted for dinner. During the evening, the young men danced, had some drinks, and asked two girls they'd met there, back to the house. Ted said he chatted with Patrick, Willy, and the girls for a few minutes, said good night and went to bed. The boys stayed up entertaining their dates and my understanding was that Willy's mother, Jean, along with his sisters, were already asleep upstairs.

Ted said he first learned of the problem the next morning after breakfast when he and Jean were playing tennis and a police car pulled into the driveway looking for William Smith. Jean said she'd get him but when they came back Willy was immediately arrested and charged with rape. Investigators later said that after William had gone to bed, his date used the phone in the den to call her boyfriend and have him pick her up. By the time the boyfriend arrived, the girl had allegedly taken two small rugs and a picture from the den which didn't sound to me like a person who'd just been raped.

Having been to the house, I was familiar with the lawn area between the pool and the house where the rape allegedly took place. It was located under the windows where members of the family were sleeping which raised the question as to why someone wouldn't have heard screaming if a rape had occurred.

At one of the parties I attended with my pal Bill Carter, he introduced me to "Brownie" McLean, a Palm Beach grand dame whose mother had owned the Hope Diamond and was one of the world's wealthiest women during the 1920s. Brownie was an old friend of Bill's and when she heard about the rape, knowing of my friendship with Ted, had one of her friends call Bill to say she'd been in the ladies room at Au Bar that night and overheard two girls laughing and saying, "Tonight, we're going to screw a Kennedy." The friend also said Brownie was willing to testify to that. Bill called me and I gave the information to Ted who passed it on to the attorneys. But it never came up in court.

By then, more than twenty television crews from around the world were camped outside the Kennedy house covering the trial. It got so bad Ted had someone call me to see if my house was available should he need to escape. It was and of course I said yes, but he never got the chance to use it

For the first and only time, I wrote a letter to a magazine, People, castigating them for their reporting on Ted's part in the incident. I believed it was not only irresponsible but jeopardizing to his personal safety. Some kooks reading that crap could have thought he was the assailant. It was never published but I still have the apology letter from People claiming they didn't print it due to lack of space. I wasn't there at the time but believed that Ted was telling me the truth. However, when he took the stand and began taking the blame for bringing the young men to the Au Bar, then for allowing them to bring the girls to the house, I was stunned. I guess he'd done that to spare his sister Jean from having to take the stand but I'm still saddened by it.

The trial cost the family over four million dollars in lawyers' fees but ultimately, William Kennedy Smith was acquitted. But when the Candle Factory deal fell through I nearly went broke. Desperately trying to hold on to my properties, I even contemplated jumping off the Sagamore Bridge! Not really. Fortunately I'm afraid of heights and wouldn't be able to even climb the fence leading to where you can jump off!

The economy was still in the doldrums but after all that drama, I decided to put the candle factory on the market anyway. When I did, some Hyannis Port residents formed a group to purchase it and turn it into a park. That didn't materialize however so one of the group, who served on the board of directors for the Hyannis Port Golf Club, offered to buy it for the same amount as I had originally paid, thinking the golf club would snap it up. As it happened, I had already investigated that option and had been turned down.

The buyer was also turned down and eventually sold the property to a local developer who eventually built condominiums far less tasteful than I had envisioned. True to form, the economy came roaring back and the builder sold all of them for big bucks. Once again proving I still had that notoriously bad sense of timing.

* * * *

When I sold The Asa Bearse House in 1989, I had taken a second mortgage on the property to get a better price. A year and a half went by with no problems but then the owners didn't pay me for six months and the bank soon began foreclosure.

I didn't want the restaurant back but when the bank scheduled an auction I told my lawyer Steve Jones, we'd attend and bid only until the second mortgage was covered. However, on the morning of the auction, the local paper ran a story giving a history of the place and my part in it, so my ego kicked in. Now that I was a millionaire, I told Steve to keep bidding until I said stop. Unfortunately the other bidder stopped first and that foolish bidding put me back in the restaurant business. Sick to my stomach with knowing I'd made a huge mistake, I offered the place back to the bidder for less than I'd paid but, infuriated that my bidding had driven the price up, he refused and stormed out the door.

Not believing what I'd done, I tossed and turned most of the night. But by the next morning, I knew I'd just have to make the best of it. Rolling up my sleeves, I made a few calls, drove to Hyannis and vowed to restore the Asa Bearse House back to the great place it had once been.

A wonderful restaurant crew was already working there so I met with them the next day to discuss my plans and they seemed re-energized. The building wasn't in bad shape but I hired a painting crew to freshen things up. I called a chef I'd heard good things about to offer him a job and also phoned Dave McKenna to ask if he would return. Both he and the chef said yes and before I knew it, the Asa Bearse House was running just as it always had.

Newspaper articles about the auction and the re-opening helped bring business back right away and soon after we were open a distinguished visitor came in to see me. Known mostly for his best-selling novel Fatal Vision, later made into a successful movie, author Joe McGinnis had also written other books with some success. His latest book, however, The Last Brother was to be about Ted Kennedy. Someone had told him I was a friend of Ted's so he arrived hoping I'd provide some information for the book. He was very pleasant but after saying hello and shaking his hand, I said I wasn't interested in talking about Ted so our conversation was brief. He had a drink, commented on how much he liked the place and left. But that wasn't end of it and the next day he appeared at my door in Hyannis Port. After apologizing for just showing up, he said "I'm here because I can't understand why Ted Kennedy's friends won't give me some good things to write about if only to offset the negative stuff I get from those who are always anxious to slam the Kennedys."

Saying I couldn't speak for anyone else, I just wasn't interested in helping him, or anyone else, write a book, especially about a friend. He thanked me for my time, shook my hand again, and left for good. I never read the book but heard the reviews were lukewarm. I was also pleased when some customers who read it told me they thought McGinnis had treated Ted pretty well overall.

That incident came to mind years later when Joe McGinnis was back in the news during the Presidential campaign of 2012. He had rented a house in Alaska next to Republican vice-presidential candidate Sarah Palin and his reporting on her personal life was criticized by many, including me. Of course most of the major media, maintaining their usual double standard, justified it. If Sarah Palin had been a Democrat and subjected to that treatment, The New York Times and feminists throughout the country would have gone bonkers!

Joe McGiness died in 2014 and when I read about it in the papers, I recalled our brief meeting and what a pleasant guy he'd seemed to have been.

As previously mentioned, when I first purchased the Asa Bearse House the Town of Barnstable had an ordinance against outside dining. I protested that and got it overturned. Now that I owned the restaurant again, I was happy to see sidewalk cafes on both sides of Main Street and knew that Hyannis had a new vitality. But I stayed with my proven formula. I hired piano players to entertain outside during lunch and had Dave McKenna and Lou Colombo back in the Reading Room most nights. The patio again became a magnet for celebrities and other musicians so I hired various trios to play during Sunday brunch and the early dinner hour.

One busy afternoon as I sat at a patio table with friends, one of my waitresses came over to ask about a credit card neither of us had seen before. It was a Platinum American Express card and I thought I recognized the name, Joseph Raposo, as a Fall River, MA guy who had become the chief song writer for the Sesame Street and The Electric Company children's shows. Earlier, as a student at Harvard he was known for songs he'd written for their Hasty Pudding Club.

Wanting to be sure I had the right man, I went over to introduce myself and asked if he was from Fall River. Grinning widely, he said, "Yah, I'm from Fall River, what about it!" After discussing the credit card, he introduced me to his wife, Pat Collins who was originally from Dedham, MA, and a former Boston television newscaster. Her parents had owned a home in Dennis for years but more recently she and Joe had purchased the former Johnson & Johnson estate in Chatham. While their official residence was New York City, they intended to spend summers and most of the fall on the Cape.

After they finished lunch, I gave them a tour of the Reading Room and when I mentioned that Dave McKenna was playing there, Joe couldn't wait to bring friends to hear him and to have dinner there. Whenever he arrived it was a treat. Dave got him to sing and play his own songs which not only meant having someone sit in for him at the piano but then he could sneak over to the television to see how the Red Sox were doing.

Besides his Sesame Street successes, Joe had also written several pop hits, among them Sing, Sing a Song, recorded by Barbra Streisand and Karen Carpenter. Four of his other songs were recorded by Frank Sinatra on his out of retirement album, Ol' Blue Eyes Is Back.

Joe was by himself one day so we had lunch together and being a huge fan of Sinatra, I asked about his association with my favorite crooner's album. He said he'd been dating Barbra Streisand at the time, which kind of blew me away. Barbara, he explained was then preparing to do a show about Ebbetts Field, the former home of the Brooklyn Dodgers. Thinking it might fit the show, Joe wrote a song for her called And There Used to be a Ballpark, which she liked but felt it wasn't for her. But, she added, "Frank Sinatra would love it!" Joe didn't know the singer personally, but a day later Sinatra's agent called to set up a meeting with his famous client and Joe.

Sinatra always said he wouldn't make a comeback unless he had new songs so the meeting was very successful and four of Joe's songs ended up on his album. Think of it Sinatra fans, if not for Joe Raposo's songs, Sinatra might never have made that comeback! Frank and Joe became good friends after that and I believe Sinatra's recording of Kermit the frog's song – "It's Not Easy Being Green," is one of his best.

In the late 1960s, I was playing piano at the Mooring in Hyannis when Bobby Kennedy announced he was running for President. The Secret Service and members of the press began staying at the Yachtsman Hotel, just as they had when Jack Kennedy was President, and since the Mooring was close to the hotel and the Compound, some reporters would hang out at the bar after work along with the entertainers appearing at the Yachtsman. During a break, I would often end up talking with various agents, actors and members of the press.

Some years later the television show M*A*S*H became popular and whenever I watched it, I thought Alan Alda, the Hawkeye character, looked familiar. I'd always figured it was just my imagination until Frank Saunders, the former Kennedy chauffeur, became a regular at the Reading Room.

One night he mentioned he'd written a book called Torn Lace

Curtain about his experiences with the Kennedys. When I said I'd like to read it, he went out to his car and presented me with a signed copy. In the book, Frank mentioned that Alan Alda used to perform at the Yachtsman Hotel during the '60s with a group called The Compass Players and the mystery was solved. I had probably met him on one of my piano breaks at the Mooring.

Joe invited me to his Chatham house one afternoon where we drank Scotch, talked about music and discussed where I had worked on the Cape. When I mentioned the Mooring and told him my Alan Alda story, he laughed and said "I'm calling him up right now! He's a good friend and we live in the same building in New York!" Alan was home and after they talked for a minute Joe put me on the phone. Alda was very cordial and after reminiscing about his days on the Cape, said he remembered the Mooring. Of course, I don't know if that was true but we had a nice conversation anyway. When Joe Raposo died of cancer on February 5, 1989, at the age of fifty-one, the world lost a wonderful man with a marvelous talent. Never forgetting his love for Cape Cod, he chose to be buried at The Union Cemetery near his home in Chatham. His music lives on to be enjoyed by people of all ages and cultures.

Foolishly believing I was finished with the restaurant business, I put the Asa Bearse House back on the market in 1991 and several buyers jumped at the chance to own the place. But no one had the money to do the deal. My bank account was still feeling the strain of the flagging economy so when a Boston broker showed up with a restaurant owner from Newton who had the necessary funds, I signed an agreement that basically let me get out with at least my original investment back.

* * * *

Those of us who knew Ted Kennedy up close saw that he could be both tough and tender. He was a man who loved to please others, but like the rest of us, sometimes stumbled. The thing I admired most about him, however, was his never-ending sense of humor.

In the years before 9/11, airlines often offered package deals to boost sales. Consequently, I always flew Delta where by purchasing a book of ten round-trip tickets I could travel anywhere and even cancel on the day of the flight with no penalty. Before flying home, I'd check the paper to see if a storm was heading for the Cape then cancel if I didn't like the forecast.

On the day before the Valentine's Day weekend, I had scheduled a flight to Boston from the West Palm Beach Airport. But seeing a bad weather report, I called Delta and cancelled the flight. No sooner had I hung up when Ted called saying he hoped I was coming home to Hyannis Port so that we could go sailing on Sunday. He was alone and needed me to crew. "And don't forget to bring some grapefruit,' he reminded me. I had business to attend to anyway so I said the hell with it, called Delta back and rescheduled my flight.

As I was sweeping up gravel the plows left behind on my driveway the next morning, I looked down the hill to see my friend with the large head and wearing a red parka, trudging up the hill to my house. I could tell something was wrong and was concerned. But when I asked what the problem was, he was still puffing a bit but finally said, "Well, my secretary really screwed up this time! I gave her a list of lady friends I wanted to send roses to on Valentine's Day a week ago but she put the wrong names with the wrong addresses on the envelopes!" Sally got roses with a card that said, To Nancy, love Ted, MaryAnn got roses with a card saying, To Paula, with love from Ted! and so on. My phone's been ringing all morning!" Divorced and single at the time, he was honestly distressed about the situation. But I couldn't stop laughing. And when I asked how many there were, he groaned a little, said "About a dozen I think" and I collapsed. By then he was laughing with me. "Never mind that, did you bring the grapefruit?" he asked and that was it. I couldn't take any more and, putting my arm on his shoulder, said "C'mon, let's have a libation and go lick our wounds!"

Moments later, sitting on my freezing deck overlooking Martha's Vineyard, both wearing red parkas and sipping on a Florida grapefruit beverage, I said, "What the hell is going on? One of the most powerful men in the world and he can't even get a Valentine's Day list right!"

There were many fun times but the burden of being the family's surviving patriarch could sometimes prevent Ted from enjoying certain other little pleasures. Cruising along the shoreline in the Mya one crisp fall day, I was smoking my usual, inexpensive Backwoods cigars when Ted yelled "For God's sake Donny, why don't you smoke a decent cigar?" I didn't smoke much but when I did, I liked my cigar to be cheap, small and mild, not the big black strong ones that made me cough. After Ted called me a cheapskate and a wimp, we sailed through choppy seas for another hour or so, tied up the boat and returned to the house for lunch.

Later, as I headed out the back door toward my car, he yelled for me to wait a minute. A few minutes passed before he came out with a cigar box which he handed to me and said, "Here. Take these. They were my brother Jack's. After Steve (his brother-in-law Steve Smith) died, the family asked me not to smoke anymore. There's only three in there and they're probably dried out. But they're Cubans, you cheap bastard!" We both laughed, but for once I had no comeback. It may have meant nothing to him but to me that cigar box was a piece of history and a gift I will always cherish.

During another party at Ted's that summer, I was getting some air on the porch when Arnold Schwarznegger came outside. As we chatted, he pulled out a cigar and offered me one. I was lighting it when Ted came outside to say, "Look at this! The only two conservatives in the house and one's even a Republican! How is it they can have a cigar but I can't?" I certainly understand a family's concern for a loved one's health regarding smoking and in the big picture, that incident was probably insignificant, but once again, Ted had to make a concession to the family and couldn't even have a cigar with friends like his brothers used to.

CHAPTER 17

IRRESISTABLE EXPERIMENTS

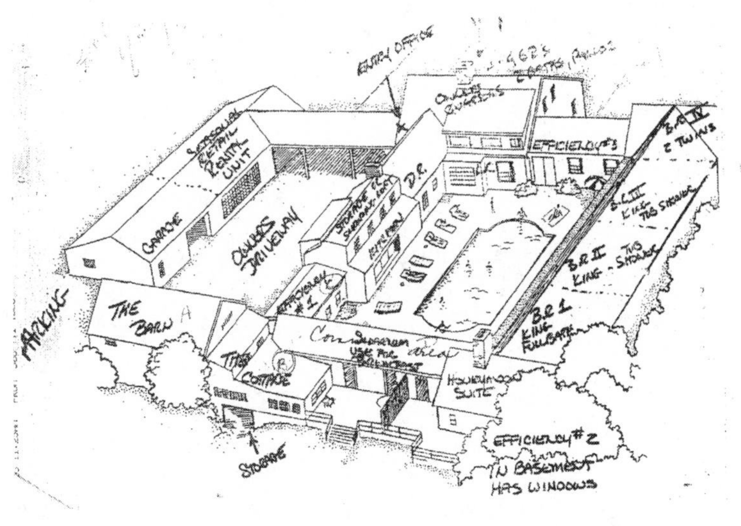

The author's 2003 innkeeping venture, the Lamb and Lion Inn, which is still located on Rte 6A in West Barnstable, Massachusetts.

After being so unhappy having to run the Asa Bearse House again, any sane person would have said goodbye to the restaurant business. But less than two years after selling the place - again - I bumped into another good friend, Jim Burke, who wanted to talk to me about The Backside Saloon, a restaurant he owned in Hyannis.

His partner's son had been leasing the place but was having trouble paying the rent and other bills. Initially Jim asked for any suggestions I might have to improve the business. I mentioned some ideas but then he paused and said, "Oh, the hell with that, why don't you just take the place over and pay me the rent!"

Instead of rushing off to find a psychiatrist, my lunatic mind blocked all my recent restaurant disasters and focused instead on the great success the Backside once was. During the 1930's, the place was a popular inn with a bar that was adjacent to a theater. Decades later, in 1965, a talented guy named Len Healey bought the property and created a unique concept: three separate bars under the same roof with customer access to each. The main bar, The Velvet Hammer, had a Main Street entrance. The other two, the Red Door and the Backside Saloon, were attached in the rear but both they and the Velvet Hammer could be entered from the parking lot. The bars offered various types of music, including rock, jazz, and solo piano. I first met Dave McKenna there years before he would be playing for me.

Len had great success with the three places for over a

decade but finally sold the place and moved to New Hampshire. Over the years, other owners operated the place with limited success until Jim bought the property, converted the first floor into offices and the second floor into apartments. That left only the Backside still open for business as a bar.

Because my other restaurants were large operations with many employees and responsibilities, I rationalized that given the relatively small size of The Backside it would be easy to run. What I hadn't calculated though, were recent changes in the industry. Tougher drunk driving laws and more sporting events on TV had seriously impacted what was once a common life style. Couples weren't going out during the week as they did in the past, people stayed home nights to watch DVDs, and happy hours had become illegal.

It was tough enough to make a profit during the good times but those changes made it even more challenging. And somehow I'd forgotten the struggle of running a year-round bar or restaurant on seasonal Cape Cod. Now though, I was trapped. One of the ways I justified the venture was having Ted's chef, Neil Connolly, join me as a partner. Obviously, Neil's first responsibility was to the Senator so I hired Sam Ricker, former chef of the Wursthaus Restaurant in the Cape Cod Mall, to do most of the cooking. Business was brisk on weekends and holidays but during the week (and especially during the winter), we lost money. Although disgusted with myself for going back into the business again, I refused to quit.

Instead I began drinking too much and like a desperate man on a sinking ship, kept pumping money into a bottomless sea.

Even so, interesting things always seem to happen in the restaurant business. And this time I was brought back to my teaching years in Rockland. One June day my bartender was ill, so I was pressed into service tending the bar. The television was on as I was setting up when suddenly the news mentioned two of my former Rockland students. The first was a horrifying report about one of them who had lived a troubled life and had just been shot by his own son. The victim's wife, too, had been one of my students and was now the mother of the shooter who had killed his father and her husband on Fathers' Day. It was a terribly sad story.

The second news report, however, was much different and involved Brian Duffy, another of my Rockland students, who had been in my English class and whom I'd coached on the high school baseball team. The television was showing the launch of the shuttle rising through the smoke over Cape Kennedy. What a thrill that was to see and Brian would eventually fly four missions for NASA, one as captain, and would spend over forty days in space before retiring in 1992.

Sometimes life delivers surprises that force us to contemplate its mysteries. There I was, a floundering millionaire, preparing to tend a bar in Hyannis, watching two young men who had once been my students, making television news at the same time. Sadly, one had shot his father; but the other was shooting through the sky as an astronaut.

* * * *

One Sunday morning, Chef Sam poked his head into my office to say there was a television crew from Channel 5 looking for me outside. They were filming a story on Ted Kennedy's thirty-five years in the U.S. Senate and a reporter was standing at the front door with a cameraman waiting to interview me. I explained I wouldn't give them an interview because Ted was a friend, but I suggested they go up the street to Puritan Clothing and ask for the owner, Howard Penn, another friend of the Senator. They thanked me, packed up their gear and left.

I forgot all about it until I was relaxing on my deck with a cold beverage and the phone rang. It was Ted who began the conversation by griping about my high wine prices and saying he was tired of me not delivering the stuff to the house on time! I had no idea what he was talking about but I have to give a little background.

Shortly after buying the Backside, I was visiting Ted's chef, Neil Connolly, at the compound when he asked where he could get some cases of champagne quickly. "I've got some you can have but why don't you order it through The Backside along with any other wines or liquor you need? I'll even deliver it myself!" Neil promptly asked Ted who immediately approved.

During that puzzling phone call to my house, Ted sheepishly admitted he was calling because he'd heard about the Channel 5 interview with Howie Penn. Now I got it. We both laughed at his little joke, but when I told him how it happened, he grew quiet and said, "Good thinking, Donny. Thanks and I'll see you this weekend." I was puzzled, but then it hit me. His call had nothing to do with wine or deliveries; it was about trust. Knowing I'd turned down an opportunity to be interviewed, to him, meant I wasn't looking for attention or celebrity by being a friend of Ted's.

On a Sunday morning, sometime later, Ted called to say he was bringing Vicky by for coffee. He also wanted to show me the new paint job he'd had done on "Old Blue," the blue 1970 Pontiac Bonneville convertible he'd had for years.

At that time, I hadn't met Victoria Reggie but knew she hailed from Louisiana and that her family was a long-time Kennedy contributor. Divorced and practicing law in Washington, she ran into Ted there as well as on Nantucket where her parents owned a house. That summer she and Ted began dating and after introducing her to me as his houseguest for the weekend, he seemed anxious for me to see the car. He wasn't too pleased when I told him the paint job was an improvement but he should get rid of that ugly brown upholstery.

Unfortunately, I'd forgotten there was a mental health facility next to the restaurant that provided daily outpatient care. On Sundays that facility provided vans which took clients on tours around the Cape. When Ted and Vicky arrived at the Backside with the top down on Old Blue, the clients waiting for the vans immediately recognized the senator. When they began shouting, Oh look! It's Senator Kennedy, Hi Teddy!, Hi Mister Kennedy!, How come you're not as good looking as your brothers, Is that your wife?, Is she your girlfriend?, Boy, she's pretty!, Teddy was taken aback but still remained gracious and patient, as did Vicky "No, I'm not as good looking as Jack or Bobby," and "No, Vicky isn't my wife, She's just a friend," he courteously replied.

As this continued, I had to bite my tongue to keep from laughing. Finally, I couldn't take it anymore but as I headed back to the restaurant, I could hear Ted lumbering up behind me saying, "What the F#%^ was that? Where the hell did they come from?" And when he followed up with, "F#%^ the coffee Donny, after that we need a Bloody Mary!!" I really lost it. The look on Ted's face was absolutely priceless and I collapsed in laughter again.

Vicky was still a little shell-shocked too and as I held the door for her trying to regain control, we slid into a booth with our Bloody Marys and I explained the situation. While both saw the humor in it, I was touched by how warmly each of them had reacted to the group.

The Backside was always busy during the lunch

hours. Prices were reasonable, service was quick, and the food was quite good. Little did I know the place was about to set the stage for a new career but also for the undermining of a friendship..

Ernie Boch, a prominent auto tycoon with dealerships in and around Boston, built a home on Martha's Vineyard and had invested in several businesses around the Cape. Often he flew into Hyannis to check out other car dealerships and somehow heard that WOCB, located in South Yarmouth and the first radio station on Cape Cod, had just come on the market. Ever eager for a challenge, Ernie decided to try the radio business and bought the place. The station was also the same one my childhood friends and I had once biked down Sea Street to examine after Hurricane Carol in 1953.

I'd met Ernie years earlier after purchasing The Flying Bridge in Falmouth. Martha's Vineyard was just across the bay so while Ernie was having his boat serviced next door at Falmouth Marine, he usually stopped in at the restaurant for lunch. Soon after he began renovating the station, he hired Cary Parhegian as general manager, a veteran of radio stations in Maine and Boston. The station was only a mile or so from the Backside so Cary soon became a regular for lunch.

When I saw Ernie with him one day I stopped by their table to say hello and they invited me to join them. As we talked, I was stunned when they asked if I'd be interested in doing a talk radio show. Given my various careers and experiences, they said I fit the talk industry profile and thought I would be a good fit. The time slot they proposed was 3:00 to 5:00, Monday thru Friday and since that wouldn't conflict with the restaurant's busiest hours, I said I'd think about it. After all, I was always willing to trying something new and never had trouble shooting my big mouth off. "But nobody will want to hear what I have to say. There'll be no feel good clap-trap and I'll be telling it like it is!" I said before they left, which made them laugh. A week later I was on the air!

A 2004 study found that only 17% of the public listens to talk radio on a regular basis and the audience is mostly male, middle-aged and conservative. Among those listeners, 41% are Republican and 28% Democrats. Forty-five percent described themselves as conservative compared to eighteen percent who claimed they were liberal.

My radio career had a shaky start when, on my second day, my co-host, Kathy Brown, had a car accident on the way to work. I was panicked and although I'd brought along extra material, I never expected to be alone when the show began. Ironically, the date was September 6, 1998, the birthdate of Joseph P. Kennedy, who would have been a hundred years old. Since that was one of the items on my list I opened the show with it. I asked the listeners if they thought having the Kennedys living on the Cape during the summer was a positive or a negative influence upon it. Was it good for business, or bad, and how long did they think the Kennedy appeal would last?

The phones stayed silent. No one was calling in and I was sweating bullets. I started talking about my history living on the Cape and described what it was like back in the 1950's. Then I mentioned what it was like for me and other residents in Hyannis Port to live so close to the Kennedys and deal with all the activity that went with that. During a break for commercials, I was at the water cooler when Cary, the manager, came from his office to tell me I was doing a great job! I was flabbergasted and said, "Are you kidding? I'm laying a huge egg! I haven't had one call!" He said, "Don, don't judge a show by the number of calls. Sure they're important, but when the listeners are enjoying what you have to say, they don't want to interrupt. Hearing that, I could have hugged him. And from that time on, I could feel my confidence grow. In the near future, and for over ten years, I would be doing a morning show with Ed Lambert from 7 until 10 a.m. five days a week

****

I had been in a relationship with a wonderful girl for two years. Everyone liked her and she was good for me. But, as usual, that wasn't good enough. I was napping on my deck one day when I heard the doorbell ring and called out, "C'mon in!" Receiving no response, I got up to find Pat, my former dining room manager at the Flying Bridge, standing at the door wearing a beautiful smile.

Years earlier, I was having lunch with my attorney at the Nimrod Restaurant during negotiations to buy the Flying Bridge and our waitress was Pat. She was so lovely I was immediately intrigued and soon after the restaurant deal went through I returned to the Nimrod alone to ask if she'd consider working for me at the Flying Bridge. That March I was pleased to see her among others applying for jobs and of course she was hired. While I had a strong attraction for her, the timing was wrong and I was still in the process of being divorced from Donna.

After the divorce we dated a few times, but by then I was running around with other women and Pat had seen enough. She took a job at another restaurant in town and we lost contact for a while. Seeing her at my door with that beautiful smile, rekindled those old passions so I invited her in for a cold drink on the porch. After catching up on the latest Falmouth news, Pat said she'd stopped by to ask if I'd be her date for the wedding of our mutual friend, Eddie Kirk.

I jumped at the chance and after having a great time at the wedding, things happened so quickly I don't think either of us knew what hit us. Excited about the future, I realized I had to end my other relationship, if I was to continue being with Pat, so I did.

The real estate market was still weak however. Banks were reluctant to loan money and my mortgage payments were draining my now limited resources. Other than the radio show and some rental properties, I had no income. Four years of waiting for the economy to turn around was enough. I still owned the Candle Factory and too much other property. Nothing was selling so I decided I'd put everything I owned on the market. Naturally, with my luck, the first offer would be on the one property I didn't want to sell. My little house on the hill!

My Hyannis realtor, Paula O'Neill (my friend Kevin's wife) received an offer on the place almost in the first week and, hoping to scare off the buyer, I tried to kill the deal. But when that didn't work, instead of just paying Paula her commission and taking the place off the market, I didn't have the guts and told myself, "Ah, what the hell, it's only a house!" and sold it. My further justification was that I had just purchased another captain's house at the bottom of Sunset Hill and could move in there.

During the winter I was spending most of my nights in Falmouth with Pat which left that house empty. I kept the heat cranked up but old houses have openings in their shingles where the combination of a pin hole and an icy wind can quickly freeze a heating pipe. Just as I was about to leave Falmouth for the radio station one morning, I received a frantic call from my Brazilian cleaning lady, who announced that my Hyannis Port house was flooded!

I called the station to say I'd be late, then rushed over to survey the damage and shut off the water main. But the burst pipe must have been leaking for days because the sheet rock, furniture and floors were ruined. I phoned the plumber but couldn't reach the insurance man. Realizing it was too late to save the pictures and family items ruined by the flood, I once again felt that Irish negativity echoing in my ears: "Things are going too well, watch out. There must be something wrong."

After the radio show I returned to the house to find the insurance adjuster waiting for me. Despite considerable damage, the adjuster stood quietly in an inch of water in the dining room making notes on a clipboard. Then out of the blue, a voice boomed behind us, "Don't give this guy a nickel! He does this all the time!" The adjuster was startled but when he turned around and saw Ted Kennedy, he dropped his clipboard into the water. Embarrassed, he explained he had to go out to his car to get new forms.

Nevertheless, I wasn't in a laughing mood and when Ted put his arm on my shoulder and said, "C'mon Donny, let's get out of here. We'll go over to Pease Boat Yard and check on the Mya," I was furious and said "Are you crazy? I can't leave here!"

Ted just looked at me and said "Yes you can, there's nothing you can do here but get more upset." I knew he was right so we jumped into my car and headed for Harwich to see the Mya and the Pease boys at their boatyard.

We rode for a while when Ted remained quiet. But finally, he turned to me and said, "Donny, you've got to learn to accept the things that really aren't important and can't be changed, anyway." As I thought about all the tragic events he'd endured, I was ashamed to think I'd let a petty, temporary situation turn me into a whining victim. Ted's example of acceptance was helping me become a calmer and more measured person. But it hadn't come soon enough.

* * * *

During our whirlwind courtship, Pat and I had a couple of serious arguments, which should have been a warning that perhaps something wasn't quite right. But I tried not to over-react and chalked it up to nerves, hers as well as mine. Losing her first husband in a car accident and having two small children to bring up was a tough thing. But I loved her and the kids and hoped our other marriages would be the incentive to try even harder this time. But each of us had been alone and in control for so long that returning to married life would be challenging, to say the least.

On the morning of the wedding the weather was windy, rainy and nasty. I was on a ladder attempting to tie down the plastic side curtains on the tent when Ted appeared. He and Vicky had taken time off from the Kerry campaign to attend the wedding and when he saw me in such a black mood fighting the weather, he insisted I come back to his house where he proceeded to cook me breakfast by himself. I was complaining about the weather, afraid the wind and rain would make the tent unusable, when once again he told me to stop worrying. He predicted it would clear and by the time we'd finished eating, damned if it hadn't. "You just don't talk to the right people Donny," he joked.

The ceremony took place in the center of Hyannis Port village at Union Chapel just across the street from my newly acquired captain's house. The Backside kitchen crew served a wonderful meal and over a hundred family and friends sat under a dry tent as Ted stood, made a toast then gave a little speech honoring the mothers of the bride and groom. Everyone had a wonderful time.

After a short honeymoon in Nantucket, we attended the wedding of Kiki and Teddy Kennedy Jr. the following weekend on Block Island. Kiki had worked for me at the Asa Bearse House, but I mention that only because her wedding provided Pat and me with a picture of what celebrities endure under the constant stalking of the paparazzi press. Young John Kennedy was attending the wedding with Daryl Hannah, the tall and beautiful actress he was then dating. The church area was filled with cameras, reporters and television crews and as we left the church following the ceremony, I had to push away several photographers trying to get to John and Daryl. The couple escaped in a car parked at the side entrance to the church for that purpose, but the photographers were like wild beasts. It was an experience I will never forget and I've never seen anything like it since.

* * * *

When Rose Kennedy died on January 22, 1995, at the age of 104, Ted's Boston office called to invite me and my wife to a private wake at the house. When we arrived the next day, a teary-eyed Ted ushered us into the sunroom where his mother lay in quiet repose. Overlooking the emerald lawn and sky blue ocean she'd enjoyed for almost seventy years, Mrs. Kennedy looked lovely and at peace surrounded by walls covered with pictures of her family. Gazing at his mother Ted choked up and said she looked just like she had when she was going to Paris on a shopping trip.

Suddenly my mind flashed back to a television interview I'd seen of her years ago. Mrs. Kennedy was sitting on a sofa, beautifully dressed in blue or pink, and when the host asked how she'd been able to cope with the tragedies her family had suffered, she looked straight into the camera and said, "We must remember that life is for the living and we must go on for those we have lost." No tears, just a simple statement stressing her faith in God.

Pat and I were part of the motorcade which was internationally televised and during the procession saw hundreds of people holding signs and crosses on the streets, highways, and overpasses. Motorists pulled over or slowed down to watch the procession slowly make its way to Boston's North End where a funeral mass was to be held at Saint Stephens Church, the same church where Mrs. Kennedy was baptized in July of 1890, one hundred and four years before.

Outside the church, sidewalks were packed with people wanting to pay their last respects. Crowds had gathered throughout the surrounding areas hoping to catch a glimpse of the hearse carrying the petite woman from

Boston whose family had achieved international success only to suffer such terrible losses. Just as her daughter-in-law Jackie had done thirty years before, Rose Kennedy set an example for a nation and for all people of faith throughout the world

* * * *

Unfortunately, it wasn't long before I realized that Pat wasn't really happy and didn't like living in Hyannis Port. In an effort to ease the problem, we went house hunting and found a rustic place on Lake Wequaquet in Centerville near where I'd summered with my aunt and uncle as a child and later lived during my first marriage. Although Pat said she liked the new house, I now realize I was too hasty in buying it. Having given up her job and moved from her comfort zone in Falmouth, I'm sure Pat felt displaced. In retrospect, I should have given her time to look at other houses on her own. I believe we truly wanted to please each other but she and I never talked about the things that meant the most to each of us. Our goals were different and I couldn't stand arguments so we finally gave up and got divorced.

Going through a second divorce churned up old memories of failure and took a real toll on me. I'd been on my financial ass for so long that not being able to sell the Backside made me wonder if the name Backside was telling me something. I wasn't drinking but I was down. Finally, a broker brought in a somewhat shady character from Boston who wanted the restaurant but could pay next to nothing for the business. I said okay but after he made the down payment and took over the place, he refused to pay the balance. When I confronted him about it, he intimated that if I tried to take him to court he would cause me a lot of trouble.

I said, "Don't hand me that bullshit," but remembering the scene in Boston when that lunatic at Sloppy Joe's stuck a Saturday night special in my stomach, I called my lawyer. He pointed out that I didn't need that problem and said there wasn't that much money involved anyway. I knew court costs would eat most of it up as well so I said the hell with it. After all, Jim Burke had given me the business for practically nothing. However, I did tell Jim about it and felt badly that as the landlord, now he would have to deal with that guy.

I was still doing the talk show but after the divorce, everything started grating on me. I argued with my co-host even more than usual and once again the success demon decided it needed a different kind of challenge. One morning, having coffee with the same friend who had found the Cash Market for me, I told him my problem. He had just listed an inn for sale on Route 6A in Barnstable, The Lamb and Lion, a building I recognized and whose name made me smile and seemed to suggest good fortune. That very afternoon we made an appointment to see it.

The Lamb and Lion is not your typical country inn. It's small enough to be intimate for singles or couples, but large enough to accommodate small groups and wedding parties. Its' size allows the guests to get to know one another if they wish but if not and they prefer solitude, an Audubon Society sanctuary behind the inn offers walking trails. The inn is also just a short walk to Barnstable Village and the harbor.

The inn also satisfied my passion for antiquity. Its New England cape-style main house was built in 1740 and sat on a secluded knoll with four acres of land overlooking the Old King's Highway where American patriots once passed on their way to Boston and the Revolutionary War. After decades with various owners, two free-spirited single guys bought the place in the 1960's, converted it into a B&B and gave it its name. Their parties, the neighbors said, were legendary.

From historic Route 6A, it's difficult to imagine how large the Inn really is. Thirteen living quarters, the five largest having two or more bedrooms, join several rambling additions, a central courtyard with a hallway past each of the five motel-style rooms, all with access to the swimming pool. Author Kurt Vonnegut's summer home was just down the street. Nearby, his daughter Edie painted an angel on the railroad overpass which became a kind of tourist attraction, especially after her brief marriage to television host, Geraldo Rivera.

Despite my varied career, I had never tried the hotel business and became so intrigued with the idea of being an innkeeper, I bought the place. Victory Chapel, a non-denominational church in Hyannis advertised on our radio show and many of their members listened every morning. Several were experienced craftsmen and after hearing me mention the new project and planned renovations they asked to do the job. The day of the closing, three women with sewing and decorating backgrounds appeared, hoping for a job. I'd never imagined I would be doing a project with a religious group, but I not only liked them, I also found their work efficient and their rates so reasonable, I was able to keep within my budget.

Even so, I soon learned that owning a B&B is neither the romantic nor moneymaking proposition it's cracked up to be. Despite the mystique of owning a historic inn, the daily work involved soon shattered that image. It's easier, obviously *much* easier, when a couple shares the load but I was alone. Granted, I had two chambermaids during the summer and on busy weekends but otherwise, everything that needed doing I did myself, often including the plumbing. The Don who scrubbed toilets didn't care much for the Don who bought the place. But I'm pleased to report that during the time I was an inn keeper, I was able to dissuade several young couples from going into that business, thus saving them a lot of money, potential marital problems, and considerable heartache.

Then there are the guests. Most are pleasant but when people pay to stay somewhere there is a tendency to think they have the run of the place. The owners' private living quarters risk constant invasion and if someone forgets or loses their room key late at night, guess who they wake up? To them, especially after a night of bar hopping, it's just an amusing adventure. But to the innkeeper, it's another loss of a good night's sleep.

Most country inns are busy during the summer season, they better be, but tourism, like the restaurant business, has changed drastically over the years. A major frustration is having to turn people away, especially on weekends, because that's often the only time they can rent rooms Today many women (mothers) work full-time and instead of being able to rent rooms for a week or two at a time, many have to divide their vacation time between family and work obligations. Another factor is the earlier starting dates for school, now often before Labor Day, which shortens the summer rental season even more.

When I was a kid, most mothers didn't work, especially during the summer, and families would rent a cottage or a double room in a motel or small hotel like the Lamb and Lion and stay for a month or sometimes for the whole summer. Fathers spent their two or three week vacation with the family, worked during the week and returned to the rental on weekends. Like so many aspects of modern family life, that, too, has changed.

Even so, the innkeeper's life gave me another opportunity to do what I like doing best -- interacting with and getting to know people. Early in July during my first summer, a group of German golfers arrived in Boston ahead of schedule and showed up at the Inn earlier than expected. They were accompanied by some attractive women who, as it quickly became apparent, were not their wives. Right away I knew this was going to be a fun loving crowd out for a good time.

Carrying two cases of fine Rhine wine, all the way from Germany, the self-appointed leader strutted into the kitchen and immediately asked for wine glasses from "Das Innkeeper." I liked him right away and he always made me laugh. Grabbing a corkscrew, I brought him the glasses and watched as the boisterous German took four bottles out of the case, opened them and filled everyone's glass. Handing one to me, he announced, "And the first thing we're going to do is make a toast to Cape Cod and to Don, the innkeeper!"

I hadn't been drinking for several years and waved the glass away. But he refused to take no for an answer and I no longer had the will to refuse anyway. I raised my glass along with the rest, and joined in the toast. With plates of cheese, crackers and sausage to go with the wine, the group got right into it and for the first time in a long while, I relaxed. The divorce was behind me and I knew I was about to have good times again.

Although I missed living in Hyannis Port, I tried to make the best of my new career. My friend Ted must have missed me a little too because often on Sundays, after Mass, he'd put the top down on Old Blue and drive over to join me for coffee and a muffin. On one such occasion, four couples from Belfast, Northern Ireland were staying at the inn for ten days. They were another lively crowd and two were fine musicians. On Saturday night we'd all stayed by the pool sipping Jameson Irish whiskey and baying at the moon for a bit too long. The starry night and full moon provided a perfect setting for the musical couple, Spencer and his wife Moira, to sing and play the Irish flute in a way that can only be described as the lilting sound of a spiritual experience. Since I had to be up to serve breakfast the next morning, I made my exit and retired earlier than the rest.

The day they arrived at the inn, they noticed the pictures of Hyannis Port and of me with Ted, hanging on the wall by my desk. They were excited and realizing they weren't anti-Kennedy, I hoped Ted might stop by that Sunday after Mass. Sure enough, just as I was putting muffins into the oven that Sunday, I heard the front screen door open and shut, then that unmistakable voice saying "Donny! Are you here? Where's the Bloody Mary mix? Heh, Heh, Heh."

After pouring us some coffee, I handed Ted a muffin and we sat in the kitchen talking about my guests from Ireland. Since he was always interested in the Irish, I told him about the beautiful music we'd heard the night before and he began plotting how we could sneak over to the breakfast room and surprise them. But that meant we had to slip by the pool, behind the gardens and around the bird feeders. I'd already set out the milk, fruit and cereal in the breakfast room but I always brought fresh coffee and boiling water for tea later on. Ted was a big man and when he said he was going to shrink down behind me and carry the basket of muffins, I had a hard time keeping a straight face.

As we began our sly approach, most of the guests were up and in the breakfast nook seated on rocking chairs or rattan sofas, reading the paper or using binoculars to watch the birds outside. After a long night of singing and sipping Irish whiskey, no one was in a hurry to do much of anything, so they paid little attention to us as we crossed past the pool, ready to spring our little surprise. I came around the corner wishing everyone a cheery good morning but didn't get much of a response. Then I noticed one of the men in a rocking chair had spotted Ted. He happened to be the Northern Ireland Minister of Dairy and when he realized it was Senator Ted Kennedy behind me carrying the muffins and toast, he couldn't believe his eyes. His chair went over backwards and when Ted said "Aaah, good morning!" the rest of the group saw him and gaped as well.

No one said a thing until I broke the silence. "Some guy off the street just came in looking for a free cup of coffee so I brought him over," I explained. Everyone laughed and babbled with excitement over meeting Ted Kennedy! They asked if it would be acceptable to take pictures and Ted said sure and was gracious about it. He even let the dairy minister take some movie film which was sometimes a no-no.

Being conscious of all the former troubles in Northern Ireland, I wondered how those pictures might be received back home. But Ted wasn't fazed. Instead, he visited with them for a while, got them laughing, said goodbye and left. As I watched Old Blue exit the driveway

I couldn't help thinking that no matter the time of day or where he went, someone always wanted something from him. And no matter how tiring it must have been, Ted usually obliged.

CHAPTER 18

AND IT ALL CAME TUMBLING DOWN

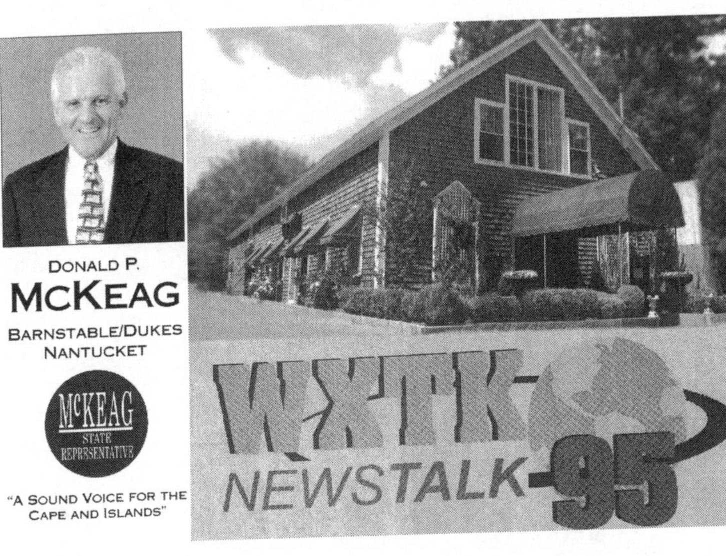

A run for office, a Carver restaurant called The Cranebrook, and an outspoken radio show formed the perfect storm for the author.

Gatherings at the Compound provided me with an opportunity to talk with other members of the family. Young John Kennedy and his sister Caroline attended very few events but having talked to John about the day at Nauset Beach in 1963 and taking him for a ride in my Dodge "Woody" fifteen years later, provided a background for conversation whenever we met.

After his mother passed away in 1995, John began spending more time in the family home in Hyannis Port. One of those visits occurred during Ted's annual Thanksgiving party. Like any young woman, my stepdaughter Alyson was dying to meet him and when Ted told me John was going to be there, I asked Vicky if I could bring her. John didn't arrive until late and I was playing the piano when he got there. As soon as I finished, I brought her over to meet him and he was terrific to her. Later, she told me John had been very nice but she was so nervous she couldn't remember anything he said the whole time they spoke!

One morning at the Inn, the phone rang and it was John saying his uncle Teddy had suggested he call. I was surprised at his candor when he said it had been almost five years since his mother's death but his sister Caroline was finally ready to deal with her estate. They had decided she would keep the Martha's Vineyard house and property and John and his wife Carolyn would have the house in Hyannis Port.

John said his bank needed an appraisal of the house

and Teddy thought I might know an appraiser who would value the property as a house in Hyannis Port, rather than the former home of President Kennedy. Flattered that he would share this with me, I told John I wasn't sure I could help because most of the people I'd known at Town Hall had retired. Nevertheless, I said I'd try but explained that finding someone willing or able to do that would be a challenge. John understood and said he'd appreciate anything I could do.

Then he started laughing and said he'd had a great time at the party and "Donny! You're a helluva piano player!" To which I replied, "Maybe for about thirty minutes, John, but then it's all over!" and he laughed again. After we hung up, I was reminded of his father's charm and wit and also of the terrible feeling of loss on that day in Dallas.

Although I was unable to find a suitable appraiser for him, during the process I learned just a little about what it was like to be John F. Kennedy, Jr.

And some of the things he had to put up with were hard to believe. For instance, anything he signed was fair game. No matter what kind of a transaction he was involved in, he had to be wary of everyone; real estate agents, appraisers, clerks, waitresses, bartenders, etc. it didn't matter. People would take the original check, bill or document, make copies, then sell the originals on the open market for a lot of money. It was really insane.

****

The day was July 16, 1999 and after finishing the radio show, I was running errands and, as usual, stopped in Hyannis Port to get my mail. I said hello to Mike Murray, the postmaster, who replied that my ears should be burning.

It seems that Provencia "Provi" Parades, John and Caroline's nanny during the White House years, had just been to the post office and was asking for me. John always invited Provi to stay in Hyannis Port for the month of July or August and when I knocked on the door she came to the door with a glass of orange juice in her hand. Looking much the same as the last time I'd seen her, Provi seemed happy to see me and after giving me a hug and a cup of tea, brought me through the house to see the renovating John and Carolyn had been doing. Jackie hadn't done anything to the house since the 1950s but now all the floors were freshly sanded, the walls newly papered, and John and Carolyn's personal paintings were waiting to be hung.

The couple was expected to arrive that afternoon to meet with Luddington, the Kennedy decorator. New red and gold drapes were stacked on the dining room table, ready to be hung when they arrived, and as we sipped our tea, Provi and I talked about old times when I lived on the hill and invited her and her friends over to sing. One time, Dave Powers, the president's advisor and curator of the JFK Library, had stopped by with her.

Billy McDonald, a former assistant at the HyPort post office and a friend of mine, had gone to work full-time for John six months earlier. He was upstairs hanging a new shower door but was having problems. Recognizing my voice, he called down, “Is that you Donny? Can you come up stairs? I need a hand?” I went up and together we hung the door in no time. Provi had poured me another cup of tea but after visiting a few more minutes, l gave her a hug and returned to my car.

Forty minutes later, around noon I think, I was driving on Route 28 in Mashpee when the music was interrupted by a news flash saying that John Kennedy, Jr.’s plane was missing! I was in shock. How could that be? I’d just left his house! Pulling over to say a prayer, I somehow knew more terrible news was to come and that my friend, sixty-seven year old Ted Kennedy, would again be needed to eulogize another member of his family. But this time, it would be the only son of a brother who had been President of the United States.

* * * *

I‘d enjoyed being an innkeeper but during the slow months of winter keeping ahead of the bills was a struggle. I was also tired of being alone. My former wife Pat was still in my thoughts and we had been talking and getting along well. But she still had no interest in running an Inn so I put it on the market where it sold in a relatively short period of time.

After I moving into Pat's condominium back in Falmouth, we seemed to be happy until the radio station asked me to return to the morning show. Pat was a private person and disliked controversy of any kind. And she thought the radio kind was the worst. One time a fellow employee came into her office to give a play by play description of my comments that day, which he thought would be a compliment. But Pat didn't take it that way and let him know it. I had been willing to give up the Inn, but not the radio show. After the disappointments and financial losses of recent years, being on the radio somehow validated me and provided a source of income. Today I realize that most of Pat's concerns were legitimate. Talk radio sometimes fueled my inner conflicts which wasn't always a good thing.

The silence at home became all too frequent and I knew we were in deep trouble again. I was in Hyannis Port getting my mail one day, when quite innocently, Postmaster Mike Murray said, "Donald, with your record of changing addresses, I think you'd be wise to keep your mailbox in Hyannis Port. It seems to be the only consistent thing in your life!" We both chuckled, but I thought about that all the way home.

Then the Falmouth Republican Party asked me to run for state representative which meant that if I became a candidate I would have to give up the talk show. By then I felt the democratic party I'd once been so proud to follow under JFK, the one that once stood for "An honest day's pay for an honest day's work," had become a mostly greedy, self-centered group willing to do anything to get elected. Granted, the republican party wasn't much better but I felt the leadership of the democratic party had lost sight of President Kennedy's "Ask not what your country can do for you" and replaced it, with support from the biased press, with a message of "Elect Democrats and your country will do it all for you!"

Pat had worked for Republican candidates in the past so I thought with me giving up the radio she would be happy and perhaps help me in the campaign. But she wanted no part of it. In fairness, knowing of what she'd gone through and seen in campaigns, I couldn't blame her.

Although we tried to work things out, nothing had really changed. Rudyard Kipling's warning that a man could never be happy as long as "his dreams were still his master" never registered with me. I guess I needed to continue reaching for that unreachable star and being desperate for adulation, had to have excitement in my life. Both my wives had wanted a conventional life with a nine-to-five husband but once again, I was too stubborn to sit down and talk about it. A rousing argument ensued and as usual, I ran from the problem and did the easiest thing. I moved out.

During the years I attended UMass-Amherst, every male student in a state college had to take ROTC. I had passed the exam for second lieutenant just as Viet Nam was heating up so when my draft notice arrived, I went to Boston to take the physical exam. I couldn't pass because of my bad shoulder, and wasn't the slightest bit disappointed. I figured it was time the high school injury that ruined my baseball career, gave me something back.

Even so, not having served my country always bothered me. As corny as it may sound, living through the Kennedy years and knowing Ted Kennedy, I thought running for office might be a way to fill that void. For years, I'd been talking on the radio about the failures of government but had never done anything to improve it. In the past, Ted and I had discussed my ideas and now I had the opportunity to either put up or shut up.

Other than electing a republican governor once in a while, the two-party system was nonexistent in Massachusetts. So after thinking it over for a while, I agreed to run for state representative as a republican and help get it back.

Surprisingly, my campaign committee raised more money than any other state representative race in 2000. Even some democrats quietly contributed. But, in addition to running as a conservative republican against a fourteen-year incumbent liberal democrat, Duke's County also included Nantucket and Martha's Vineyard where I didn't stand a chance. That was also the year George W. Bush was so low in the polls even some Republicans didn't turn out to vote.

At least I tried. I had the opportunity to state my views on important issues and met some remarkable people. For the most part the campaign was a worthwhile experience. But I'd be lying if I didn't say how disappointing it was to meet the greedy and self-seeking individuals along the trail. I had run for office hoping my varied life experiences might help serve the people in correcting a failing system. Instead, I found myself talking to people more interested in my party affiliation than in my credentials. It was a first-hand lesson in why politics is such a nasty business and why more experienced and qualified people won't run.

When I left Pat's condo, I had moved into a friend's apartment and the day after the election results were posted, and I lost, she stopped by to say she'd voted for me and was sorry she hadn't been more supportive. It was so nice to see her and after hearing her words, believe it or not, we tried living together again!

But this time, something happened beyond our control. I was diagnosed with prostate cancer and while the operation went well and was supposedly a success, I refused to acknowledge the psychological as well as physical effects. Pat was supportive but I wouldn't talk about what was going on in my head and began getting home late in order to avoid both the subject and her. Radio had finally lost its attraction and the tension at home was carrying over on air. Rather than seek professional help or talk to Pat about it, I began searching for answers elsewhere.

After finishing the show one morning, the

receptionist told me a real estate broker in Plymouth had left a message to call him. Returning the call, I learned a restaurant I'd looked at so1me months earlier in Carver and thought had sold, was back on the market. For years, my accountant had kept reminding me I still had a large tax credit on the books, much of which could be reclaimed if I bought a business or piece of real estate in Massachusetts, fixed it up, and sold it at a profit. Pat and I were working on us again, so I mentioned the phone call to her and we drove to Carver to look at the restaurant. She said it was nice but was smart enough to know my getting involved in another restaurant was risky business to say the least.

Talk about a masochist! Despite all the personal and financial damage I'd suffered in that business, I still hadn't learned a thing. Somehow I was always convinced that this time would be different and I'd be successful again. The demon had me again and I was on another mission. Without telling Pat, I went to the banks to see if they would give me a mortgage and if they did, planned to make a deal with the owner to buy the restaurant. Before I had a chance to tell her about it however, Pat learned about my plans from a friend at work who saw an article mentioning the potential sale in the newspaper. Furious and justifiably upset, she couldn't believe I'd done such a stupid and inconsiderate thing. I knew I wasn't thinking straight but in my escapist frame of mind, that was all I needed. This latest disagreement provided me with all the justification I needed for moving on once again. And this time it would be permanent.

* * * *

The Crane Brook building was a classic New England structure that fit all the criteria I had loved for the past thirty years. Located on Foundry Pond in South Carver, it dated back to the pre-revolutionary era. Built in 1757, it was used to smelt local iron deposits called "bog ore" and dubbed Charlotte Furnace in honor of Queen Charlotte, wife of George III, King of England. In 1762, it became the first foundry in the country to produce iron tea kettles and other iron products including cannon balls to supply the USS Constitution, "Old Ironsides," throughout the War of 1812.

Over the years, it had been a cranberry separating building and used for storage. Still later it opened as an antique shop before becoming a tea room that evolved into a restaurant in the early 1990's. By the time I looked at the place it was in need of some improvement. But I had also remembered when Pat and I looked at it, there were spacious and attractive living quarters upstairs overlooking the water which was where I was going to live

After leaving Falmouth under a cover of darkness, I immediately began renovations to the interior which were mostly cosmetic and quickly accomplished. Then I hired a talented young chef who, along with his wife, assumed the most critical parts of setting up the kitchen, helping to hire staff, and creating a new menu. The Crane Brook was up and running in no time at all and that certifiably crazy Donald P. McKeag was off to the races -- again!

The restaurant did pretty well for almost three years but my heart wasn't in it and I knew I'd made another mistake. I had purchased the property with the idea of following my account's advice by creating a successful business, then selling it at a profit to get the tax benefit. But now it was 2005. I was sixty five years old, skittish about being on my own again and wondering what I'd do after I sold the place. Adding to my dilemma was the property next door being suddenly for sale and included a wonderful stone building twelve feet from the water which I envisioned as my future home.

In keeping with my original plans, my young chef found a buyer and potential partner for the Crane Book. But despite the fact I was now having health problems, I decided not to sell. I would stay and buy the property next door. Knowing it was far too ambitious at my age and that I was not thinking straight again, I rationalized the move because the restaurant needed extra parking spaces!

Deciding to build three condominiums on the property triggered my usual poor sense of timing and after turning down my potential buyer, I also lost my talented chef. The economy went into a downturn and the restaurant's remote location, coupled with severe winter weather and power outages, especially during the busy Christmas season, cost me desperately needed revenue and signaled the end.

I was still doing the radio show to help pay expenses. But even though I'd stayed current with my bills, taxes and mortgage payments, the bank refused to help. I remember thinking of my father when he told me years before, "Remember one thing about banks Donny. They'll always give you an umbrella on a sunny day."

Then the President's stimulus money, supposedly available to small businesses like mine, proved to be a myth and although I've never liked that saying, "things can always be worse," but that's just what happened. That summer, after letting my landscaper go to save money, I was taking care of the lawn and gardens myself when my cancer returned. While having radiation at Cape Cod Hospital and still doing the radio show in Hyannis, I was bitten by a mosquito that just happened to be carrying the West Nile virus. (There were only eight cases in the entire state and one was a baby who died). Sweating and soaking through three or four T-shirts every night before that diagnosis, I thought I was dying. But by this time, things had become so bad it was almost like a comedy show so I kept on going.

In 2008, Ted Kennedy was diagnosed with brain cancer and I was crushed. Years earlier I could always get him laughing as we sat outside on the porch. Or he'd have me come inside to sing and play the piano for a while. It killed me to know that, because of a meaningless radio show, I couldn't be there to help when I'm sure he could have used the music and laughter. However, I still called the house every week to tell his Irish nurse's aide, Caroline, to let him know I was thinking of him.

Those who knew me and my political views have always wondered how I could have been such a close friend of the man commonly known as the U.S. Senate's "Liberal Lion." Well, the answer is pretty simple. I was just extremely fond of the man. Although I didn't always agree with him or his politics and said so, he was a man willing to debate both sides of a political issue, a friend who once pretended to be the waiter for my guests at the Lion and Lamb Inn, an avid sailor who playfully called himself The Commander, a man who cared deeply about others no matter what their side of the political spectrum, a jokester who loved to tease others, a raconteur who laughed at his own stories, and finally, a brother who had endured the unspeakable tragedies of others as well as his own, but also a man who ultimately regained his personal balance.

Like me, he was far from perfect, but knowing Ted and seeing the way he lived day to day, made me a better man. He once told me, "Donny, I haven't got time for whiners and moaners." It was a lesson I learned only gradually and have to still work on, but with his death on August 26, 2009, that didn't seem to matter anymore. All those lessons and good times with him were gone and nothing would ever be the same for so many of us.

With most of my retirement nest egg gone up in smoke, and after more than forty years of paying taxes and employing hundreds of people, this one-time-big-shot decided it was time to fold up his tent for good.

* * * *

It had been almost two hundred years since Charlotte Furnace had been supplying ships with cannon balls for the Revolution but I still wasn't done shooting myself in the foot. The night before I shut the doors for good, I threw a party for my employees and other special guests. But with free drinks and the knowledge that it was over, a few employees went overboard and the night turned into somewhat of a disaster.

The next day found me standing alone on the deck of that old foundry, looking out at the pond, preparing to file for bankruptcy and wondering what happened. While pondering my unimagined fate, I heard wings flapping and saw a familiar visitor flying in to join me. A blue heron landed under a spotlight originally meant to illuminate the pond for guests dining outside and began using it to preen his feathers and give me the eye.

When watching that water fowl up close, you'll see a tall, slender creature standing in water or in a marsh searching for prey. But when in flight, soaring over various wooded areas, the size and sound of its wings creates a prehistoric feeling of total freedom and timelessness. One morning, while watching the aloof head and confident aura of that majestic bird, my mind somehow pictured the figure of George Washington and from then on, I called him George.

On this particular day however, it occurred to me that even though George kept glancing my way every now and then, he really didn't give a damn about my predicament. I laughed at the thought but as he continued to preen, pose, and look for fish, I felt comfort in his presence. But when Mother Nature summoned him back to the wild as she always did, I was jealous. Watching his wings unfurl, I envied his freedom and wished I could join him as he soared off into the mist.

A strange thing however is that the poorer I have become, the richer my life has been. For over forty years, I've experienced the highs and lows. I have known wild success and dismal failure, both in business and personally. But through it all, I have relished the excitement and joy of meeting so many wonderful people along the way. I hope my life's journey of always searching for something better is finally over.

But what if it isn't?

EPILOGUE

HELP WANTED

NO IRISH NEED APPLY

ABOVE: The Old Candle Factory on Scudder Ave in Hyannisport used to be the Hyannisport Garage (shown 1941). Joseph P. Kennedy's car is in front of the gas pump.

BELOW: One of many signs that were hung in stores and factories in the early 1900s.

Every now and then, when I want to take a trip down memory lane, I'll drive through Hyannis, past the former Asa Bearse House on Main Street, the now long- gone building once the Backside Saloon on Pleasant Street, and continue down to Baxter's Boat House. Then I'll head over to Hyannis Port, passing the houses I once owned, the site of the Candle Factory and the village chapel where I once got married. Finally, ignoring the signs, I head down Marchant Avenue and sit for a moment in the driveway of that famous and familiar house where I spent so many wonderful times. Its glory days are gone now and even the window shades seem different. They remind me of eyelids now closed to the events of a world that once embraced the house and all who lived there.

Since Ted's death the Kennedy homestead is no longer a residence or an exciting destination. The house is now part of the EMK Foundation and will be used for meetings and private tours only. Ethel Kennedy still spends summers next door in the house she and Bobby bought in 1959. And behind her, on my former street, Irving Avenue, Teddy Kennedy, Jr. his wife Kiki and their children now own and spend summers in the house that was once the President's, then his son John and wife Carolyn's before their tragic deaths in 1999.

In this book I occasionally mention that sardonic Irish saying "When things are going too good there must be something wrong!" yet I never thought it ever applied to me. Despite having two failed marriages, four or five careers, seven businesses, eight or more residences and all the cars and boats, I never understood I had become the poster boy for that message of self- sabotage. My father had been gone for years but every now and then I could still hear his voice saying "Keep it up Donny and you're going to lose everything!" Maybe I was so angry at him for saying that, I subconsciously went overboard every now and then, just to prove him right.

But who cares? All I know is the choices and mistakes I made weren't my father's fault nor my ex-wives. That saying "Easy come, easy go" and "Having money burn a hole in your pocket" certainly applied to me. Through high school and college I was always restless and couldn't "go with the flow." Staying with one project for long was always a challenge. But I've been fortunate to have had the opportunity to restore several buildings and create successful businesses that other talented people enjoyed doing with me. I think that part of my life, working with others, has probably given me my deepest satisfaction.

After filing bankruptcy, I lost my residence in the restaurant but the condo property next door was a separate entity the creditors couldn't touch. The mortgage holder is a friend who suggested I live on the property and maintain it for her until such time as the real estate market improved. I've done that and have also converted the former gift shop attached to the condos into an apartment where I now live, among my pictures and artifacts. It's been said that when you're unable to live with anyone else you had better learn to live with yourself and I think I've managed that pretty well.

Thanks to help from Steve and Pam Dane, I still do a radio show on WXTK Saturday afternoon from 11am - 1pm, a public television program in Plymouth, Thursdays at 6:00 pm on PACTV., and continue to enjoy watching the avian activity on and around Furnace Pond and at the old foundry.

Once in a while, as I watch a beautiful sunset, I'll think back to that day on the deck when I felt lost and my mind was racing through a million memories; most good but some not so good. But when that happens now, I feel a smile come over my face and addressing no one in particular, I'll look up at the sky and say "Well! At least I owned a Rolls Royce!"

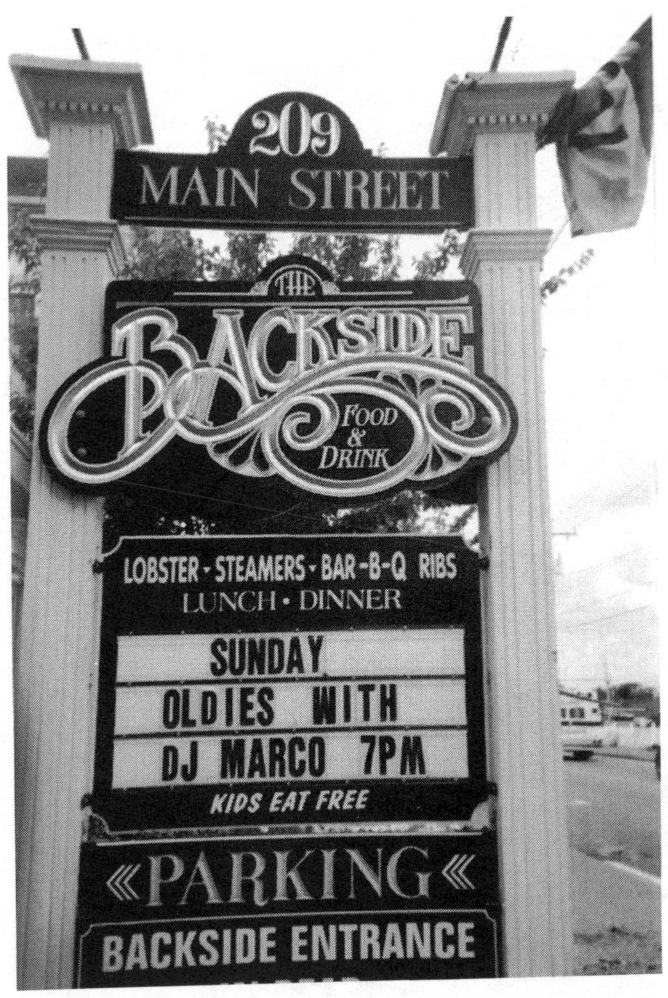

The Backside Restaurant from the 1990s on Pleasant Street in Hyannis.

ABOVE: the author's beloved Rolls Royce.

LEFT: The author and good friend, Ted Kennedy

L to R: The author, Don McKeag, along with Gail Kirk, wife of former Senator Paul Kirk, and Charles Haughey (former Prime Minister of Ireland) enjoying a party at Bobby Kennedy's home in the mid-1980s.

ACKNOWLEDGMENTS

It can take many years to learn that if your dreams for the future don't work out, you must move forward and refuse to let disappointment turn you into a victim.

Lost dreams will be an incentive rather than a detriment to success when you roll up your sleeves and work hard. But of course, that will depend on whether your definition of success is a personal thing or just a financial matter.

In my case, the financial success I achieved was lost through a combination of poor decisions, bad timing, and most of all, an impatience and unexplained discontent with anything I'd ever worked for or accomplished.

Why that happened is still a mystery to me but I'd like to think and hope that my life, overall, has been successful. I've written this book as a thank you to my family, friends, coworkers, teammates, coaches, teachers and students, employers, employees, customers, bankers, lawyers, politicians, radio and television viewers and listeners. In other words, to all those who have played a part in the journey and gave me so much to remember and be grateful for.

I also want to thank the library staffs in Plymouth and Carver, Massachusetts for their kind assistance throughout this endeavor and special thanks to Michael Foley for his many hours of encouragement and invaluable computer knowledge that helped me to continue on.

Finally, my appreciation also goes to the successful, wonderful authors, Nancy Rubin-Stuart and Kate "K.R." Conway for creating the final product I hope you will enjoy

THE WHO'S WHO

MARTHA RAYE, (1916-1994), Margaret Reed, and Rosemary Clooney remained life- long friends and 1992, after her long career in both movies and television, Martha was awarded the highest honor any private citizen can receive, the American Medal of Freedom. President Bill Clinton presented it to her even though she was a life- long Republican!

ROSEMARY CLOONEY, (1928-2002) Rosemary used to be the spokesperson for Coronet paper products on television for years and appeared in several episodes of the popular television show ER starring her nephew George Clooney in 1994. She was married to dancer Dante DiPaulo from 1993 until her death in June of 2002.

LEE REMICK, (1935-1991) Grew up in Quincy, Massachusetts and had originally trained to be a dancer. But her mother was an actress in New York and when her parents divorced, Lee and her brother Bruce went to live with her. Lee's film career included an Academy Award nomination for her role in Days of Wine and Roses,with Jack Lemon, and other co-starring roles opposite many of the top male stars in Hollywood, including James Stewart, Gregory Peck and Richard Burton. During a difficult first marriage, she had two children and her life had its share of troubles. But after marrying British director Kip Gowans, those personal matters seemed to calm down and she continued on to better things. The house on Sepuit Bay was sold back to members of the Mathison family from whom they had purchased it and to whom I had delivered groceries when I owned the Cash Market in Marstons Mills.

RITA MORENO, (1931-) was a fine singer and became

a well-known actress. But she was also the first Latina to win an Oscar - for Best Supporting Actress in the movie West Side Story. Like many who are envied by the public however, she also had her bad times. While making that movie, she'd been living with actor Marlon Brandon and when he left her, she tried to commit suicide. She eventually returned to her career, married Leonard Gordon a heart surgeon, and they had a daughter.

EDWARD MC CORMACK, (1920-2005) and the McCormack family had wanted the Senate seat as much as the Kennedys and felt Ed the qualifications that Ted didn't. During their debate, however, when he said, "Teddy, if your name was Edward Moore instead of Edward Moore Kennedy, your candidacy would be a joke!" the comment made Ed look mean spirited and ended any small chance he might have had to win.

EDWARD M. KENNEDY, (1932-2009) My times with Ted Kennedy dealt more with the person than the Senator. But seeing him in action and listening to his speeches, I came to believe his politics were a direct result of the tough road he'd traveled as the youngest of nine in a highly competitive family. He wanted to be his own man but couldn't escape the family's control. Hearing people idealize his brothers over the years and seeing the heroic stature they'd assumed must have elicited mixed emotions. Obviously he was proud of them but it must have been difficult to handle and painful as well. Once they were gone, the pressure on him to continue the political dynasty had to have been a burden.

The tragedy of Chappaquiddick, closely following the deaths of his brothers Bobby and John, all in the 1960s, changed everything for him. And people tend to forget the plane crash he was in on June, 19th of 1964, just seven months after Dallas. Two men were killed, including the pilot, and he was given the last rites. His back would never be the same but during the recovery time he learned how to paint and re-evaluated what he wanted to be as a senator. Chappaquiddick made him more vulnerable to people and issues than before and while his political success and popularity came from both sides of the aisle, I suspect certain factions in the Democratic party, as well as other personal and political forces, now knew his Achilles heel; which wasn't just Chappaquiddick, but also his love for the Senate. I believe the fear of not being re-elected and thus letting his family down kept him at the mercy of others as well as the press and public opinion.

Interestingly, the only time Chappaquiddick came up during our times together was in reference to his Presidential campaign in 1980. Fifteen years after that race we were sitting on my deck when the subject came up. I was surprised when he said that neither Chappaquiddick nor his divorce from Joan had impacted the campaign anything like his fall from grace with the National Rifle Association. When they withdrew their support, he knew he was done.

DAVE MCKENNA (1930-2008) was considered a piano genius by other more famous pianists and after deciding to concentrate on playing solo piano, became a favorite of many other top musicians and entertainers throughout the world. I've mentioned going to St. Martin one winter and taking the crew from "Monkee Business" out to dinner. The place was called "The West Indian" and when I told their Bahamian piano player I had Dave McKenna playing in my lounge, he was bowled over. Dave appeared in Carnegie Hall more than any other solo pianist but being shy and never properly marketed, he remained relatively unknown to many who considered themselves piano enthusiasts even in Massachusetts and on Cape Cod. Most musicians would kill to appear in Carnegie Hall. But Dave called it the "Sweatbox" and told me he never liked playing there!

HAROLD RUSSELL (1914-2002). Despite having won two Academy Awards, Harold only appeared in three other movies. Director William Wyler told him to go back to school because there'd never be enough roles for a man with no hands and he took his advice. After attending Boston University, he entered a career of helping the handicapped and after serving three terms as the National Commander of the AMVETS, retired to the Cape where we became good friends

SAUNI RILEY (???), won a beauty contest during the 1960's to become Cape Cod's "Princess of Indian Summer" so it was expected she would marry her handsome, Notre Dame footballer, Marshall Riley. They got married before Marshall graduated and she moved to Indiana. Unfortunately, unlike the Ken and Barbie fairy tale, after graduating and moving back to the Cape, things didn't work out and they got divorced. They had two lovely daughters but like so many of us living on the Cape during that time, many marriages didn't last. Sauni still lives in Palm Beach and Marshall's on Cape Cod. We are still good friends and I have coffee with Marshall almost every Saturday before I do my radio show.

MICHAEL DEELEY, (1932-)produced "Close Encounters of the Third Kind" and also a well-received television production of "Young Catherine (the Great)" which was intended to star fellow Osterville resident and friend, Lee Remick. But Lee was battling cancer at the time so the role went to Vanessa Redgrave.

BILL CARTER, (1919-1995) had always refused to take any of his wife's "John Deere" money. He paid family and personal expenses with his own earnings and didn't like kowtowing to New York Society. They had two children but in less than ten years, the marriage was over. Bill had fallen in love with, Elaine Stewart, an actress from his Hollywood days and when he and his wife split up in 1953,"Trink" was so angry, she quickly married a millionaire in his own right, William Wakeman, the Chairman of the Republican Party of Palm Beach and very popular in the community. After a cocktail party, one night, Trink shot her new husband. The story was she had learned he was involved with her and Bill's daughter and although still alive and able to talk after being shot, he refused to name his wife, or anyone else, as his assailant before dying in the hospital. Following a long and highly charged trial, "Trink"Wakeman was acquitted of the crime. When Bill and Elaine Stewart divorced not long after, he soothed the pain by living on the French Riveria for six months with actress Bridget Bardot, then referred to as the sexiest and most desirable woman in the world!

Bill was also a close friend of America's most decorated soldier in WWII, Audie Murphy. He had written a book after the war called "To Hell and Back" and when actor James Cagney read it, he brought Audie to Hollywood to try acting. After appearing with Bill in two low grade "B" movies, his career stalled until he played himself in a movie named after his book "To Hell and Back". It was Universal Studio's largest grossing movie for thirty years, and. from then on he would appear in forty films and become a star. Audie was on his way to meet Bill at LaGuardia Airport in New York, when the plane crashed and he was killed.

He and Andrea had come to Hyannis Port to attend my second marriage and shortly after, my new wife and I took a mini-vacation to Florida to stay at my unit at the Palm Beach Hotel. We visited with them at that time and I was so glad to have spent some time with him not long before he died.

THE ROLLS ROYCE – (1992- 1997) -. I had considered taking that beautiful machine up to the Cape to rent out for functions and wedding parties. But driving a Rolls around Hyannis Port and over to the local watering holes was a bit too ostentatious even for me. There was an after- hours joint in Palm Beach called, Lulu's, that opened at 11:p.m. and closed at 3:00 a.m. And as I pulled up to the valet station one night, a German couple was just exiting their cab. The young woman went crazy over the Rolls and her escort said, "I must have that car!" I told them I had just arrived and couldn't talk to them at that time, then went inside. Later on, I saw them dancing but nothing further was said until the valet was handing me my keys and I was about to leave. The bald German fellow and his lovely friend came rushing up, pleading with me to sell them the car, but I just figured they'd had too much to drink. He insisted on calling me the next day so I gave him my number; figuring that was the end of it. Wrong. He called at nine the next morning, brought a mechanic with him and after examining the car, said he wanted it. As usual, I didn't think it through and probably charged him too little. He agreed to my price and was back in an hour with his giggling little blond girlfriend and a certified check. I shook my head, wondering why I'd sold it, and then watched as they drove happily away.

One of my favorite movies is "Arthur", starring Dudley Moore and Liza Minelli. Although dark blue, the Rolls Royce in that movie was the same model and had the same interior as my white beauty. Of course it always brings back those memories and, ironically, Dudley Moore's favorite piano player was Dave McKenna, and Liza Minelli spent two summers in Hyannis Port on my street, Irving Avenue.

ABOUT THE AUTHOR

Although Don McKeag has retired from the restaurant business, he continues to do a talk radio show and occasional piano playing gigs on Cape Cod. He lives on Foundry Pond in South Carver, Massachusetts and enjoys spending time with family, friends, and former associates in the sports and restaurant world. *Well, At Least I Owned a Rolls Royce* is his first novel, and he hopes to continue writing and return to teaching in some capacity.

The author, age seven.

Made in the USA
Middletown, DE
01 October 2015